EXECUTIVE'S

GUIDE

TO

EFFECTIVE

SPEAKING AND WRITING

EXECUTIVE'S

GUIDE

TO

EFFECTIVE

SPEAKING AND WRITING

FREDERICK C. DYER

PRENTICE-HALL, INC., ENGLEWOOD CLIFFS, N.J.

Sixth printing ....*July, 1967*

PRINTED IN THE UNITED STATES OF AMERICA
29442—B & P

OTHER BOOKS BY FREDERICK C. DYER

EXECUTIVE'S GUIDE TO HANDLING PEOPLE

PUTTING YOURSELF OVER IN BUSINESS
(in collaboration with Ross Evans and Dale Lovell)

THE PETTY OFFICER'S GUIDE
(in collaboration with Rear Admiral Harley F. Cope)

ACKNOWLEDGEMENTS

Acknowledgements for a book like this are difficult to make because so many people have helped me directly or indirectly by their comments, their teachings, and their examples. The books and articles I have most depended on are identified in the text or listed in the Appendices. Among the persons who have most influenced me in recent years are: T. Bagg, W. E. Blasingame, S. F. Block, C. M. Boyer, T. Clark, Ross Evans, Noel Gayler, Shy Greenspan, Richard Jackson, J. J. Killeen, P. J. King, J. C. Lang, Ray Leavitt, Dale Lovell, Robert E. Merriam, J. V. Noel, J. J. O'Connor, N. J. Pope, Henry Roberts, Herb C. Rosenthal, W. J. Saylor, J. V. Smith, R. H. Stevenson, W. W. Strong, W. T. Sutherland, R. J. Tartre, B. D. Tillett, J. A. Umhoefer, J. E. Walters, T. W. Waters, E. A. Woody, and Alan Young.

PREFACE

"Why can't my people speak more to the point?"

"Why can't I get a presentation organized quickly?"

"Why are our reports so unpredictable? Some cost a lot of money and look like junk."

"Why do we lose our tempers over badly written letters? Why are our feelings hurt when someone criticizes our writing?"

"What sort of production rates can I expect of myself and others when something has to be written?"

This book has been written to answer the foregoing questions and a thousand others like them.

Specifically, it is the executive's guide to:

Organizing presentations, reports, studies, and letters.

Speeding up the creative process—how to get started and how to work more easily.

Using participative techniques—how to lead conferences, stave off hecklers, and enjoy it.

Using humor effectively; speaking and reading at the same time; developing aids and illustrations.

Handling artists and other creative people with skill—and with firm kindness—capsulizing lengthy documents; keeping control over grammarians and punctuation experts.

And above all, how to improve your skills and those of your assistants in the practice of *effective* speaking and writing.

TABLE OF CONTENTS

PART I

EFFECTIVE SPEAKING
FOR EXECUTIVES

1

THE EXECUTIVE'S VIEWPOINT OF SPEAKING AND WRITING

THE WHY AND HOW OF THIS BOOK

The Executive's Most Needed Skills

In his article on "How to Be an Employee" (*Fortune* magazine, May, 1952) Peter F. Drucker stated:

As soon as you move one step up from the bottom your effectiveness depends on your ability to reach others through the spoken or the written word. And the further away your job is from manual work, the larger the organization of which you are an employee, the more important it will be that you know how to convey your thoughts in writing or speaking. In the very large organization, whether it is the government, the large business corporation, or the Army, this ability to express oneself is perhaps the most important of all the skills a man can possess.

Of course an executive must be able to speak and write clearly and forcefully; how else could he obtain action? But how well does the average executive communicate? How well does he teach his assistants and subordinates to communicate?

Dr. Julian A. McPhee, President of California State Polytechnic College, concluded after interviewing more than 100 top executives:[1]

The one consistent criticism made of business graduates of all colleges is that they do not know how to communicate their ideas effectively in speaking and writing. I have heard this criticism from every executive I have talked with during the past five years. The road to the top in any business or profession requires technical know-how, but it also requires the ability to communicate with others.

[1] *Associated Press*, June 2, 1957.

3

Most businessmen recognize the importance of speaking and writing ability to their *personal* advancement; not so many, however, realize the importance of communicative techniques in the whole process of management. Let's say a word about "communication feedback" before going further.

Communication Feedback and Management Action

I was once asked to write part of a manual on handling rejections of a certain product. About halfway through I came across an illustration of a form that was to be sent to the home office. I asked, "Who will process that form?"

"What do you want to know for?" snapped the assistant manager in charge of the project.

"So I can word the instructions more intelligently."

"Well, you just write what we tell you, and we'll worry about the system."

I shrugged my shoulders and walked away. A week later he invited me back with many apologies; he had run into a snag. There had been at least 10,000 rejections that year; handling reports on each would have meant processing 10,000 pieces of paper, and, with his system, would have required four additional people for several months —something for which there was no provision in the budget. A new system was worked out, and I had no trouble writing about it. In other words, a weakness in the written materials revealed the weakness in the management method.

After many writing and editing assignments I have also learned that if you tell a man bluntly, "Your material is badly written and poorly organized," you will make an enemy or hurt a friend. Telling a man his writing is full of errors implies to him that he cannot think clearly and that his education has been deficient. Moreover, generalities do not help him, because if he had known how to organize his writing better, he would have done so.

But when you say, "This report does not have a neat summary. How about a statement of the one, two, or three things you have set out to prove, propose, or comment on?"—the writer returns to his office thinking he has only an easy literary flourish to make. Usually, however, when he starts looking for the "three points" he finds a vital element missing. The parts do not add up, and the request for a "neat summary" often brings additional data and important information as well as a better order of presentation.

Ineffective articles, letters, reports, and presentations usually are so because the data are incomplete and the thinking is unclear—not because the "English" is incorrect or the charts badly colored. Few salesmen can sell a bad product; few writers or presentation experts can make a good case out of a pile of confused and incomplete ideas. (I know, because as a writer I have often been called on to help "present a case" that was, in fact, no case.) Just as the salesman can *feedback* to his company the customer's objections and desires, so the writer or presentation middleman can feedback to his client the needs and desires of the intended reader or listener.

THE TARGET: MORE EFFECTIVE SPEAKING AND WRITING

This corrective feedback process is analogous to that which occurs with accounting and statistical techniques. At one time people considered accounting and statistics to be just collateral functions, required by the Government, the labor unions, the stockholders, the trade associations, and by the bankers who wanted "some figures." But over the years brilliant men like Foulke and Shewhart have developed the figures into important management tools.

We take for granted the ratios of receivables, of profits on investment, of sales, etc.; but they are recent inventions. The first statisticians may have been mere counters of personnel employed and materials in inventory and similar raw data. But once the figures were collected the mathematicians could work on them, and now there are all types of statistical tools—from the Gross National Product (GNP) to Statistical Quality Control (SQC).

Note the alternation between requirements for a service and its invention, then the invention and its uses, and then more requirements and more inventions. Sometimes the numbers people acted as though the business existed simply to produce data for them; at other times the production people have acted as though a report would cause the roof to fall down. But the process has worked to everyone's benefit: new methods have called for new kinds of data; more and better data have led to better "datamation" systems, and to charts, graphs, and indexes, all of great assistance to the executive.

The science and art of *business communications* are about 30 years behind accounting and statistics in the cycle of demand and invention, invention and demand. To some people the term *communications* connotes mysterious skills, "Madison Avenue," or the half-forgotten complexities of grade-school grammar. Similarly, to the "horseback managers" of years ago, accounting and statistics were arcane subjects for the "longhairs." Nowadays most executives have no fear of accounting and statistics, but few have acquired enough familiarity with modern theories and practices of communications to know when to cooperate with, and when to object to some of the proposals to "improve company communications." To begin with: you don't improve something called *communications,* or a *corporation's communications*; you improve an *individual's* ability to speak and write!

There are, and probably always will be, people who will fuss over a rule of grammar more than over the meaning of a sentence. They equate better communications with correct spelling, or with the location of a preposition.

This Book's Purpose

The executive's view, however, and the approach of this book, is that communicative skills are to be used to advance the business, not to become ends in themselves. This book, therefore, is about the rules and techniques of effective speaking and writing as they are applied by the executive. Sometimes he hires or assigns others to do the speaking and writing; sometimes he must do it himself, but he is always responsible for the success of his subordinates as well as for his own success.

What You Should Bring to This Book

You will get more out of this book if you bring the following three attitudes to it:

1. *Be willing* to accept criticism. Anything in this book that seems new to you will therefore be, to some extent, a criticism of your way of doing things. At least try an idea before you reject it.

2. *Be willing* to criticize others gently, kindly, and helpfully. Be tough on yourself, allowing yourself no excuses; be easier on others.

3. *Be willing* to accept the fact that the burden of being worth listening to belongs on the writer or speaker, not on the reader or listener. As Reginald O. Kapp points out in his *The Presentation of Technical Information*: "An author with unique and indispensable information has his readers at his mercy. . . . (They) must quarry hard . . . (to understand him) . . . (They) are turned into quarry slaves. . . . But as soon as a better expositor comes along with the same knowledge the slaves will turn to the new one and be free of their slavery."

The consumer of your communications is the ultimate master. If you want to be heard and read, you must change yourself, not the listener or the reader.

How To Use This Book

You can start either with **Part I** on **Speaking**, or with **Part II** on **Writing**. For most business men and women, the chapters in **Part I** on **Speaking** will also serve as good introductions to modern writing practices which are described in the latter half of this book.

Wherever you begin, you should start by skimming the pages for general content; then read more leisurely for the details. Naturally, you will make quick decisions as you go along: "I agree with this," "I can use that." "I don't see the importance of this point." "I'll skip that idea until later." And so on. Later, however, you should re-read the whole book because:

1. You will find that you have consciously or unconsciously changed your mind about some things you had thought unimportant or with which you disagreed.

2. Those items with which you agreed, or whose applicability was immediately evident to you, will be found to be even more useful to you on the second or third reading. Just as the rich usually are the first to get richer, so the experienced speaker and writer is often the one to gain most from advice which to some extent was already known to him.

One learns best through a combination of study and practice. Take advantage of every chance to observe others—in conferences, meetings, conventions, and daily interviews. Watch what the other fellow does; decide which of his methods you like; compare them with the ones discussed in this book; and, as the opportunities arise, try them yourself—and, of course, avoid the mistakes against which this book and your own observations warn you.

Remember the woodman who was always too busy chopping trees to sharpen his axe. Remember Mr. Kapp's warning: If you do not improve your ability to express your ideas, someone who has improved his will come along and people will turn to him instead of to you.

2

SPAIBASCATH

HOW TO REMEMBER THE GOOD ORGANIZATION RULES
OF AN EFFECTIVE PRESENTATION

Spaibascath

SPAIBASCATH is simply a mnemonic device—a memory aid—
to help you put together a presentation or to review, assist with, or
approve another man's presentation. It can also help you check a
written report or article for effective content and organization. See
the chart on this page and the next.

This chapter will explain the meaning of the letters S P A I B A S -
C A T H; the next chapter will describe the three essential elements
of an *effective* presentation, and the two chapters after that will
explain the other important elements of a presentation.

S P A I B A S C A T H

GUIDELINES FOR EFFECTIVE ORGANIZATION OF A PRESENTATION

SPAIBASCATH (BUSINESS PRESENTATIONS)			TOMIPASTA (TEACHING TERMINOLOGY)	
1. *S*	Subject	What the presentation is about; a label to identify the message.	*T*	Title or Topic
2. *P*	Purpose	What the *audience* is to learn, think, do, or feel. Why the presentation is to be given.	*O*	Objective
3. *A*	Aids	References, notes, props, handouts, films, charts, equipment, etc., needed or helpful.	*M*	Materials

8

4.	*I*	Intro-duction	Preparation of *audience* to receive the message; stimulate interest; give them a roadmap of where you will take them.	*I*	Intro-duction
5.	*B*	Body	The message itself; the argument; the demonstration; the "pitch."	*P*	Presen-tation
6.	*A*	Audience Action	Participation on part of *audience*; something for them to do; drill; tryout; practice; etc.	*A*	Appli-cation
7.	*S*	Summary	Restatement of main points; tying ends together; summing up in easy-to-remember form.	*S*	Summary
8.	*C*	Check-Up	Checking for understanding and re-tention of message; did the *audience* really get it loud and clear?	*T*	Test
9.	*A*	After-math	Something for the *audience* to do or think about in days to come.	*A*	Assign-ment
10.	*TH*	Take Home	Handouts; samples, reading lists; something for *audience* to take away.		

NOTES:

1. The essential elements are: Introduction, Body, and Summary.
2. The above order need not and often should not be followed in that order when writing the speech or on delivering it.

   The above form is intended as a *memory aid* and a *guide*; as a *stimulus* for new ideas to put in your presentation; and as a *checklist* for review-ing presentations for completeness and effectiveness. Departures from it can often be worthwhile, but first make sure that the departure is consciously made and really will increase effectiveness.

(Copyright, F. C. Dyer, 1961)

Why the TOMIPASTA?

The TOMIPASTA chart (Topic, Objective, Materials, Introduc-tion, Presentation, Application, Summary, Test, and Assignment) is included on the SPAIBASCATH Chart, because the concepts that have gone into developing effective teaching methods have provided much support for those developed for effective presentations.

Isn't there a substantial similarity between *teaching aids* and *pres-entation aids*? A salesman is really trying to teach the customer to know and remember the good points of the merchandise. The office manager tries to teach procedures and rules to his clerks. The fore-man seeks to instruct his workmen in the tasks to be done. The essence of teaching is to impart to others certain knowledges, skills, or attitudes. The methods are to lecture, to demonstrate, to illustrate, to discuss, and to practice—all with the aid of charts, tapes, films, etc.

The business presentation also seeks to explain, to demonstrate, to convince, and to stir to action. The methods are talking, showing, discussing, demonstrating, and practicing, and these with or without aids are combined to form business presentations.

Steps of a Modern Teaching Session

Let's follow a modern teacher through a session before we take up a business presentation. The teacher has a lesson—the *Topic*, with the title—for example, "The Pythagorean Theorem." His *Objective* is "To explain how to find the sides of a right-sided triangle." The *Materials* are "chalkboard, chalk; class text on geometry; film strip on visualization of the abstract; sample problems."

In the *Introduction*, the teacher explains what the session will be about, why the topic is important to the students, how and when the knowledge will be used in other courses, and what the students are expected to accomplish by the end of the session. ("Be able to solve for any side of a right-triangle, given the other two.")

The teacher moves into the actual teaching and *Presents* the instruction to the class—using the chalkboard, the visual aids, and several demonstrations. Then comes the *Application*: the students go to the chalkboard, or use paper and pencils at their desks, and work several problems. After they have applied themselves, the teacher *Summarizes* briefly the main points of the lesson and runs a little *Test*—perhaps by asking questions or by giving a problem for all to work. From their answers, the teacher finds out how much the students learned, and perhaps where and how he or she may improve future instruction. Lastly, the teacher gives the class an *Assignment*—perhaps to read a chapter on how to find square roots, or perhaps some more problems that illustrate the Pythagorean theorem and its various uses.

The purpose of all these steps is to ensure that the instruction is focused on what is to be taught, that the proper materials are at hand, that the students actually practice what they are supposed to learn and that there is some "feedback" to ensure continued good work.

The Steps of a Business Presentation

Look again at the chart on pages 8-9. You begin with a Subject—it might be a presentation on Safety in the Welding Room; Checking for Account Errors in the Billing Department; Installing New Budgeting Procedures; and so forth.

Next, you state the Purpose of the presentation: why you will be saying or showing or demonstrating this Subject to this audience. What are they to end up knowing, thinking, doing, or feeling in its regard?

The Aids include the facilities, equipment, and props, as well as any reference manuals, charts, files, or even just speech notes. By listing them, you make sure they will not be forgotten—also you encourage more use of potentially valuable aids. (More about this in Chapters Four and Eight.)

The Introduction tells the audience why they should listen and what they can hope to learn and to profit from what you will say.

The Body is the message which you want to put across.

To make sure the audience takes the message to their hearts you try to include some participation—the more the better.

After you have made your points, you gracefully Summarize, reminding the audience of the important points, and buttoning down any that were left a little loose.

But did the audience really get the message? To find out, you Check them for their understanding and retention. If you find out they missed parts, you are warned against similar failures or weaknesses in future presentations.

Will you allow the audience to go home and forget about you and your message? Not if you can help it. You make some suggestions about what they can do to continue their interest in the subject of your presentation.

Finally, you press upon your hearers something they can Take Home—some handouts or samples that will reinforce the message and serve as reminders of the presentation.

Does the foregoing mean a lot of work? Yes and no. If you described a walk across town in terms of each step taken and each street passed, it would sound like a task of 10,000 steps.

The full treatment of a presentation according to SPAIBASCATH sounds complicated, but each step is not necessary every time. Often one or more of the steps can be considered briefly and then left out or handled briefly. As you gain familiarity with the use of the steps, they will seem so natural and easy that you will not understand how a person could ever want to avoid even one of them.

How to Use SPAIBASCATH

First, don't think of SPAIBASCATH as a fixed, rigid form. You don't have to follow the order of steps as given when thinking up or preparing a presentation. You can freewheel all around its chart. However, you will find it a pretty good map with which to orient and organize your freewheelings.

Don't think that you must do everything listed on the chart every time you make or give a presentation; but do be willing to consider each item. When you leave one out, do so because it isn't applicable or because you don't like it—not because you didn't think of it!

On the positive side, use the SPAIBASCATH chart for improving your own presentations and those of others in these three ways:

1. *Use it as a stimulus.* After you have roughed out your ideas, glance at the SPAIBASCATH chart and ask yourself: "Do I have the right aids? Could I use another chart? Can I work in some audience participation before the end? What can I use as a handout?" And so on.

2. *Use it as a checklist.* Before a presentation, you can refer to the SPAIBASCATH chart to see if you have the right aids. You can check: "Is my purpose clear? Have I a good summary to drive home the main points? Have I overlooked a chance to refer the audience to other explanatory materials? Do I have a good introduction?" And so on.

3. *Use it as a guide.* Often the hardest job of preparing for a presentation is to organize a mass of information into a 30-minute talk. If you hold SPAIBASCATH in front of you, you will find the job of packaging your message for a specific audience or audiences that much easier. Stating your purpose, your aids, your summary, or your handouts, and so forth, will help you build a pattern of what you are to say, what to show by charts or other aids, and what to give to the audience or refer them to.

Chapter Three will explain the three essential elements of an effective presentation—the Introduction, Body, and Summary. Chapters Four and Five will explain and show how the other elements can add the smoothness and polish which can turn an otherwise ordinary talk into a powerfully effective presentation.

3

THREE ESSENTIALS OF AN EFFECTIVE PRESENTATION

Note the word *effective* in the title to this chapter. To guarantee an *effective* presentation, you need at least three parts:

1. Introduction
2. Body
3. Summary

This chapter will tell you what makes effective *introductions, bodies,* and *summaries.* Subsequent chapters will help you round out the picture of *thinking up, writing down,* and *giving* these essential elements of an effective presentation.

I. THE INTRODUCTION TO A PRESENTATION

A good introduction accomplishes three things:

1. Arouses attention and focuses the audience on you the speaker.
2. Motivates the audience to listen to your message.
3. Provides the audience with a roadmap of where you are going to take them and why.

Here, we are talking about the introduction to the body of a presentation, not the introduction of a speaker.

Obtaining Attention

This matter of gaining audience attention has often been over-emphasized. All too often a speaker strains to be dazzling with some opening pyrotechnics, or struggles through some old jokes in order "to get the audience on his side."

Of course, you have to get an audience to look at you and to listen to you. On a few occasions—and these will be rare—you may have to fight for attention. The people have come to hear you, or you have the floor, and they will at least start to listen. Let's look first at the danger of an overly exciting introduction.

Take, for example, the man who removed his trousers. He gained a lot of interest. People are still talking about him and his daring beginning. But when you ask them what he said in his speech, all they remember is that he took off his trousers. Surely his purpose had been to do something else than leave them with the memory of knees and underpants.

Unfortunately, some public speaking teachers have gone so far as to recommend: "Do anything you can to gain audience attention —set off a bomb—slam a book on the table—jump up and down— shout—anything to get attention." Such advice is dangerous, because it over-dramatizes the problem of gaining attention. A loud crash, a wild shout, or a fancy gimmick will indeed shock an audience and bring them to the edges of their chairs. But it also distracts them from your message, and it can leave them too confused and excited to pay thoughtful attention to the real purpose of your presentation.

Probably this emphasis on grabbing attention is because of the fact that most authorities on public speaking have spent a lot of time on the "platform circuits." They have talked to conventions, dinner meetings, large luncheon meetings, and to diverse crowds. On such occasions it is difficult to get an audience to settle down and listen. One has to bang with a gavel, clink a knife against a glass, call for attention over the public address system, and so on. Half the audience are still drinking coffee; waiters are running to and fro; some men are looking around for the rest room; others are remembering unfinished business. Naturally, speakers who have lived through such experiences tend to emphasize the problem of gaining attention. When you are in a noisy situation, you may have to bang a gavel, or do something dramatic to catch people's attention.

The primary focus of this book is on the *business presentation*— when you speak seriously to an important audience on an important subject. On such occasions you have only to stand up, or take your place at the rostrum, pause a moment, and begin with what you have to say. Usually, a simple pause is enough to gain attention. As any practiced salesman can tell you: when the customer looks away, just stop speaking, and he'll look back at you. If you are at a large meeting, the spotlight will be on you, or the chairman will have introduced you. If you are in a small office meeting, either you are the boss and the others are already listening, or you are called on to speak by your boss, and you have his attention and your colleagues' attention without having to resort to gimmicks. However, once you begin to speak, your words should hold the audience's attention to what you have to say, not to how you say it. You will sell yourself better, when you concentrate on putting over a message rather than on selling yourself!

Gaining Their Interest

The secret of motivating an audience to listen is to show them why or how your words will profit them. Richard C. Borden, in his excellent book, *Public Speaking—As Listeners Like It* (Note his title: *As Listeners Like it*—not as speakers like it!), says there are four stages of audience reaction:

1. Ho hum!
2. Why bring that up?
3. For instance!
4. So what?

The *Ho Hum* has to be broken through by the speaker's opening actions and sentence. Mr. Borden explains: "Don't open your speech on Safety First by saying: 'The subject which has been assigned to me is the reduction of traffic accidents.' Say, instead: 'Four hundred and fifty shiny new coffins were delivered to this city last Thursday.'"

Next, says Mr. Borden, "Your listener admits, 'Yes, you caught my attention by an intriguing opening sentence. But in the cold light of second thought—why bring up this subject anyway?' You must build a bridge, from your subject to the island of your listener's interests."

In other words, how will your speech affect the life, fortune, and sacred honor of your listener? How will your message help his health, peace of mind, and family security? How will you give him the jump on his competitors, help him face creditors, and save him from the tax collector?

The important fourth stage. Most speakers go through three stages, the good speakers achieve a fourth. First, they struggle and strain to prepare a speech; second, they get to their feet and give it; third, they settle back relieved that *they* have expressed *their* thoughts on the subject. They have gotten the job off their chests; they feel much better. But a fourth step remains: it is to examine the speech from the other fellow's viewpoint: Does it tell the audience what that audience wants to know? With this question in mind, the speaker should rewrite the speech, and if he has another chance, give it in a way that helps the audience accept the ideas into their minds—not just in a way that makes him feel he had unloaded his painfully formulated thoughts. As Mr. Borden points out: the audience asks, "Why bring up this subject anyway?" It sounds like a selfish statement, but that's the way most audiences are. They think, "What's in it for me?"

For examples of opening sentences that grip a reader's attention and at the same time personalize the subject so that he feels it relates to his private life, see almost any issue of popular magazines like *Reader's Digest, Saturday Evening Post,* and so forth. Read the first sentence of almost any of the articles and you'll find your attention gripped. Start that first sentence, and you'll read on into the article. Note, too, how often the writers begin with a question; a practice that can be overdone, but when you cannot think of a better way, try a question. It automatically calls for audience interest.

Or, suppose the publisher of this book began an advertisement with these words: "This book discusses many of the elements of effective writing and speaking." Would that motivate you to read it in the same way as would the following sentence? "This book will help you earn more money by enhancing your ability to write and speak more effectively."

Three tips for gaining an audience's attention and interest:

1. Show immediately why the audience will gain by listening to you. "What I say here tonight will save you money. . . ." "Do you want to cut costs and improve sales?" (Who will not listen to your next words?)

2. Study the *Reader's Digest* technique of opening a topic without a bang, flash of color, or fancy gimmick, but with a question, challenging statement, or promise of profit and benefit to the reader.

3. Be quick to answer the audience's—not your own—unspoken question: "Why bring that up? Why should I listen?" The real issue is not that you should unload your mind, but that you should present to them what *they want* to hear or *ought* to hear.

Give Your Audience a Roadmap

The third element of a good introduction is a hint or explanation of what you are going to say, what your presentation will consist of, and what you expect to accomplish. You need not provide a long, complete, or detailed roadmap, but do say enough to prepare the audience for what is coming.

Over 150 years ago, Henry Taylor, in his famous little book, *The Statesman,* (reprinted in 1958 with an introduction by C. Northcote Parkinson—of "Parkinson's Law"), explained that one should distinctly announce the tenor of one's argument from the outset in order to help the hearers. He wrote:

"These are well-known rules, which were superfluous to cite . . . but examples may be occasionally observed . . . of juvenile orators who will keep the secret of the end they aim at until they shall have led their hearers through the long chain . . . in order that they may produce a sort of surprise by forcing a sudden acknowledgment of what had not been foreseen. The disadvantage of this method is that it puzzles and provokes the hearer through the sequence, and confounds him in the conclusion: the only advantage is an overcharged impression of the orator's ingenuity. . . . It is a method by which the business of the argument is sacrificed to a puerile ostentation in the conduct of it—the ease and satisfaction of the auditors to the vanity of the arguer." On the other hand, the lack of a roadmap at the beginning often indicates the speaker does not have a clear idea himself where he is going and what his stages will be along the way.

Let's return to our school teachers for examples of good and bad roadmaps. Did you like the teachers who started off on a ramble and when they finished a topic rambled onto another? They depended too heavily on transitions such as, "Well, now let's show the movie." Or, "It's about time for a test, so break out paper and pencils." Their students cannot be sure which books to have ready, must less which mental gears to keep enmeshed, as teacher jumps from topic to topic.

Similarly, don't you prefer the business speaker who gives you at least a one-sentence explanation of what he is going to do? For example: "In my talk today, I'll spend about five minutes on budgeting, five on reports to top management, and the remaining five minutes for questions from the audience."

Or, "Our presentation will start with an introduction by Mr. Black. Then Mr. Brown will show the slides of Factory ABC's layout. Mr. Green will explain the costs involved. And I'll return for the summary and questions and answer period. The whole presentation will take 45 minutes."

After such an announcement, an audience can pay attention to what is being said, and not fret about how soon they can leave, or sit wondering if they are going to hear about a facet that interests them. Just letting people know you'll answer questions later can be a great reassurance to many of them.

The Shorter the Introduction the Better

Professor Henry Roberts, a leading public speaking teacher of Washington, D.C., has said that in over 30 years of helping business and government executives write speeches, improve speeches, and give speeches, he has noted again and again that the introduction tends to be too long. He has said, in effect, "When I'm handed a speech to read I skip the first paragraph and sometimes the first page, and I've yet to miss anything important. When asked to edit a speech, I usually begin by cutting out most of the opening remarks."

The reasons in favor of a short introduction are:

1. The longer version is rarely needed.

2. Your reason for speaking is the message in the body of your presentation. The more time you save for it, the better.

3. Some important members of your audience or group may have to leave early. You want to give them as much of your message as possible before they go. Don't take up their time with a long introduction.

But, whether long or short, one sentence or ten, be sure your Introduction includes a word, a phrase, a question, a statement, or a comment to accomplish each of these three elements:

1. Catch the audience's attention—but with something related to the message that is to come.

2. Give the audience a reason why they should listen to you. You will make money for them, solve their family problems, help them understand the world situation, improve their health, mental well-being, etc.

3. State a simple guide or roadmap to what you are going to do. Tell them what they can expect you to do, and what you expect them to watch for, listen for, or be prepared to accept, or cooperate with.

II. THE BODY OF A PRESENTATION

The patterns of a presentation are: narration; cause and effect; contrast and comparison; enumeration; argument; demonstration; illustration; discussion; definition and description, problem, investigation, solution.

Sometimes the subject matter governs the choice of pattern of presentation, sometimes the needs of the audience, and sometimes the choice is based on the conscious or unconscious predilections of the author or speaker. In fact, all too many men automatically commit themselves to one pattern and use it repeatedly—ofttimes blindly and awkwardly. When you next prepare a speech ask yourself, "Could I use another pattern to good advantage instead of the pattern I automatically selected first?" Such a checking will take only a minute or so, and may give you several ideas on how to organize your presentation or on how to re-organize segments of the presentation.

Narration is an easy and natural pattern to follow: you tell the story in chronological order. For example: "Last year we had a call from the building inspector. He told us to repair the chimneys on the XYZ plant. We obtained the services of the ABC Construction Company." And so on. The chronological pattern has the advantage of being easy to remember when you are on your feet. It has the inherent danger of leading to rambling and extraneous detail. Too often the speakers sound like school boys telling how they spent their vacations: "And then . . . and then . . . and then . . .and then . . ."

Hint: Keep the story about past events short and succinct. Avoid the natural tendency to talk about what happened to you; cut short the history; and concentrate on the present and future, which are more likely to interest the audience. A *business* audience is interested not in the history as history, but as information that helps them understand the present and helps them chart the course of the future. *You* may enjoy recalling events you have lived through, but you should control the urge to tell about any events except those which relate directly to what the *audience* needs to know in order to make *their* decisions. The secret of being boring, said a sage, is to tell everything. For our purposes let's add: everything of interest to the speaker but not really needed by the audience.

Definition, description, and *enumeration* are alike in that you try to identify to your audience exactly what you are talking about.

Don't use "definitions" or "getting the terms straight" as crutches or stalls from facing the real issues. Too many speakers begin by saying, "Let's turn to the dictionary for our definition of our subject today. When I looked up *Leadership,* I found that Webster said . . ." and so on. Usually, these episodes of definition in a speech are just padding which at best fool only the speaker and some of his audience into thinking for a while they are really digging into the accurate facts. Most of the time, however, they are simply getting or giving a verbal massage using tautological terminology. A good parody of this approach was given in "The All-Purpose Management Speech" by Vivienne Marquis (*Supervisory Management.*[1]) The "All-Purpose

1 April, 1960, pp. 27-31.

Speech" is supposed to be on "Trends, Aspects, and Implications," and the speaker is supposed to say:

Now Webster says a trend means, and I quote, "to have or take a particular direction."

In other words: *Where do we go from here?*"

Webster defines an aspect as "appearance, view—of objects, etc." And an implication is "the act of implicating or state of being implicated."

Finally, Webster says a challenge is, and I quote, "an invitation to engage in a contest; specif., a summons to fight, as a duel; also, the message conveying the summons."

The "All-Purpose Management Speech" in Vivienne Marquis' rendition rambles on in an inspired series of cliches and confused repetitions of the type which are all too common. The foregoing excerpt shows how useless to an audience a dictionary definition can be. However, when special terms are used, or when a new process or product or problem involves special terminology, then a word or two of informal, practical "for instance" type of definition is worthwhile. But a definition should not be a crutch or a gimmick on which you support your whole talk.

Similarly, a speaker can too readily deceive himself into thinking his careful description of details, or his enumeration of materials, items, or "factors bearing on the case" are advancing the purpose of his presentation. Often when the time comes for description or enumeration, a visual aid can do the trick in a minute—for example, a photograph or two of the materials or objects, and a chart of the items of real importance—and save five minutes of verbiage.

Hint: Don't be too insistent on "defining the terms." If the terms are easy to define, your speech probably is not necessary! Indeed, if your speech is really needed, it is probably because the terms are hard to define. And, if you give a good presentation, the audience will understand the terms in the right context, which is something a dictionary cannot do for them. Test your own descriptions and enumerations with these questions: Are they simply padding? Are you piling up words because you cannot think of a sharper way of presenting the issues for information and decisions?

Demonstration and illustration involve the use of presentation aids. Note the distinction between *speaker's aids* and *presentation aids*. A speaker's aid might be his script or a card with notes on it—something he uses to help him give the presentation. A presentation aid is, for example, a chart or film which the speaker shows to the audience. The presentation aid carries part or all of the message to the audience.

Demonstration includes the actual operation of devices and equipment, whether models, mock-ups, or actual equipment to be used in a process. Illustration includes visual and audial aids—films, strips, charts, photographs, tape recordings, drawings, etc. (More about these in Chapter Eight.)

Argument and *reasoning* patterns can be pretty dry even to lawyers and professors who are perhaps more used to them than anyone else. For most audiences you should dress up your arguments with stories, examples ("for instances"), and visual aids. The more abstract a line of argument, the more you have to try to express it in visual terms; "visualizing the abstract" will be a continuing challenge.

An old theory—it goes back to the ancient Greek rhetoricians—held that you should start with a strong argument, sandwich your weaker argument in the middle, and then finish with your strongest argument. Proponents of this arrangement believe that the weakness of the argument in the middle of your speech will be overlooked, and by having the "killer-diller" at the end, you will leave the audience convinced. The purpose of the strong argument at the beginning is to hold their attention, start them with a favorable feeling toward you, and to help hide the weakness of the argument sandwiched in the middle.

A newer theory recommends you begin with your strongest argument. It is based on the findings of some psychologists that the average person is most impressed during the first ten minutes or so of a discourse, after which his attention begins to wander. Also, the proponents believe if you use your strongest argument and convince the hearers from the outset, then they are on your side and accept all your subsequent statements more readily.

There are merits to both approaches, and no doubt, the types of arguments, the nature of the subject and the audience and the speaker can make a difference when deciding what order to follow. For *business presentations*, the new theory is probably safer to follow, though not necessarily for the psychological reasons (which may or may not be possible to prove). What governs the choice in a business presentation is the factor of time and the possibility of losing your audience. The modern executive considers ten minutes a long time for a speech; usually, too, he has three more appointments and is late for them. If you want to sell something to the chairman of the board, president, vice-president, and general manager, you had better state your strongest argument immediately. If you hold it back for five minutes, you may not get the chance to use it. The phone may ring, another caller may show up, or they may decide not to listen to you any further. So lead with an ace.

Even if you have no fear of losing your audience—physically, that is, for their minds may leave you—and have been promised no interruptions for 30 or 40 minutes, the fact remains that modern audiences are conditioned to the TV and radio 15-minute and 30-minute programs. After allowances have been made for station breaks, introductions, and commercials, the speaker actually has 12 minutes or 24 minutes in which to speak. In so short a time, one can develop only two or three major points. The safest procedure is to start with your strongest argument and work down to the weaker ones.

As a matter of fact, since the time is so short, it is probably a good idea to leave out the weak arguments altogether because you will barely have time to get the strongest and stronger ones across! In the ancient days "orations" lasted an hour or two hours (sometimes even longer) and there was time to tell everything about a subject. But, as Carlyle has said, "There isn't time to read all the good books; there is only time to read the best." Nowadays, we can paraphrase that statement thus, "There isn't time to give all the good arguments; just barely time enough to state the best."

Discussion and conference techniques and patterns are covered in Chapter Nine. Here, we will simply point out that a whole presentation can be developed using a conference method, or part of a presentation can be built around discussion. The important thing to remember is what sort of conference method you are using and to warn or explain to your audience what you are doing and why.

Problem, investigation, solution is an obvious pattern requiring no explanation. Our hint here is: Go easy on your description of the problem and investigation and use the time to explain the solution and tell how it can benefit the audience.

Use Plenty of Examples

Mr. Borden (*Public Speaking—As Listeners Like It*) says that the body of your speech must be keyed to one relentless audience demand —*for instance!* By this he means that you bolster each statement, each point by an example, a story, a statistic, or an anecdote about a famous or important person.

Build the Body First

Usually the best approach to a presentation is to build the Body of it first. (More about this in the chapters on writing.) Get your message organized and clearly stated, and you will find that the Title, Materials, Introduction, and Summary will become that much more obvious to you. The worst three words to the speech writer, says Henry Roberts, are "Ladies and Gentlemen." The writer puts those words at the top of the page and then sits staring at the blank page wondering what brilliant introductory words must come next. Alas, he often ends by writing, "As I drove here today, I thought . . ." or, "I saw . . ." or, "So and So said to me. . . ."

If you jot down what you want the audience to learn, the introduction and summary and other parts will flow from your message. Above all, when cutting to save time, cut first the Introduction, then the Summary, and finally the Body. If you have to cut out much of the Body, then you started with too much fat, or you are talking on the wrong subject, or to the wrong audience.

But let's assume you have a good Introduction and a good Body, and you are ready for the third essential element: a good Summary.

III. THE SUMMARY OF A PRESENTATION

A summary does one or all of the following:

1. Reviews salient points of a presentation.

2. Reminds audience of major points and related points as necessary.

3. Emphasizes particular points *this* audience is to remember.

A good summary is brief, to the point, hits the right spots, and *does not contain anything that was not stated or implied in the body of the presentation.*

Father Daniel Power, S.J., Director of the Georgetown University TV and Radio Forum, once described a good summary in terms like the following: Assume there is a TV listener watching your program. As he watches your picture fade from the screen, or as he gets up to turn off the TV set, what do you want him to think? What two or three main ideas should he retain? What should he walk away saying to himself? You should decide what you want the viewer to think or do and then make those key points your summary. Be sure the body of your presentation builds toward them, and that your introduction leads into the structure that builds toward them.

Think about that comparison for a moment. When you finish a speech, what final words do you want your audience to carry away with them? When you dim out of their mental TV screens, what statements, what ideas, should they hear ringing in their ears?

Mr. Borden expresses the idea in the slang phrase, "So what?" He says that the conclusion of your speech must be more than a graceful leave-taking, more than a review, more than a reminder—it must answer the audience's question: "So what?" In other words, you should seek some action from your audience, some action response which is within their power to give.

Business presentations range over many types and purposes, and often they are intended—on the surface anyway—simply to impart information or explain rules and procedures. Often there are implied requests for action, trust, confidence, or more support, but just as often you cannot ask for what you really want in blunt words. For example, you have explained a new budget procedure to a group of peers and superiors. You may want to cry out: "For heaven's sake, now, remember this procedure, follow it, publicize it, and give me the credit for it!" But all you can do is end by asking, "Any questions?"—and you hope that the beauty and clarity of your presentation as well as the inherent merit of the procedure will get across to the group and you hope that they will do all the things you cannot openly demand of them.

It is also just a matter of terminology whether you consider an "action demanding summary" as part of the summary or as part of the body of your presentation. One might well argue that the body should include the "so what" conclusions, findings, and recommendations, and then the summary need only restate and reemphasize them.

The main thing is to have a summary. Most beginning speakers, and many who think themselves quite advanced, all too often miss the chance for a final few sentences to button up and button down their presentation. Look on it as your last chance to remind the audience of the main points you have made, to recall the places you and they visited on your roadmap, and tell them what they should have gotten out of your presentation—and what they should do about it, if anything.

The main error in most summaries is to drag in a new topic, start off on a new tangent, or put forth statements you have not mentioned in the body. In the speaker's mind the "extra added" conclusions and recommendations may be clear, but if he has not talked about them, or explained them or argued for them in the body of his talk, how is the audience to know what they are and why they should be accepted?

Hint: Check your presentation to see if you have a good Summary at the end of it. Does this Summary leave the audience with a restate-

ment of the vital parts of your message? If it doesn't, go back to see
what was wrong with the body of your presentation. If you cannot
write or speak a good Summary, there must be something wrong with
your presentation. Check also to see that statements in your Summary have really been supported in the Body of the presentation. In
short, a Summary in addition to being a convenience for the audience
is a measuring stick by which you may check the completeness and
orderliness of the statement of your message.

SUMMING UP THIS CHAPTER

This chapter has discussed the three essential elements of an effective presentation—the introduction, body, and summary.

A good introduction should arouse attention, motivate your audience to listen to you, and provide them with a roadmap to see where
you are going to take them.

The body, the message you intend to give, is the truly vital part of
the presentation; if you must cut the length of your speech, cut into
the introduction and then the summary before you touch the body.

The summary serves to remind the audience of salient points, to
emphasize special features, and to repeat requests for action or
decision.

Some things to remember especially are:

1. Keep the introduction short; don't use gimmicks that shock
or fascinate an audience to the extent that they are distracted from
your message; and do give them reasons why *they* will profit if they
listen to you.

2. Expect your mind to have its favorite pattern of presentation,
but be willing to check this pattern against other possible patterns.
There may be a better one for *this subject* and *this audience.* Reread
this chapter to remind yourself of the various possible patterns.

3. In a short business presentation, start with your strongest and
most effective arguments. If you save the best argument for last, you
may not get a chance to use it.

4. The introduction and summary will come much more easily
if you prepare the body first. Of course, you can always begin the
job by stating the main points you want to make: These will turn out
to be your summary as well as the core of your presentation.

5. Consider the summary your last chance to tell your audience
the most important features of your message. Think of it, too, as a
check on your presentation: what is vital in the *body,* ought to re-
appear at least briefly in the *summary;* whatever is in the *summary,*

ought first to have been explained or proven in the *body* of the presentation.

We are now ready to take up the other steps of a presentation, which though not so vital as the Introduction, Body, and Summary, yet contribute immensely to the effectiveness of a presentation. Indeed, they often make the difference between failure and success. The next chapter will explain why this is so, and what you can do about it.

4

THREE STEPS THAT HELP YOU ORGANIZE A PRESENTATION

The previous chapter explained the *three essential* elements of an effective presentation: Introduction, Body, and Summary. The SPAIBASCATH chart gives *seven* more steps, which though not absolutely essential, can make the difference between a poor presentation and a great one.

In this chapter, we will discuss the three steps which help you organize an effective presentation. These are:

1. *Subject*—the topic and its label or title.
2. *Aids*—materials, references, props.
3. *Purpose*—statement of the objectives you have in mind for the audience in question.

These sound simple, but are too often overlooked. The speaker who knows how to use them, and who begins by checking them off on the SPAIBASCATH chart, will find his presentations easier to prepare, to give, and to get results with.

The next chapter, Chapter Five, will cover the remaining four steps: Audience Action, Check Up, Aftermath, and Take Home.

The Subject—How to Get a Good Title

Quite often an inexperienced speaker remembers that his school teachers of composition and public speaking told him: "Get an interesting, a dynamic, a provocative title." So he struggles to think of something clever. Perhaps you have noticed that a wet blanket can be cast over a person by demanding of him: "Say something funny." The same deadening effect can happen to you, if you begin by telling yourself, "Think of a clever title."

27

Hence, the SPAIBASCATH chart uses "Subject" where it might have used "Title" or "Label" or "Provocative Title." Yes, you want a good title, but you will find one more easily if you back into the search for it. Let's explain.

The simplest way to get a good title is to write the whole speech first. When you have it prepared, and perhaps have rehearsed it once or twice, you need only look closely at the purpose of speech and the summary, and the title will practically write itself.

Suppose you are assigned to talk on the budget for your department for the next year. There is your general subject, the budget for the coming year, so label the file "Budget Presentations." Or, suppose you have been asked to address the PTA or your Trade Association on the Business Budgeting Processes of your own advanced and enlightened company. You may expect to make such a talk only once in your life; even so, you should file it. The very fact that you are asked to speak on a certain subject indicates you must be identified with that subject, and if so, you can expect to be called on again to tell about the same or a related subject. Don't throw away your old speeches; keep them plainly labelled so you can find them quickly and save the work of relocating references and data. Moreover, if you know what you have said before, you can more easily add on or switch to new ideas. Many men do not realize how much they repeat themselves until they see their speeches in writing or hear them played back on tapes.

While you may use different titles on different occasions to interest a certain audience or to emphasize a special slant, you should file the speech by *subject*. Don't be like the plumbing engineer who titled his talk on new developments in jubilee pipe patches as "A Dream Come True." How could anyone guess that that presentation was on pipe patches? It could have been on almost any topic in the world. Thus you label your subject "Budgeting" rather than "The Paperwork Route to More Profits"—though you might use that more provocative heading as the *title* to your speech. A complete title might be "Business Budgeting—Paperwork That Earns Profits." Now, your hearers will know what to expect of your presentation, and will have a hint about your approach to the topic.

Five Hints for Getting Good Titles

Let's recapitulate our suggestions for handling the matter of a good subject/topic/title:

1. Prepare the whole presentation, then pick a title for it.
2. Decide on the general subject area; your title should have at least a word to indicate the subject area; next think of the specific

audience and of the aspect of the topic you will emphasize; and, finally, try to put into the title something to indicate the importance of the subject to the audience.

3. Don't try too hard to come up with a short "punchy" title. You are not writing newspaper headlines with limitations on space. Use a long sentence, if need be. Be grammatical.

4. Although you may not think so, there may be other occasions when you will talk on the same subject, so label and file the presentation.

5. Be sure your title actually covers the subject matter—that it does not promise more than you can produce, and that other strange bedfellows do not creep under the same tent. If new topics belong in the presentation, expand the title to cover them.

Purpose or Objective—Focus the Message, Avoid Rambling

You may or may not state out loud in your Introduction your exact purpose or objective in talking to the audience. You will, as we said earlier, give them an idea of what you are going to talk about and why they should listen. In a teaching situation, you almost always can state your objective in open terms. For example: "The purpose of this chapter and the next chapter is to explain the seven valuable, but not essential, parts of a presentation and to give hints regarding their effective use." Or, "The objective of this session on safety is to demonstrate the mouth-to-mouth rescue breathing method."

However, for certain subjects and occasions you cannot be so blunt. For example, you may not want to say out loud: "The objective of this talk will be to convince you people that you have been stupid blockheads and that you must now reverse your prejudices and act another way."

But, for your own effectiveness, you should state at the head of your speech or notes the purpose of your speech. Don't try to get away with a vague objective like, "I'll tell them something about the new budget." Or, "I'll jolly them along a bit and then slip in a few digs about coming to work on time." Such casually stated purposes lead to rambling and clumsy speeches.

If you cannot state your purpose clearly and in terms of what the audience, as a consequence of your presentation, is to learn, think, do, or feel, you are not ready to give the presentation.

I mentioned earlier an experience with the Georgetown University Forum. On another occasion, I assisted with the plans for a program which was to involve a discussion on "Can Engineers Make Good Managers?" About halfway through the planning, the director, Professor Power, asked, "Just what is the purpose of this program?"

One of the participants, a distinguished engineer, but a man inexperienced in public appearances, replied, "What purpose? Why do we need a purpose? I thought we were just to sit around and discuss what certainly sounds like an interesting topic."

Professor Power replied patiently, "The audience will want more than that, even if the audience doesn't realize it immediately. Just aimless discussion is not enough. You need some objective or purpose about which to build the discussion. Even if you cannot agree on a final conclusion or recommendation, you should state for your own clarity of intent and organization that the objective of the program is to discuss two, three, or four aspects of the issue, and to inform the audience of the state of the question, factors bearing on it, and probable future consequences and related matters."

The engineer thought a moment, and then agreed whole-heartedly. The planning of the program went quickly ahead as soon as the participants had formulated a purpose for it.

It is a lack of a stated objective that makes so many teachers ramble through their classes. Similarly, many a business presentation is ruined because the speaker stands up "to say a few words" and goes on and on. He should have stood up to say words whose purpose was to inform the audience of such and such a fact—or to alert them to such and such a danger or opportunity—or to persuade them to adopt such and such an attitude.

Returning to the presentation on budgeting: Suppose you stated your purpose as: "To inform the ZYX Department of the new budget requirements, to obtain their cooperation in adhering to the new standards, and to list for them the nine changes to make and the six possible errors to avoid." Now what you say can be focussed towards accomplishing those objects—and you can measure each word, gesture, joke, and chart that goes into your presentation on the basis of: "Will it advance the stated purpose of my talk?"

Five Hints for Formulating Your Purpose or Objective

1. Jot down your *general purpose*—what you hope to accomplish —and leave this aside until you have roughed out the whole presentation. Then go back and examine your statement of your purpose. If you have gotten new ideas that are worthwhile or important enough to include, you can incorporate the requirement for them in the statement of purpose. On the other hand, if your statement of purpose remains the same, check the presentation to see if it really will accomplish your purpose. Also, see if there are any loose ends extraneous to your purpose.

2. Try to state the purpose in one clear, complete sentence. "The purpose of this presentation is to show the members of the Accountants' Association how the ZYZ Company handles its budgeting process."

3. If you have any hidden objectives, state them in the *purpose*. Check to see if your presentation will get the hidden objectives across in an unwarped, unconfused fashion. If you intend just to "play some mood music" for your audience, be sure to state the fact plainly to yourself. Otherwise, you may just kid yourself about your chances of obtaining the effects you desire.

4. The same *subject* matter can be used in connection with many different *purposes*. The subject and title are not the same as the *purpose* of your presentation, but they certainly should hang together.

5. When a presentation, your own or someone else's, doesn't seem "to jell," or if it rambles or leaves questions floating in the air, start your diagnosis and treatment by looking at the *purpose*. If the purpose is clearly stated, and kept in front of the presenter, the other parts of the presentation will fall more easily into place. And, each word, chart, action, or "gimmick" can be more easily justified—or eliminated.

The Place of Aids in the Presentation

The use of *aids*, such as charts, in a presentation is explained in Chapter Eight. Here we will show where they fit in your outline and in the organization of your speech.

Obviously, an *aid* appears during a presentation at the point where it is needed or will do the most good. A chart can be used in the Introduction, Body, or Summary; a tape recording, film, or blackboard can be used in the main parts of your presentation or can be saved for the Audience Action or even Aftermath portions. On the SPAIBASCATH chart they are listed ahead of the Introduction where they will not be overlooked.

Among the *aids* you might list are:

1. *References*—books, dictionaries, handbooks, manuals; and reference material to bring with you for use during the presentation or for assistance in answering questions.

2. *Visual Aids*—charts, graphs, pictures, films, transparencies, photographs. (Don't forget chalk for the chalkboard, or crayon for the easel board!)

3. *Devices*—models, cutaways, actual pieces of equipment.

Four Hints for Organizing for Aids

1. Jot down possible *aids* as you think of them. You can discard the unsuitable ones later, meanwhile keep a list lest you forget a possible aid.

2. Before giving a presentation, check your list of *aids* to see that you have everything ready. Somebody might have borrowed that excellent chart on the budgeting process from your file and forgotten to return it!

3. After you have roughed out your presentation, check the list of possible *aids* again. Check to see what reference materials might be included; where a chart or drawing might be shown; where a device or model could be demonstrated; or if some audio-visual equipment might be employed to good advantage. If you have thought of the use of an aid, and decided against it, that's fine; but if you aren't using one simply because you failed to think of the possibilities, you may be missing a good bet. Most inexperienced speakers tend to think only in terms of what they will say; it usually takes months, even years, of practice, and considerable coaxing and coaching, to persuade them to replace some of their wordage by pictures and by demonstrations. Whenever I have challenged a student (and the students were all over 30 years of age, and already in the middle-management bracket) to think of a possible aid to use with his presentation, he has been able to think of a good one; and, after developing and using it, has admitted it improved his speech. *But he had to be reminded of the existence of the aids.* Do this reminding for yourself and for others whose presentations you are called upon to review or criticize. At least think of the aid before you decide not to use it.

4. Don't adopt aids solely to "pretty up" your presentation. Each one should do something specific and helpful to carry forward the *purpose* of your presentation.

This chapter has covered the place of Subject, Purpose, and Aids, in your SPAIBASCATH plan of a presentation. Later chapters will cast more light on the use of these elements in written as well as in oral presentations.

Now, let us go to the next chapter for the discussion of the four elements: *Audience Action, Check Up, Aftermath,* and *Take Home.* At the end of that chapter we will sum up both these chapters.

5

USING THE AUDIENCE TO ENSURE SUCCESS: FOUR STEPS

The remaining four steps or part of our SPAIBASCATH Chart are:

Audience Action—participation or application on the part of your audience, whether one or many persons.

Check-Up—testing the effectiveness of your way of making the presentation.

Aftermath—message reinforcements for a later date.

Take Home—handouts for audience to take with them.

These steps involve the audience and therefore have immense leverage with respect to ensuring your success which, in the last analysis, is dependent on the audience's *acceptance* of you and your message.

AUDIENCE ACTION—SUCCESS INSURANCE

Return, for a moment, to the third grade. After Miss Brown, the teacher, had explained long division, she said, "Now, children, go to the blackboard and work the following problems." Or later in high school, when the math teacher said, "Break out paper and pencil and try your hand at the algebra problems in your textbook." And, in college, the chemistry professor may have said, "After my lecture today on titration, we will go to the laboratory and work the experiments on the analysis of solutions." In the language of the educator, the teachers were making the students *apply* what they had learned.

If you took military training, you may remember how range practice was taught: the instructor explained the method of aiming the
rifle and squeezing the trigger. Next, half the group fired the rifles
while the other half stood by as "coaches"; each "coach" watching
one of the "doers" fire a rifle. Then, the coaches and doers changed
places. Classroom teachers use this method when they assign half
their students to work on the blackboard while the others watch for
errors.

Can you bring *application* into a presentation? Into a public
speech? Should you try to do so? The modern answer to these questions is an unqualified yes, you ought to try and to keep trying. Indeed, a good presentation lacks something if it lacks *application*, i.e.
audience action or *participation*. On the other hand, a poorly organized presentation can be saved, and even turned into a success by the
use of *audience action*.

On our SPAIBASCATH Chart, *Audience Action* comes after
"Body" and before "Summary." Normally, the participation is part
of the main body of the presentation. You tell or show the audience,
then you have them apply or practice what they have learned; later
when you sum up you remind them of what they have done. However,
participation and *audience action* can be, and often should be, used
in the Introduction and in the Summary as well as anywhere in the
Body of the presentation. Some form of participation can be very
effective in the Introduction to warm up the audience, increase their
interest, and start *them doing their own thinking* about what they
are to hear. Audience Action in the form of discussion can be most
effective in the Summary. Whenever possible get various members
of the audience to help you sum up the presentation. They can be
guided into doing a good job and the impact becomes double on them
when they hear themselves expressing your key points.

Why is Audience Action so Important? If you have ever read a
book or an article or heard a lecture on human relations and communications, you know that "getting people to express themselves"
and to put a message "in their own words" is considered vital for
obtaining their cooperation. Unfortunately, too many people inter-
pret this concept too narrowly: they assume it is only applicable to
small groups and to supervisor-subordinate relationships; they do not
think of its potential with large groups—indeed, with any audience,
whether you are meeting with them on a first or last occasion.

Everyone likes to participate, and the speaker who can get the
other fellows into the act is always that much more interesting to them.

Moreover, as teacher knows, an audience has not really learned
until it has tried out the new knowledge. You can not say you know

how to fire a rifle until you have pulled the trigger and hit the bull's eye yourself. You do not know how to calculate a budget estimate until you have tried it on the company's forms. An audience has not come to grips with new ideas and attitude until its members have formulated the arguments in their own words, have expressed them out loud, and have tested them with questions and answers.

Once you have led a good discussion or question-and-answer period and have seen people's faces light up with interest, and have heard them state your case for you, you will be sold on the practice. At the next meetings you attend, note which method is more interesting to you and to the others: the one where the speaker gives his prepared address and sits down, or the one where the speaker gives a short talk and then holds a question-and-answer period. Note, too, how the professional speakers, the politicians have tended more and more in recent years to depend on the question period rather than on long formal speeches. Mr. Clayton Fritchey, formerly Deputy Director of the Democratic National Committee, says, "The Q and A, once merely a nonfunctional appendage, is rapidly becoming as large as or larger than the body of the speech."

"Sure," you may reply, "Discussion, participation, demonstration, and so forth, make for a more interesting class, conference, or TV program. But I can't use participative methods in my presentation to the board of directors, to the executive committee, or before a large audience of 500 people at an annual meeting."

"Can't you?"

I have asked this question of group after group of persons I have taught or worked with to improve their presentations and speeches.

"No, because . . ." Their voices trail off as they begin, perhaps for the first time in their lives, to think that there are ways of obtaining participation even when speaking to the top executives and before large audiences as well as small ones.

"How about suggesting a way?" I ask.

One man replies, "You could hand the members of the board of directors a piece of paper with the figures on it and suggest they see if the percentages you predict will come out."

Another man says, "Even with a large audience you could call for a show of hands on some issue."

So they go on until they have discussed the following methods:

1. Actual experience with a device, formula, gadget, or product.
2. Questions to the audience.
3. Questions from the audience.
4. Audience demonstrations; if all can't do it, then one or two rep-

resent the audience in manipulating a device or writing some on a chalkboard.

5. General discussion—guided by the speaker.

When we finish the list I point out to them that I have actually conducted an Audience Action session with them. Instead of handing them a prepared list, I had had them think of the items and had accomplished four things: (1) they had paid better attention, enjoyed the session more than they would have, had it been a straight lecture; (2) they had visualized each method as it could be used by them in a specific situation—with seniors, with juniors, with large outside groups; (3) they had actually participated in an application session and now could see better the value of Audience Action in a teaching or speaking period; and (4) they had broken through the unconscious barrier that had kept them from thinking of using participative methods in their own speaking situations.

Three Hints for Audience Action

The first hint, of course, is to keep Audience Action on your check-list, and try to figure out ways of obtaining it—not excuses for avoiding it.

1. Try to put some participation in the Introduction and Summary, as well as in the Body of your speech.

2. Don't let the size of the crowd scare you. Some "experts" on group dynamics say that conferences and discussions should be limited to 9 to 15 persons. But I know many discussion leaders who have regularly obtained excellent results with groups of 100 persons and more.

3. When in doubt, schedule *twice* as much participation as seems adequate. Most speakers err on the side of too little participation rather than too much. The audiences love it; they enjoy it; they will never protest against too much talking or action on their part, but they will regret too little. One often sees speaker evaluation sheets with the comment, "not enough group participation; too much monologue." One never sees the comment, "too much group participation."

CHECK-UP, AFTERMATH, AND TAKE HOME

So far, we have covered the SPAIBAS of SPAIBASCATH—that is, we have explained the purpose and use of:

Subject (Title, Topic)	Body (Main Part)
Purpose (Objective)	Audience Action (Application)
Aids (Materials, Props)	Summary
Introduction	

Now, we will take up the last three elements:

Check-Up (Testing)

Aftermath (Assignment)

Take Home (Handouts)

These can play very valuable roles in your presentations. Because they are often overlooked, we will give them added emphasis here.

Check-Up—Did the Audience Get the Message Loud and Clear?

There can be confusion between *Audience Action* and *Check-Up*, but if there is, no harm will be done. In the course of a discussion or question-and-answer period, you can often detect the hazy spots in the audience's understanding of the message you have given them. However, there is a difference which is worth bearing in mind. The purpose of *Audience Action* is to give the audience a chance to practice *their* skills, to use *their* knowledge, to express and formulate *their* thoughts for *their own benefit*. The purpose of Check-Up or testing is for you the speaker to find out how well *you* put the message across.

The purposes, therefore, of attempting a Check-Up on your presentation are:

1. To find what the audience has learned from you, what they have gained, and what they have missed.

2. To find out the errors or weaknesses in the presentation so that you can correct them.

3. To obtain criticism with regard to your speaking and presentation ability so that you can improve your presentations on other subjects to other audiences.

How can you run a Check-Up or Test during a speech? Again, the average man's first reaction is to say: "It can't be done. A teacher can say 'break out the blue books, we're going to have a test,' but I can't do that with the executive council or before a convention meeting."

"Can't you?" I have asked, and after awhile the objectors began to think of ways that they could use even in the "impossible" situations. Here are some of the techniques that have been proposed:

1. Questions oral and written on the points most likely to have been missed or misunderstood by the audience.

2. Recognition methods—for example, you hold up a picture of something or a large card with a term, diagram, formula, etc., on it and ask the audience to identify the parts and purposes.

3. Demonstrations by all or part of the audience. One or more men explain or demonstrate different segments of your presentation.

How well they do, and how the audience reacts can give you samplings of message penetration and dissemination.

4. Observation of faces and attitudes. While this is not too accurate a method, it is the most available. Some audiences are experts at keeping dead-pan faces (many executives fall into this class because they have spent years learning to appear noncommittal); others will beam with interest and approbation simply because they are polite. But during your summary or while you fire some test questions at them, you should be able to discern on their faces signs of understanding or of puzzlement.

5. Recording devices—for example, the testers of movies, advertisements, and TV shows use a set of push buttons connected to a computer so that an audience can register their reactions to each stage of a performance or commercial. Similarly, tape recorders and hidden cameras can obtain evidence of audience reactions.

Three Hints for Obtaining Check-Ups

1. The first hint, of course, is to try to think of some way of testing your audience to see how you have done. Devise your test so that it will answer the three questions: What has the audience missed; what do you need to improve the presentation; and what can you do to improve all your presentations?

2. Don't go on the offensive or defensive when the criticisms roll in. Remember the humbling rule of the professional educator: If the student has not learned, the teacher has not taught. Thus, if your hearers have not heard, understood, or bought your message, that is *your* fault, not theirs!

3. Keep trying to find ways of testing—each bit of information you obtain is vital feedback; it can lead you to all sorts of improvements.

Aftermath—How Long Will the Audience Retain the Message?

Remember how teacher said, "During the coming week, your study *assignment* will be to read the next two chapters in your textbook."? His or her purpose was to reinforce the lesson you had in class, or to prepare you for the next class.

Wouldn't it be wonderful if you could get the customer to learn more about your product on his own time? To get your subordinates to study more about the rules and procedures you are trying to teach them? To get your audience to recall your message and to think about it and to study subjects related to it during the days after they have heard from you? These are difficult things to accomplish, but such *Aftermaths* of your presentations are certainly worth thinking about.

The first objection, of course, is: "But I can't assign *homework* to my hearers! Imagine telling the boss he has to write a theme paper over the weekend!"

Are you sure you can't?

In the course of a talk you can recommend or praise a book, an article, or a report that helps carry your message or provides more background. You can say that you are available at such and such a time in your office or at home to discuss the matter further; you can recommend certain of the handouts, or you could even mail to the key members of your audience copies of the things you hope they will read. You can recommend future meetings, you can leave interesting questions to be answered later. The important thing is to try to think of something, and then think of ways of motivating your hearers to do that extra "homework." Remember, you motivate them by showing them why *they will profit* from the *assignment,* from the *aftermath,* you propose. Don't ask them to do it for your sake, show them how to do it for their own sakes.

For example, after I have finished a course or session on presentations, I discuss what the participants can do in the way of follow-up to reinforce what they have learned and to keep them improving without having to have a teacher standing by—or without having to spend more money or attend more classes. How can they go ahead on their own? They always think of the following methods, and they usually promise themselves, each other, and me that they will do some or all of the assignments. The ideas are:

1. *Further study*—readings in various books on how to improve one's speaking ability. (E.g., read the rest of this book; and also *Putting Yourself Over in Business* and *Executive's Guide to Handling People,* both books available from Prentice-Hall, Inc., Englewood Cliffs, New Jersey.)

2. *Practice*—one can practice SPAIBASCATH at work, at home, and even at play. Try the different steps when next you explain something to your colleagues, to friends, to your children.

3. *Observations*—observe the good points and mistakes of others, at work, at home, at play, at other meetings, and also the behavior and techniques of speakers on TV, radio, the cinema, and the stage. Once you start looking, you can learn much.

4. *Other teachers*—one can often take advantage of courses pro-

vided by a company, or held in the evenings nearby, or provided informally by organizations like *Toastmasters, Inc.*

In other words, if the audience has come to hear a presentation on a subject, one can reasonably infer that they want to know about the subject or ought to know about it. Therefore, there must be additional sources of information to them, and there must be reasons why they should make the effort to seek or accept the additional sources.

Five Hints for Obtaining More Effective Aftermath Cooperation

1. No one, or very few persons, can learn from or be sold by the "one-shot" exposure of a speech or presentation. Follow-up is necessary or greatly to be recommended. Before you decide it is impossible of attainment, try to think of something. With practice you will find the problem of *assignments* easier to solve.

2. First, pick what *you want* the audience to do in order to enhance their acceptance of your mesage; whatever Aftermath you give them ought to be to your advantage; but show them why *they will profit* from doing what you recommend.

3. Make sure that what you recommend will be available and interesting. Don't recommend books that are out of print, reports that are secret, or visits, trips, and courses that cost too much, or materials which the average person cannot understand or use without an instructor.

4. Be specific—don't just stir up a vague desire for future action; give the audience the exact things they can do to reinforce the message they are supposed to receive.

5. Above all, because Aftermath is something most people don't automatically think of by themselves, you should always check your own presentations and those which you supervise or advise on, for the inclusion of some Aftermath. Don't take the first "No, it's impossible; it won't work" for granted. Make yourselves or others think for at least five minutes—and try to prove something can be used, don't just try to prove nothing can be done in the way of Aftermath.

Take Home—Are Your Handouts Effective, or Are They Junk?

One rarely attends a meeting nowadays without being given a handout of some sort, from a sample product to a plastic briefcase full of booklets, charts, letters, and brochures. Obviously, the purposes are good, and the practice is to be recommended. The *Take-Home* materials can help with the *Audience Action*, though at a later time, and with the *Check-Up*, and *Assignment*. The handouts can help the audience do the things you didn't have time for them to do during the meeting. With a "mail-back" or "report-back" sheet, form, or card, you can test the audience's grasp of the subject and thereby help your *Check-Up* on the success of the presentation. By giving them something to use at a later time, you are assisting the *Aftermath* process.

Therefore, nearly everything we have said so far in support of *message reinforcement* goes double in favor of the use of Take-Home materials. In addition, the following quotation from Henry Taylor ("The Statesman") shows the importance of having carefully thought-out take-home or "leave-behind" materials to serve as reminders and as sources of further information. Taylor, discussing the matter of having a personal interview with an important person, e.g., a minister of State, says:

> ... In the rapid succession of topics which chase through the mind of a minister of state ... words spoken are for the most part as evanescent as those written on a running stream. ... But even if he should recollect what has been said for a day or two, with sufficient precision to give effect to it in business, that effect must be in writing. ...

Taylor adds that the minister will not have time to write the projects himself, so the man who wants the projects done should also bring the written resolution of it. This is obviously good business practice, and any successful executive knows that he is expected to bring an answer all worked out at the same time that he brings a problem or decision to his superiors. Strangely enough, the same man, when talking to an audience will not remember that 1,000 things chase through their minds, and that they will not recollect beyond a day or a week what he has said. Hence, he should leave with them reminders of his talk—an outline, or materials that continue presenting in permanent form the ideas and proposals he has made.

What's wrong with so many handouts? No doubt many of the handouts you have been given have seemed "junky," and you have dumped them unread. How can you avoid having the same thing happen to your handouts?

There are three main reasons why handouts become junky: (1) the men who make them do a poor job; they produce junk, just junk; (2) the items are well made and good in themselves, but do not belong with the subject matter; and (3) too many handouts are used and the audience is overwhelmed by them.

The answer to the first reason—poor workmanship—is to obtain better materials. If the handout does not have a quality appearance, don't use it. Don't let your people dump shoddy stuff on an audience.

It is all too easy for a speaker or for those who help him to think, "Let's gather some stuff and pass it out; maybe it will do some good." Unfortunately, such stuff may do some harm. In any case, the important thing to remember is that a handout should have a purpose, and to carry out its purpose it needs to be read and respected. If difficult to read, or unattractive in appearance, it defeats the purpose. A ten-cent item left unread is more costly than a fifty-cent one which is read and admired.

A more subtle trap consists in using nice-appearing but unsuitable handouts. The items are expensive, impressive, and excellent, but do not fit the purpose of your presentation. Again, the tendency to "dump on any audience" must be avoided. If you have one item that the audience could use and would use, then distribute it by itself, don't add five other items which can distract the audience from the significant item, or—worse—cause the audience to discard the useful piece along with the ones which are just padding.

You need discernment and firmness in avoiding these errors with regard to the use of handouts. The temptation is strong to overload on the excuse that "here is an opportunity to get the word around." A parallel with advertising practices and a parallel with public relations practices may make this warning clearer. The sophisticated advertisers allow for a lot of "white space" in their advertisements, and in each of their advertisements, they focus on *one* product and on *one or two* aspects of that product. The less expert advertisers try to make the same space carry all sorts of messages. Their advertisements become so crowded that a reader misses an item of real interest to him, because it is lost in the other sales copy. The latter type of advertiser can not overcome the tendency to think, "Since I'm paying for a half page, I might as well fill it up."

Similarly, a public relations manager likes to look busy and successful. But how does one measure success in public relations? One false but tempting way is by keeping count of the number of releases mailed each week. Thus editors of thousands of newspapers and magazines throughout the country complain about the useless mail which comes to them. For example, the editor of a medium-sized magazine reports an average of 75 pieces of public relations materials come in the mail to him every day. Of these, less than 10 actually relate to the type of things he prints, and of the 10 he can use perhaps one. The public relations people who send him these releases know, or should know if they are really professionals in the game, perfectly well that his magazine does not print the type of stories they send him. (For example, a news story on earth-moving equipment sent to the editor of a cosmetics magazine!) Why do the public relations people send the stuff? Because they can tell their bosses, "We sent out 100 pieces of public relations mail today. Got to keep our name before the editors." They don't admit that they ought to have sent out only 10 pieces to 10 carefully selected editors. They may impress their bosses, but they annoy the editors who have to wade through the useless mail before throwing it in the wastebasket.

All the foregoing is equally true when applied to a presentation: somebody will always think it is a good idea to slip a few extras in with the handouts you have prepared. "After all," they'll say, "why not? The pieces look pretty nice, and we might as well use them up. Always give the audience something to carry away, so let's give them a lot."

Yes, it is a good idea to give the audience something to carry away, but that something should be carefully selected and should be designed to be read by the particular audience. Otherwise, it will not be worth the weight of the paper and the cost of the ink.

Finally, even good handouts, when they are collected from many sources can form a pile that appears junky. The answer to this is to seek for a "family resemblance" among them. Note how many modern companies have developed a "family style" among their products, their buildings, their packages, and their advertising. They have variety, and yet there is a consistency, a repeated motif, or emblem, so that you know all the boxes belong to a certain company. As far as possible you should seek variety among your handouts, so they don't appear to be the same identical chart, brochure, or manual, but you should strive for a "family resemblance," a consistency among them that keeps them from appearing to be a hodge-podge of things thrown together.

Five Hints for Effective Handouts

1. Look for the possibility of a handout before you decide—out of ignorance, laziness, or inertia—that there are no handouts available or useful for the occasion.

2. Call attention to the Take-Home materials during your speech. Don't apologize for them or boast about them, but do explain what they are, where people in the audience are to pick them up, what their general contents are, and why the members of the *audience will profit* from taking the items (name the pieces, specifically) with them. Explain the purpose of the handouts, how many to take, and what other persons can use them so that the members of the audience will know to whom they might pass their copies.

3. Avoid a junky pile, seek pleasing variety within a general "family style."

4. Keep in mind the *presentation purpose* of the handouts—the message they are to carry or reinforce. Keep this purpose fixed clearly in your mind and you will avoid forgetting the handouts, misusing them, or dumping the wrong ones on an audience.

5. Combine them, where appropriate, with the *Aftermath* and *Check-Up* parts of your presentation. While they don't have to be correlated, it is reasonable that some of the "homework you assign" to the audience could involve the handouts, and some of the *testing* can make use of the handouts. In particular, certain handouts should contain mail-back cards. The return of these cards, and the orders, requests, complaints, or remarks on them, can help you check the successes and failures of the presentation—and of the handouts.

SUMMING UP THIS CHAPTER AND THE PREVIOUS CHAPTER

This chapter and the one before it have covered seven vitally helpful elements of an *effective* presentation: *Subject, Purpose, Aids, Audience Action, Check-Up, Aftermath,* and *Take Home.* Because these aspects are often overlooked or not developed fully, we have given them special attention and emphasis. The key rule with regard to all of them is: Don't overlook them; check them off on the chart; at least think about each one, and do not discard its possibility until you are sure you are not acting from ignorance, laziness, or inertia.

Key rules for each of the steps are:

1. *Subject*—stick to one subject, one topic in a speech. Decide on the title after you have written the speech.

2. *Purpose*—state the purpose, the whole purpose, and nothing but the purpose clearly for *your own use*: What you want the audience to learn, think, do, and feel.

3. *Aids*—look through your presentation to see where you could use an aid—chart, film, device, prop, reference—to good advantage. Pick those that carry the message, not those that simply "pretty up" the presentation.

4. *Audience Action*—include something for the audience to do, say, or respond to, in the introduction, body, and summary. When in doubt add more, not less, participation.

5. *Check-Up*—try to include some testing techniques to find out how much of the message sank into the audience. Use this information to help you improve all your presentations.

6. *Aftermath*—don't be "one-shot" with your presentation. Figure out some follow-up so that the audience will reinforce your message at a later date themselves; but give them reasons why they should make the effort.

7. *Take-Home*—by all means include handouts so the audience can take away permanent reminders of your message. But be sure the handouts are attractive, are focussed on your message, and are neither junky in appearance nor distracting from the main points you want to get across to the audience in question.

Finally, when developing the parts of your presentation, and when giving it, you need not follow rigidly the order given in the SPAI-BASCATH chart. The purpose of SPAIBASCATH is to help stimulate you to think of good ideas, to help you develop a complete, fully effective presentation, and to serve as a check-off and reminder list.

6

HOW TO SPEAK — READ A SPEECH

Never Read a Speech?

The basic rule of public speaking is: *Never read a speech*. Experts say it is better to fumble for words, back track, and give an unpolished, but human, personal, and direct talk. They advise you not to bury your head in a manuscript—even though your prose becomes thereby more meaty and your voice more sure.

A second rule is to prepare your own speeches. Don't parrot someone else's words.

But what about the busy executive, politician, or scientist who is invited to make a speech, outline a program, or report on the status of his research? He knows the audience prefers not to be read to. He's been in too many audiences himself not to realize that fact. However, he doesn't want to stop his work while he spends days, even weeks and months in preparation for a speech—though that speech can be vital to his business, his political party, or his research hopes.

Fortunately, there are techniques of "speak-reading" which enable you to save time and yet please an audience. We will explain these here, but first let's discuss audience boredom and adequate speech preparation.

What Not to Do

The chairman of a convention introduced the speaker, Mr. Brown, with fanfare and flourish. It was a special event to have him at the convention and those present were really going to hear the latest and best information.

The men and women in the audience leaned forward. They knew that Mr. Brown was president of the largest corporation in their industry and that he was a director of many more. They wanted to hear him.

He took the rostrum. He put on his heavy, horn-rimmed glasses. He took a sheaf of papers out of his pocket, placed them before him, and without looking up at the audience, began: "Well, let's see what my writers have given me to say today."

The audience sank back; their eyes glazing, their interest wilting along with their spines. They had not come to hear Mr. Brown read a speech prepared by underlings—they could skim the mimeographed releases later.

Suppose Mr. Brown had said, "You are such an important audience, and the subject is so important to all of us, that I asked the best brains in my outfit to come up with latest information. I've written down their ideas as well as mine, and today I'm going to make sure that I give you the best I can by keeping to this carefully written speech." With such a beginning, he would have gained better audience interest, for they at least would have started with the idea that he was going to read something worth while. But, of course, he would still be *reading*, and being read to does not hold audiences the way *speaking* to them does.

Mr. Brown, having downgraded his speech content by admitting it had been put together by underlings, and having downgraded the importance of the audience by admitting he had not taken the trouble to prepare for them, tried to regain their interest by a "gimmick." After reading a few pages, he suddenly stopped, pretended to glare at the page, and then said, "Well! That's what my speech writers wanted me to say. I'm not going to endorse those ideas. The facts as I see them are. . . ." The audience perked up while Mr. Brown spoke "extemporaneously" for a moment or so. Then he returned to reading the speech.

What was the effect of this bit of "showmanship"? One man who had been in the audience told me, "When Mr. Brown departed from his script, we all got interested. I guess many of us kept listening after that to see if he would do it again."

"Did he?"

"No, but we kept hoping he'd get his head out of his script and say something to us."

I asked, "Can you remember anything of what Mr. Brown said? Can you remember his message to your audience?"

"No, but I sure remember the way he got mad at his speech writers."

What was the point of the speech? To tell the audience something they needed to know or could profit from? Or to amuse them with a gimmick? I've known speakers to perform magic tricks—to take off their coats—even to take off their shirts—and one man took off his trousers "so the audience would never forget him"—all to gain attention. People remember such stunts, but they rarely remember the *messages* they were supposed to receive.

The purpose of a business, political, or professional address is to impart a message; the test of success is the degree of reception and retention of that message. To obtain these goals the speaker ought to have a real message, and he ought to present it in a form that does not disappoint the audience. The more the presentation can please the audience, the better, but the cut-off point comes when the entertaining reduces the effectiveness of the message.

Why Most Speeches Should be Written

A good speech can take a long time to prepare. By reducing your ideas to writing you make them easier to organize, remember, check on, and clear with others.

A corporation executive—or the head of a Government agency or military department—wants to be sure his speech will reflect the corporate view. There may be times when he wants to speak in opposition to or beyond the limits of the "party line," but even then, he has to know the "party line" in order to agree or disagree with it.

By writing out a speech one goes a long ways towards ensuring not only a well-organized and carefully "critiqued" speech, but also a speech directed towards audience enjoyment. The first stage a man goes through in preparing a speech is to search his mind for "what he wants to say on the subject." He should spill such first thoughts onto paper rather than onto an audience. After he has allowed the paper to sit awhile, and after it has collected some comments from available experts, and he has developed some second thoughts, he can look at the speech with the question in mind: "What will the audience want to hear?" "What parts of this speech answer their needs, what things are missing which this audience would like to hear?"

If a man makes only a few speeches and is not a practiced public speaker, then he needs a written version to give him confidence, to assist his memory, and to prevent stumbling. If a man makes a lot of speeches, then he needs a written version lest he fall into the errors so ably described by Dr. Henry Wriston in his wise and witty book on the art of being a college president, *The Academic Procession*, namely, that the expert can err in having too much confidence in expecting himself to be able to deliver a new, thoughtful, interesting, well-organized speech without preparation. Or, he prepares a "standard speech" and repeats it over and over again. Eventually the audiences note the repetition, or the speaker gives the same tried-and-true message long after the basic information has changed—and the audiences know it! Writing out a speech helps one check it for out-of-date information and hackneyed phraseology.

Now, we have returned to the dilemma: the busy executive needs a written speech; the audience wants to hear a speech as well-prepared as a written one; but the audience doesn't want the speaker to bury his nose in his script. The answer to the dilemma is to develop the ability to "speak-read" a speech. Fortunately, this ability is not one that only actors and TV announcers with long practice can acquire. The average man can learn it quite rapidly. Here is the technique boiled down into a set of simple rules.

Six Rules for Speak-Reading

The first and basic rule is: 1. Don't speak while looking down at the page. Read silently to yourself, and then look up, face the audience, and speak to them.

To perform this essential act smoothly and effectively, follow these secondary rules or principles:

2. Don't try to photograph in your mind's eye a whole sentence, much less a whole paragraph. Just get the thought. You know enough about the subject already (or you should not be speaking!) and you should have read through your speech aloud at least once so that you have an idea what the segments of thoughts are.

3. Don't speak while looking down. Just read to yourself while your head is down. Raise your head and gain eye contact with a person in the audience before you open your mouth.

4. Hold eye contact at the end of a thought. That is, don't keep speaking—or "slur down"—as you lower your head to read another line.

5. Read one idea, one thought, at a time. Raise your head and speak one idea at a time into the audience's ears.

6. Above all, don't worry about the time it takes you to look down and read. Don't panic. Don't start reading before you look up. With

practice you'll find yourself "head's up" more often than "head's down." The silent time may seem long to you, but it won't be to the audience. *Have a full thought ready before you look up and speak. Leave a full thought with the audience before you lower your eyes. Their minds will be kept busy with that thought while you are reading the next one to yourself.*

Five Tips for Preparing Your Script for Speak-Reading

To speak-read smoothly, try the following tips which have been culled from the professionals:

1. Type the words in large type on only one side of a page. Make sure the paper is opaque—flimsy paper may be easy to fold into one's pocket, but it is hard to read from.

2. Don't clip or staple the pages together or place them in a binder. Keep the pages loose so that you can slide them rather than turn them. Turning the pages forces you to make an awkward arm movement or to show too plainly that you are reading from a "book." Sliding the pages allows you to move the top one off with a small motion of either hand.

3. Have the typing double spaced or even triple spaced. Better yet, use a sort of "verse style" so that the lines represent complete thoughts, and your eye is guided to the segment to read at any one glance.

4. Mark off the main ideas and phrases with a slant (/) or dash (—) or an asterisk (*) or other sign (e.g., #). Underline key words. These signals will speed your reading and also warn you when you are coming to a pause, change of mood, or thought, or special emphasis.

5. Practice breathing at the breaks, that is at the slants (/), dashes (—), or asterisks (*) which mark off the main ideas and phrases.

Use Notes With a Flair—Use Them as Props

When you speak from notes, or have to refer to them, do so with a flair. Don't try to hide them. A speaker is all too obvious—and often clumsy—when he tries to hide his notes in his palm, or on the rostrum, and tries to steal surreptitious glances at them.

If you need notes, be above-board with them. Hold them up to eye level so that you can maintain eye contact with your audience with the least interruption. Most of the time you don't have to mention the notes. People expect you to use memory aids for important matters—just as you use a laundry or shopping list. If you feel you must say something about your notes, don't apologize, but say something like: "I wanted to be sure I had the right information for you, so I wrote the facts down." Or, "To be sure I wouldn't overlook anything you might want to know, I made a list." Look at your notes—held high—and when your memory is refreshed, start speaking again.

How to Practice Speak-Reading—Easily

Can you learn to speak-read smoothly overnight? To look down; take a paragraph at a glance; look up; regain eye contact; and then speak directly to the audience?

No, you can't learn overnight, but you can in a week or a month. Fortunately, the first big step is just to know what to aim for. Once you get the picture in your mind, you can quickly learn to live up to it. The picture is: You look down at the page, you read the thought marked off by slants or asterisks, you raise up and speak the thought to your audience. Each time you do it, it becomes easier—and each time you also become more effective with an audience. In other words, you please as you learn.

The polish really comes when you can take your breaths as you glance down to read a phrase, and when your eyes learn to encompass the next section so that you are prepared for what you will be saying next. Finally, you will find yourself able to prolong the heads-up periods and to decrease the heads-down periods. Eventually, the heads-down periods will be no longer than those required of any speaker who must pause for breath, for emphasis, and to give an audience time for his words to sink in.

Can you practice between speeches? Yes, because each day will provide opportunities. Try it when you read a story to your children or when you read an article or news item to your wife. Practice when you read a letter, a budget report, or other business matter to your fellow workers. Each time you try to speak-read, you will not only build towards smoother performance, but you will also make that moment of communication with others more satisfying and more effective—both for them and for you.

SUMMING UP THIS CHAPTER

Writing out a good speech is only half the job; next you must re-phrase it to fit the audience's needs, and you must deliver it in a way that audiences like—which means: don't read it.

Yet there are many occasions when you must follow a script rather than talk off-the-cuff—or pretend to talk off-the-cuff!

The following steps will help you solve the dilemma of reading and not-reading at the same time:

1. Prepare in advance by reading the whole speech through as many times as you can; mark reading directions on it; and have it typed in an easy-to-read fashion on pages that are easy to handle.

2. Hold eye contact until the end of a spoken thought; that is, don't "slur down" as you lower your head to read another line or two.

3. Don't speak while looking down at the page; take in a section, a whole thought, at a glance at the same time as you take a breath; then face the audience when you speak. Don't try for exact wording.

4. When you use notes, use them as props; don't try to hide them; act as though they are to help the audience, not you.

5. Practice the speak-read technique every day—every time you have occasion to read anything out loud, from a budget report to a bedtime story.

7

THE USE OF HUMOR

A TOOL THAT CAN CUT TOO MUCH

Should You Tell a Joke?

The question, "Should I tell a funny story?" always comes early in any class on public speaking.

Before we go further, let's answer the question right off with "No." If a man has to ask if he should tell a joke, then he is not yet skilled enough in public speaking to tell one! With him doing the telling, it probably will not be funny or appropriate.

The average person tends to identify something called public speaking with the "performers" he has seen do their stuff at a head table. These "performers" are primarily "entertainers" and they tell many jokes, because it is their *forte* to do so.

Others who ask the question are thinking of a toastmaster or master of ceremonies, whose success is measured by the laughs he obtains. Thus, they equate "public speaking" with an "image" of a smooth, smiling fellow who, standing with one hand in his pocket, tosses off a series of stories. Because they have seen such speakers at Kiwanis, Rotary, Lions, etc. luncheons and at civic banquets, or because they have been greatly impressed by a man who can tell a story to break the monotony of dull meetings, they assume that *all* public speaking occasions should include a humorous story.

Many teachers of public speaking and many authors of books on the subject have also assumed the "need to tell a few stories to warm up an audience." Teachers and writers on public speaking are themselves often in demand as speakers; they know they are expected to entertain their audiences; so they naturally tend to use the stories which they have found will please an audience.

It is not surprising that the average man when first planning a talk thinks to himself, "I suppose I've got to have a joke to start with. Now, what is a funny one which will make the audience laugh?" Hence, we all sit embarrassedly, if not wearily, through so many occasions when a novice toastmaster or inexpert speaker doggedly runs through a repertoire of forced and labored anecdotes.

The relief of some men is unmistakable when they hear the blunt advice: "No, you don't have to tell a joke. If you are good at telling stories, and if you have a story that makes a point to help your talk along, by all means use it. But there is no law, custom, or necessity of any sort that a speaker must tell a joke."

As a matter of fact, most of the speeches one hears could be improved by dropping the overly long introductions and far-fetched efforts to drag in a joke. At least half of all speech makers would do better if they spent more time improving the content and delivery of their message, and less time struggling with the mistaken notion that all audiences must be told jokes.

The Three Crucial Principles for the Use of Humor

When you have an occasion to tell a story—either because your presentation needs some livening up, or because you happen to have a joke that you would like to tell—check to see if: (1) it helps make a point for you; (2) it is humor, wit, or wisecrack; and (3) who the butt will be.

1. *What point does it picture?* If your job is purely to amuse or distract the audience, your only concern will be to tell a joke that will make the people in front of you laugh. But if you are making a business presentation or a serious speech, your joke should illustrate or highlight a point you are trying to make. If you use a joke that pictures or emphasizes your message, you need not worry whether the audience has heard the story before, or whether it will bring a big laugh. For, if the joke pictures your point, you are still ahead, even though the joke has been heard before, or you "goof" it.

Senator Thomas Corwin once said to President Garfield: "It was the greatest mistake of my life that I ever cracked a joke or made a funny speech, for people never believe that a funny man can have solid abilities, and if I didn't make a funny speech, my audience was disappointed." Of course, you want people to know you have a sense of humor, but don't put laughs ahead of business—or your audience will do the same thing. People will take a laughing message in a laughing way; and this can be a terrible thing for you, if you had wanted them to accept the message in a serious way.

2. *Humor, wit, or wisecrack?* Rudolf Flesch, in his book *A New Way to Better English*,[1] describes humor in this fashion: "You might call it humor, you might call it the light touch, you might call it grace. It's the perspective in which the subject is seen, the smile that seems to hover over everything that is being said, the nice sense of seriousness without solemnity." Clayton Fritchey pungently describes the distinction between humor and wit and wisecrack, in these terms, "Think of Lincoln as humor, Stevenson as wit, and Clare Booth Luce as wisecrack."[2]

Humor, in our terminology, is a friendly, serene, not-too-critical poking of fun—and mostly at oneself. It is an attempt to be light, to be pleasant without dazzling others and without hurting anyone. It can help the audience enjoy you and your presentation without distracting them from the real message.

Wit involves clever and ingenious play of thought and words. When well done it impresses others with your intelligence and insight and focuses a point of your message into unforgettable phraseology. But when poorly or unsuitably employed, it alienates some by making them feel inferior, and it distracts others from your basic message— it gets people thinking *how* you say something, rather than *what* you say.

Wisecracks are only for professional comedians or for occasions when no serious messages are intended. When well done, wisecracks come close to wit and serve a useful purpose in releasing tensions or in satirizing and ridiculing actions you can attack in no other way. When made at the wrong time and place, wisecracks may make the audience laugh, but they always distract people from the primary business of your presentation, and they often make people afraid of your "biting" tongue.

3. *Who will be the butt?* Usually the butt of *humor* is oneself or some strong and solid institution that "can take a joke." The butt of *wit* may be oneself, but more often it is the other person or the cherished belief of another person. The butt of a *wisecrack* is all too often someone you are trying to take down a peg, or someone below you who is easy to hit. In general, try to tell the joke on yourself. But don't repeat so many jokes on yourself that you begin to sound

[1] New York: Harper & Brothers, 1958, p. 150.
[2] "A Politician Must Watch His Wit," *New York Times Magazine*, July 3, 1960.

like a bumbling oaf! In all things, stop and think who will be in your audience and who might hear the joke at second hand.

In the old days, audiences were usually homogeneous. A speaker could be sure that the men had the "same school tie" and belonged to the "right church and club." In many cities, a man could be sure that he faced an audience made of "white Protestants of English descent" to whom dialect stories were funny. Nowadays, however, audiences have become complex groups, and one finds among lawyers and doctors, among businessmen and farmers, men and women of all nationalities, races, religions, and backgrounds. It's best, therefore—and just good manners—not to joke about race or religion, about crippling diseases or accidents, about mental or physical defects, or about localities, trades, or professions. Your speech might be televised or reported on the radio and people in all walks of life all over the country might hear your jokes—and not find them or you a bit funny.

Two Jokes That Made Their Points

Here are two jokes that put a point across in a way that both pleased the audience and saved a thousand words of difficult explanations. (Remember, a story ought to support your presentation and by its ability to picture a point should *save time*, not just serve as *padding*, as a *distractor*, or as a *time-filler*.)

Colonel C. M. "Count" Boyer, USAR (Ret.), for years Executive Director of the Reserve Officers Association, was called to testify before a Congressional Committee about a proposal to extend Reserve Duty requirements for all draft-eligible men to ten years. The Reserve Officers Association, however, believed that six years was long enough.

"Mr. Congressmen," he said, "the proposal reminds me of the time a man was convicted for stealing. The judge in sentencing him stated, 'It looks to me like I'll have to give you ten years for one theft and maybe ten more for the other theft. Before I pronounce sentence is there anything you would like to say?" The man replied, 'Yes, sir, judge, I would like to say that you are making yourself mighty free with somebody else's time!' "

The Committee rejected the proposal for an extension, and "Count" Boyer credits his story with focusing the issue for them in his favor. (As might be expected, "Count" Boyer is a professional public speaker and story teller. His booklet, *Laughing with Count* (3518 South Utah Street, Arlington, Va.), contains 60 jokes and epigrams, and a page of suggestions on how to tell a joke.)

During the Truman administration, Mr. Frank Pace (later Secretary of the Army and President of General Dynamics) was Director of the Budget. While Director of the Budget, and on the firing line between the White House, Congress, and other Government agencies, Mr. Pace made a speech to the Washington Chapter of the Society for the Advancement of Management. When he finished, the chairman said, "Now, I am sure Mr. Pace will gladly answer any questions."

The audience, mostly Government administrators or executives doing business with the Government, moved forward on their seats, visibly prepared to pounce on the opportunity to grill the Director of the Budget.

Mr. Pace replied that he would indeed be glad to answer questions, but first would like to tell a story that came to mind.

"A man was reading the newspaper one evening," said Mr. Pace, "when his little boy asked him: 'Pop, what makes the sun shine?'

" 'Now, son, don't ask me that. I'm not an astronomer or astrophysicist. You'll have to ask that of one of those guys.'

"There was silence for a while, then the boy asked, 'Pop, why is the grass green?'

" 'Son, I don't know. You've got to ask a botanist or chemist about things like that.'

"A little later, the boy asked, 'Pop, what makes my skin bleed when it's cut?'

" 'Now, boy,' snapped his father, rattling his newspaper in annoyance, 'You know, I don't know the answer. I'm not a doctor or physiologist. Let me read my paper in peace and quiet.'

"The boy replied wistfully, 'You don't mind my asking questions, do you, Dad?'

" 'Of course not!' exclaimed his father. 'How else are you going to learn, if you don't ask questions?' "

This story broke the tension; the audience laughed; and thereafter, no one minded when Mr. Pace answered a question only in part, or begged off answering it altogether. At the same time, no one tried to ask him nastily worded questions. They were able to identify themselves with the scene between a father and a small boy and they appreciated the neatness of his use of the story to establish the point that he could not be expected to answer the "impossible" questions.

A Joke That Made a Point—But Hurt

We are all familiar with the fellow who asks long, complicated questions that are half query and half speech. When he finally comes to the end of his harangue, he asks something like, "Don't you agree?" or "What do you think of the matter?" Perhaps he deserves charity and perhaps he does not. In any case, at a large dinner meeting one night, after the main speaker had finished, a man in the back of the room stated a very long and complex half speech, half question.

The speaker, obviously, had been unable to follow the question and had no desire to untangle it, so he replied, "Your question reminds me of the letter a girl wrote to a Miss Lonely-hearts Column. In the letter, she said that her boy friend kept asking her to say yes. She had gone with him for years and she had several good things to say about him and several less good things to say. Her mother thought he was a fine fellow, but was not quite sure he was the right man. Her friends were equally divided; some thought she should say yes, others were not sure. She herself sometimes thought she would, and other times thought she wouldn't. So, would Miss Lonely-hearts, in view of all the facts, please help her make up her mind about saying yes to the boy friend.

"Miss Lonely-hearts replied with one line: 'What is his question?' "

The audience laughed and applauded this answer. The chairman smoothly moved on to another speaker, and the matter appeared to have been neatly disposed of. But had it? Yes, if the questioner was an unimportant person who had been so out of place in his ramblings that he deserved the public humiliation. Suppose, however, he had been an important person who had trouble expressing himself in public, and was in a position to take revenge on the "smart-alecky" speaker? Or, suppose the man had had the germ of a good question, which the speaker in his desire to "use his good story" had refused to discern?

The story by Mr. Pace shifted the joke onto himself; the story about Miss Lonely-hearts made a member of the audience look foolish.

This also gives us another distinction between humor and wit and the wisecrack. You don't have to try to be a good sport if the *humor* is about you. On the other hand, if the *wit* or *wisecrack* is directed at you, you may have to try very hard to be a good sport. Don't expect others to readily be such good sports.

By All Means Use Humor—and Wit, and Even Wisecracks

What has been said so far has been intended to warn you to use humor, wit, and wisecracks with caution. By no means should you always avoid being witty, mocking, satirical, or even buffoonish. Heaven knows the world needs more humor and wit and wisecracks.

The crucial point is that you should recognize what type of humor you are using, how suitable it is to the occasion, and how it will help or hurt the primary purpose of your presentation.

The 13 Rules for Telling Humorous Stories, which end this chapter, are based on the principles expressed so far, and sum up the advices which have been compiled from a large number of expert speakers and toastmasters.

HOW TO TELL A HUMOROUS STORY—13 TESTED RULES

In addition to suggestions on how to tell a joke in the booklet by "Count" Boyer, already mentioned, you can find in Herbert V. Prochnow's book, *The Toastmaster's and Speaker's Handbook*,[3] 20 basic rules for telling stories. The following 13 rules include most of Boyer's and Prochnow's rules, as well as several of my own. Here they are:

1. Be sure the story makes a point connected with the message of your presentation. That way, even if the story has been heard before or it doesn't get a laugh, it will make a worth-while point.

2. If you are going to tell a story, practice telling it. If possible, practice under the same conditions you will have to face. A story that sounds perfect around a campfire can be difficult to put across when you stand on a large stage, with a spotlight in your eyes, and a microphone to talk into.

3. Don't praise the story before or after you tell it. Tell it because it illustrates a point, not because it is "so funny." That is, never say, "I have a howlingly funny story to tell you folks tonight"; but rather something like, "The problem before us reminds me of the time . . ."

4. Write the story out before you tell it so that you can see how it appears in writing. This will show up the extra words, paddings, and repetitions. Don't add extraneous trimmings or lots of local color.

5. Unless you are an expert—and have practiced to perfection—avoid dialect stories.

6. In general, choose the shorter stories rather than the longer stories. A long story takes that much more time from the "meat" part of your talk. Moreover, the final denouement must be extra good in order to warrant the long suspense. In my experience, most long stories are that way because of rambling on part of the speaker. (Always see how much wordage you can cut from any story that takes more than a minute to tell.)

7. Keep your stories clean. If your story is "dirty" and gets a tremendous laugh, then its "shock" value must also be great, or the

3 New York: Pocket Books, Inc., 1955.

audience has a lot of tension that explodes along such lines. If the shock value or the tension is so great, then the very "success" of the story argues that it will distract the audience from your message. On the other hand, if the story lays an egg, then you have lost on a double count: (1) you lose as a poor story teller, and (2) you lose in not getting a point across. Finally, there will always be a number of people who will not like a dirty story, nor respect you for telling it, even if they laugh momentarily; among these persons may be the ones you wish to impress. In short, you have everything to lose by telling an off-color story, and rarely anything to gain.

8. Choose stories that will please your audience. This sounds obvious, yet many speakers pick their favorite story, rather than the one related to the time, place, and interests of the audience. In other words, don't tell golf stories to a meeting of tennis players; or anecdotes about famous explorers to a meeting of beauticians.

9. People like jokes, they like to be amused—to forget their troubles, to relax, to ease tension, and to stop thinking about difficult things. Thus, your stories can be two-edged swords: on the one hand, they increase audience attention and pleasure and serve to revive interest and quicken spirits after some difficult or tough explanations; on the other hand, the ready acceptance of a story, the loud laughs, and the applause can tempt you into taking the path of entertainment when perhaps you should be holding to the roadway of your message.

10. Make your stories as extemporaneous as you can; that is, don't say (or act as though you are saying): "Now, it's time for a joke, and here's a good one." Rather, come upon the story because that part of your presentation appears to generate the story as a fitting illustration.

11. With regard to telling stories about personalities, remember:

    a. If the story is critical, make it about yourself rather than about someone else. However, don't tell a string of self-deprecating stories, because too many can have a cumulative effect upon your audiences. The first one or two stories may make them love you for your modesty and humility; after that, they may become convinced you are a constant bumbler.

    b. Don't make fun of people who have physical or mental disabilities—don't make fun of the blind, the crippled, or those who have harelips or who stutter. You can joke about common, take-for-granted ailments like near-sightedness, far-sightedness, and an "aching back." But don't joke about baldness, toupees, falsies, or false teeth.

Too many of the people in your audience have to take such things all too seriously—and unhappily—and they don't like being reminded of their personal defects, much less being embarrassed about them.

c. Be careful with jokes that assume that a race, a nation, a class of people, or a religious sect are not as bright or as clean or as honest or as patriotic as they might be. Nowadays, members of many minorities are taking their place in all levels of our society, and while they have the ability, education, and influence to take such positions, many do not yet have the sophistication to absorb without flinching jokes about the groups to which they belong or from which they have just graduated.

d. If possible, connect your story with a distinguished person so that the story takes on the aura of that person. In general, a business audience would prefer a story about a president of General Motors to one about a minor Government official; a woman's club would prefer one about a famous artist or author to one about a farmer.

12. When telling the story, remember:

a. Pause before starting into the story, and then speak the opening lines with extra clarity so that the audience is sure to hear the beginning.

b. Speak the punch line clearly, and don't repeat it. When you reach the end, stop. If the audience doesn't laugh, go on to the next paragraph of your presentation. If the audience does laugh, don't try to keep milking the same joke by repeating the punch line or explaining it. Wait until the laughter stops; then go on to the next paragraph.

c. Try to believe in the story yourself as you tell it. Picture the situation to yourself, and enjoy it again no matter how many times you have told the story. Your feeling, or lack of feeling, for the story will be transmitted to the audience.

13. Finally, remember Corwin's Law, Markel's Law, and Fritchey's Law:

a. Corwin's Law: "Never make people laugh. If you would succeed in life, you must be solemn, solemn as an ass. All the great monuments are built over solemn asses." (More accurately, "Never try to make people laugh at the wrong time or just for the sake of being entertaining—make the joke teach a point.")

b. Markel's Law: "Humor is okay; wit can be dangerous; wise-cracking is disastrous."

c. Fritchey's Law: "If you can't take it [humor] or leave it alone, don't touch it at all."

This final law leads us back to the opening paragraph of this chapter, where we said that if you cannot tell a story with aplomb and flair, don't tell one. Stick to your business and let the toastmaster or master of ceremonies supply the entertainment.

But, why not practice until you can tell the right story in the right way at the right time?

8

USE OF CHARTS AND OTHER AIDS

Special Purpose of This Chapter

There are a thousand ways to discuss the use of aids—props, materials, audio-visual aids, presentation aids, and sales promotion aids. Books have been published on the use of films, on the design of charts, and even on the use of blackboards (or chalkboards as they are now called). For instance, *Putting Yourself Over in Business*, (Dyer, Evans, and Lovell)[1] contains chapters on "How to Select Presentation Aids," "How and Where to Get Your Aids Easily," and "What to Do When You Need Aids in a Hurry." Charles B. Roth's book *Successful Sales Presentations, How to Build Them . . . How to Use Them*,[2] explains how to fit a presentation to the customer, and provides six demonstration presentations with the instructions to the speaker placed in the margin to show what the speaker is to do and say. A subscription to a magazine like *Advertising Requirements*, or a few hours spent in a library with its back issues, will bring you up to date on available modern presentation aids.

Our special challenge here is to focus on what the executive, the manager, the actual speaker needs to know in order to pick his way through the different kinds of aids and, more importantly, to employ an aid so that it helps him drive home his message. Like *humor,* an *aid* can become a distractor rather than a point-maker.

[1] Englewood Cliffs, N. J.: Prentice-Hall, Inc., 1957.
[2] Englewood Cliffs, N. J.: Prentice-Hall, Inc., 1960.

Which Comes First, the Script or the Aid?

Formerly, most, if not all, the teachers would say that a speech should be prepared first and then examined to see where an aid might be used to advantage. They believed, and probably the majority still do, that an aid is just an *aid*, a supplement to what is being said. In essence, this attitude amounts to one of: "You can take an aid or leave it alone; because the aid is an added attraction, an optional way of facilitating the giving of your message."

On the other hand, a growing number of practitioners believe you should decide first on your aids and then write the script. Herbert Rosenthal, Director of the Graphics Institute in New York City, has lauded what he calls the "Kopy Killers Klan." By it he means you should seek ever less and less wordage in every presentation and, conversely, more and more visual and aural aids.

Similarly, Theodore Maynard, of Washington, D. C., who is a nationally known lecturer on the "Presentation Middleman" regularly states that the charts should be designed before the spoken script of a presentation is prepared.

And, Shy Greenspan, President of Blair Associates of Alexandria, Va., and Washington, D.C., while not being so blunt as Herbert Rosenthal and Theodore Maynard in demanding that the *visuals* or *aurals* take precedence over the *spoken* or *written copy* of a presentation, is outspoken in recommending more, not less, aids in all presentations.

That the trend is toward more aids, and that the old-timers are not always ready to go along, is indicated by the following excerpt from Mr. Burnham's article in the *Wall Street Journal on* "Corporate Ghosts":

Ghosts complain that speech making today often requires frills and extras seldom needed in simpler bygone days.

"Films, slides, mockups, and other demonstration tools make speeches a dramatic performance today," says a former scientist, now a ghost writer and public relations counselor. "I'm getting a lot of work from executives who have given up on working out the theatrical intricacies."

One could question the assertion that aids are "frills" or that in bygone days men used "simpler" types of speechmaking. Perhaps the good old speeches were harder to give and understand than the modern charts? Shouldn't even a chartless, simple speech contain enough drama to please the most old-fashioned audience?

A balanced presentation is the executive's responsibility. The executive remains in the middle, and he must balance the arguments of the *aids-men* against the claims of the *script-men*. Moreover, he must be alert to his own prejudices and preferences; his goal ought to be what will carry the message to the audience, not what he likes best himself.

Assuming you are the executive, you will find yourself able to make better decisions if you keep the following principles in mind.

1. Some men naturally tend to think in visual terms and in terms of gimmicks and devices. They will always want many charts and gadgets. Men who are in the business of making presentations or who are company artists and draftsmen will naturally try to sell you more artwork. Just because a man obtains personal satisfaction or profit out of making charts, or selling a film strip or transparency, doesn't mean he gives biased advice. But it could.

2. Other men are unable to think in terms of aids; they can't visualize a chart; and they are afraid to operate an overhead projector or tape recorder, so they sneer at "frills." Perhaps they are right in any given instance, but it never hurts to make a doublecheck to see if a picture worth 1000 of their words is available.

3. In general, the use of *aids* is still new to many beginning speakers; therefore you can expect them to shy away from *aids*. If so, don't let them rationalize their reluctance by saying "they won't work" until they have actually employed some aids in their presentations over a six-month period.

4. On the other hand, if your organization is one that has been richly endowed with artists, draftsmen, and presentation experts, you had better look carefully at proposals to "dress up a talk with some color." The people may be using expensive visuals and other aids simply from habit or from a mistaken assumption that aids are always required. Or, they may be using the aids as expensive crutches. Perhaps the only thing a speaker needed was a card file of notes; instead he paid $500 for a set of easel charts which actually did nothing more than provide him with a blown-up outline to follow!

Making the decision. Finally, with regard to which comes first, the script or the aid, the sensible thing is to jot down the purpose of the presentation and the main points you want to put across. Study them to see which can be carried by aids, and which can be carried by your voice. Then write the final script.

When you are dealing with people who don't like aids, ask them to decide first on the aids they could use. This may prevent them from casting their ideas in the concrete of prose so that they will refuse to drop a page for the sake of a chart. On the other hand, if you are dealing with people who believe a presentation must be built around a series of dazzling charts, ask that the presentation be written first. After the script is on paper, you can decide which point would be better shown on a chart, and which could be left to the speaker to put across with words.

PRESENTATION CHARTS

Technical Charts vs. Presentation Charts

Many speakers are confused by contrary advice such as the following. One man advises them: "Don't over-decorate your charts, keep them simple, avoid the frou-frou. Don't show the details!"

Another man recommends: "Make your charts accurate to the decimal point. Show the details and sources of information."

A third man says: "Put some life, and color, and designs into your visuals. Fancy them up to please the audience."

Such contrary advice arises because people confuse *presentation charts* with *technical charts*. A technical chart is the type that you use in an operation, process, or laboratory to record data or to find data. It can and should be detailed, accurate, and authoritative. The user expects to refer to it many times, and he expects it to be accurate. It belongs in the appendix of a technical book, or on the pages of a handbook. *The user has plenty of time to study it and to work with it.* Hence it can be in great detail.

On the other hand, a presentation chart is intended for a brief exposure to any one audience. It is not to be spread out on a laboratory table, or on an accountant's desk, or in the appendix of a book. It is to be displayed in a room at a distance from a number of people. Accordingly, a presentation chart should contain only one idea, it should avoid details, and *it should be designed to be displayed for one minute at the most.* Hence, the fewer details on it the better.

Consider the men behind these two opposite types of charts. Engineers, accountants, and other technicians have grown up with technical charts. They naturally look for charts that are accurate and detailed and can be used for finding much data. They expect a chart to have several curves on it, and they expect to be able to read specific information off it. The engineer will feel at home with a chart that has logarithmic progressions and some square roots on it. The accountant will feel better if the chart resembles a bookkeeping form. In other words, you can expect the technicians to want charts to resemble those in their textbooks and manuals.

The type of person, however, who becomes a presentation expert had a flair for art and will think in terms of color, contrast, mood, and esthetic effect. He will want four colors instead of three, and three instead of two. He will want to remove data that fails to plot prettily or casts an unattractive shadow. He will want lots of "class" where only a few figures are needed.

It is the job of the executive to maintain the balance between such conflicting desires. What the average man—speaker and executive— wants to know about technical charts can be found in *Communication Through Reports,* by Paul Douglass.[3] For an excellent explanation of presentation charts he can turn to *Presentation of Ideas,*[4] which was published by the Navy Department (under the aegis of the Ted Maynard mentioned earlier in this chapter).

Ten Characteristics of a Good Presentation Chart

1. A presentation chart, by definition, will be displayed before an audience gathered to hear a presentation. This means that the chart has to be big enough to be seen from all corners of the room and it should be focused on one specific point.

2. It should be designed for a *reading time of one minute* at the most. The audience is not going to use it to solve accounting, laboratory, engineering, or shop problems. If there is more on it than can be read in one minute, you will lose part of the audience; some will read too quickly, some too slowly; and some will dawdle on one topic, others will focus on another topic. So, design your presentation charts for 15-second, 30-second, 45-second, and at most 60-second viewings.

3. It should have only one main thought. If you have more than one main thought, add another chart.

4. Details should be left off. If a member of the audience does not trust you and wants the exact figures, the sources of data, and all the other refinements of technical chart, tell him to see you later. Don't clutter the chart with details which others don't care about.

5. The chart in essence should show a *relationship of interest to management* or to the decision-making function of the audience. That is, the chart should focus on showing *too much, too little; on time, behind time, ahead of time; materials on hand; materials needed; materials in excess; usage this period vs last period,* and so on.

6. A presentation should have a simple declarative sentence by way of title or explanation to tell the audience what the chart is intended to illustrate.

[3] Englewood Cliffs, N. J.: Prentice-Hall, Inc., 1960, chap. 5-6.

[4] Available from Govt. Printing Office, Superintendent of Documents, Washington, D. C.

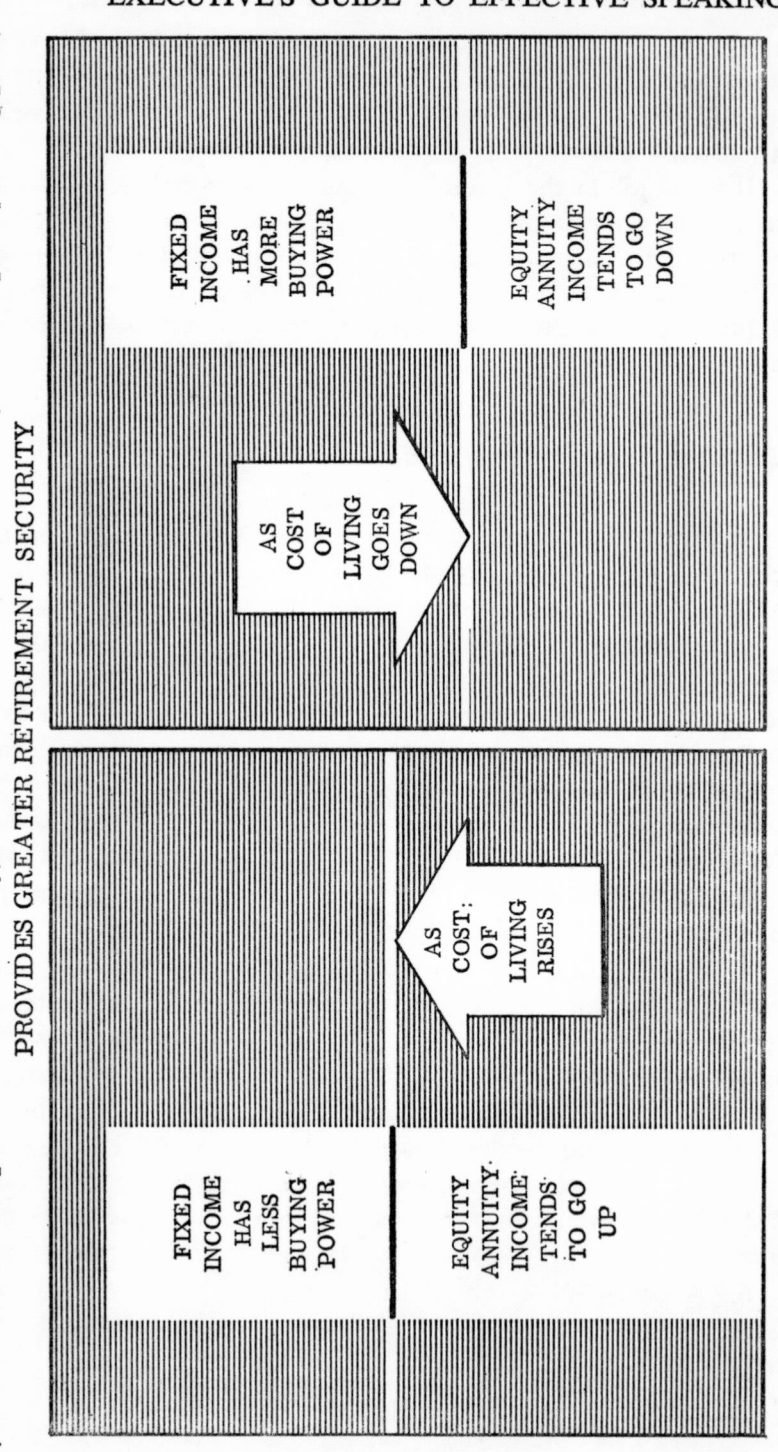

RETIREMENT INCOME BALANCED BETWEEN FIXED DOLLAR INCOME

(from the retirement plan and social security) AND EQUITY ANNUITY INCOME (from the profit sharing plan)

PROVIDES GREATER RETIREMENT SECURITY

FIXED INCOME HAS MORE BUYING POWER

EQUITY ANNUITY INCOME TENDS TO GO DOWN

AS COST OF LIVING GOES DOWN

AS COST OF LIVING RISES

FIXED INCOME HAS LESS BUYING POWER

EQUITY ANNUITY INCOME TENDS TO GO UP

A typical presentation chart with a heading which is a simple, declarative sentence. Note the lack of scales, complex figures, or numbers. The chart concentrates on the crucial message — showing the relationship between cost of living

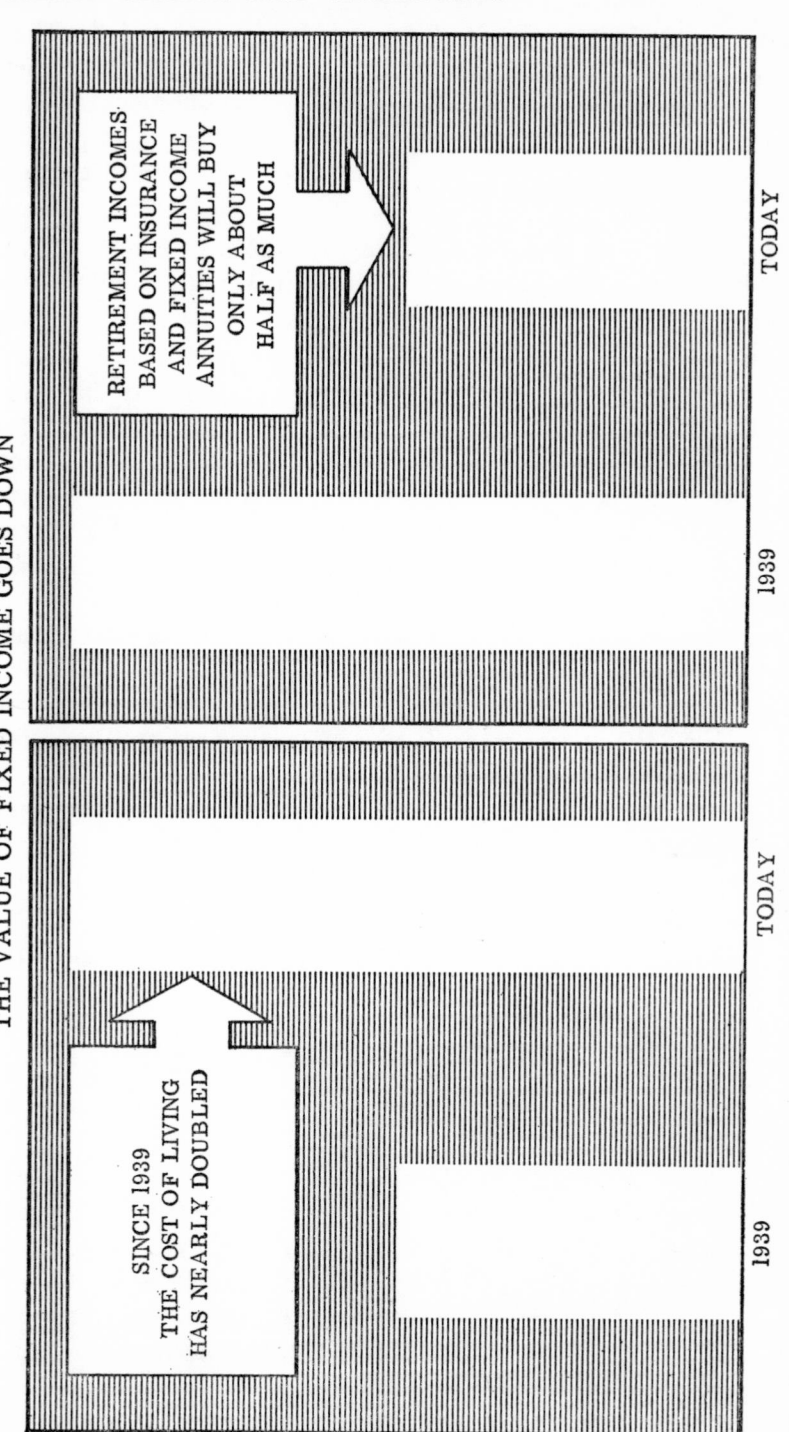

AS THE COST OF LIVING GOES UP
THE VALUE OF FIXED INCOME GOES DOWN

SINCE 1939
THE COST OF LIVING
HAS NEARLY DOUBLED

1939   TODAY

RETIREMENT INCOMES
BASED ON INSURANCE
AND FIXED INCOME
ANNUITIES WILL BUY
ONLY ABOUT
HALF AS MUCH

1939   TODAY

Another presentation chart with a general family resemblance to the chart shown on page 68. Note the use of arrows to emphasize the line dividing fixed income from equity income. (*Courtesy of The General Tire & Rubber Company.*)

7. Extraneous information and designs should be avoided. They may be pretty and they may be correct and interesting, but do they focus on the one main thought of the chart? You should use color codes to highlight certain facets, and pointers or arrows to emphasize trends, levels, significant dates, and so forth, but avoid the frou-frou and the gingerbread.

8. In general, soft pastel colors are preferable to bright colors, because under most conditions of illumination the bright colors can cause annoying or at least distracting contrasts. Also, the strong colors may make a viewer feel he is being high-pressured.

9. As with handouts (see Chapter Five), you should maintain a general similarity or "family appearance" among the charts of the same presentation, but with enough variety so that one chart is not confused with another. While you are on one subject, the charts should follow the same format. When you change topics, the charts should change format. For example, suppose you have been discussing plant materials costs and have been using bar charts drawn on a light green background, with block lettering, and a squarish format. When you change to a discussion of personnel costs, you might use a light yellow background, and a more rounded format, with less stolid lettering. When you change to a discussion of the financial aspects, you might use a pink background, an oblong format with rounded corners, and a lettering halfway between the other two styles. In this way, the audience can "feel" the change, without being confused by a kaleidoscope of colors and shapes splashed up in front of them on a screen or easel board.

10. Above all, remember that the chart, or other aid, should carry an important segment of your message, or help build towards one. Otherwise, you should question its use. Like humor, if an aid does not help the message, it distracts from it.

Costs of Aids for Presentations

Good aids for presentations almost always are *high-priced*. Note the term *high-priced*: an aid is not costly or expensive if it does a job better than anything else could. A $100 chart that saves 10 minutes of discussion on the part of 100 people, or that convinces an important man who would not otherwise be convinced, or that can be used over and over again with many audiences, can be a tremendous bargain. A good aid will be high-priced because it will either have been done by a professional who must be paid accordingly (at least $50 a day), or by someone in your organization, and that someone must be diverted from other money-making enterprises in order to plan or make the aid.

In general, it seems a good idea to call on professionals, whether outsiders on contract, or insiders on loan, to prepare charts and other aids. The reasons are, principally—and they also apply to the use of ghost writers: you avoid taking your people away from their basic jobs and you probably get better workmanship. Here are three principles to help you decide when aids are worth their price:

1. If the chart is to be shown only once, or to an austere or knowledgeable group, rough and ready charts will be suitable. (See Chapter Ten of our book *Putting Yourself Over in Business*[5] for "What to Do When You Need Aids in a Hurry.") For instance, when you are explaining a program to the *Budget Committee on Cost Reducing,* you would not use charts which appeared expensive.

2. If the chart is to be shown to a large audience, to a mixed audience or to several audiences, it is worth being made with care and with good materials and design.

3. Aids should be developed for only the vital and most suitable parts of a presentation. There is no need to have a chart for every statement and for every column of figures. Don't let the chartmakers include the first chart, which has just the title of the presentation on it, at the same price as the rest of the charts. Avoid charts which have only one or two words on them. As we said before, charts can be nothing else but high-priced outlines to jog the memory of the speaker. The presentation aid ought to carry the message to the audience, not remind the speaker of it.

How to Convert a Technical Chart for Presentation Use

Suppose you want to illustrate a point but do not have the time or the money to arrange for a specially made presentation chart. You have a technical chart which makes the point, but the technical chart is too small, too crowded, or too detailed to be used for a one-minute display before a large group. Can you adapt the small technical chart to serve your presentation?

Yes, and the method is simple. Fix the small chart onto a large sheet of paper or cardboard, write a caption to tell what the chart is supposed to show, and then draw a "blow-up" on the sheet of the point you want to show. You then have a chart which can be used to good advantage in a presentation.

[5] *Op. cit.*

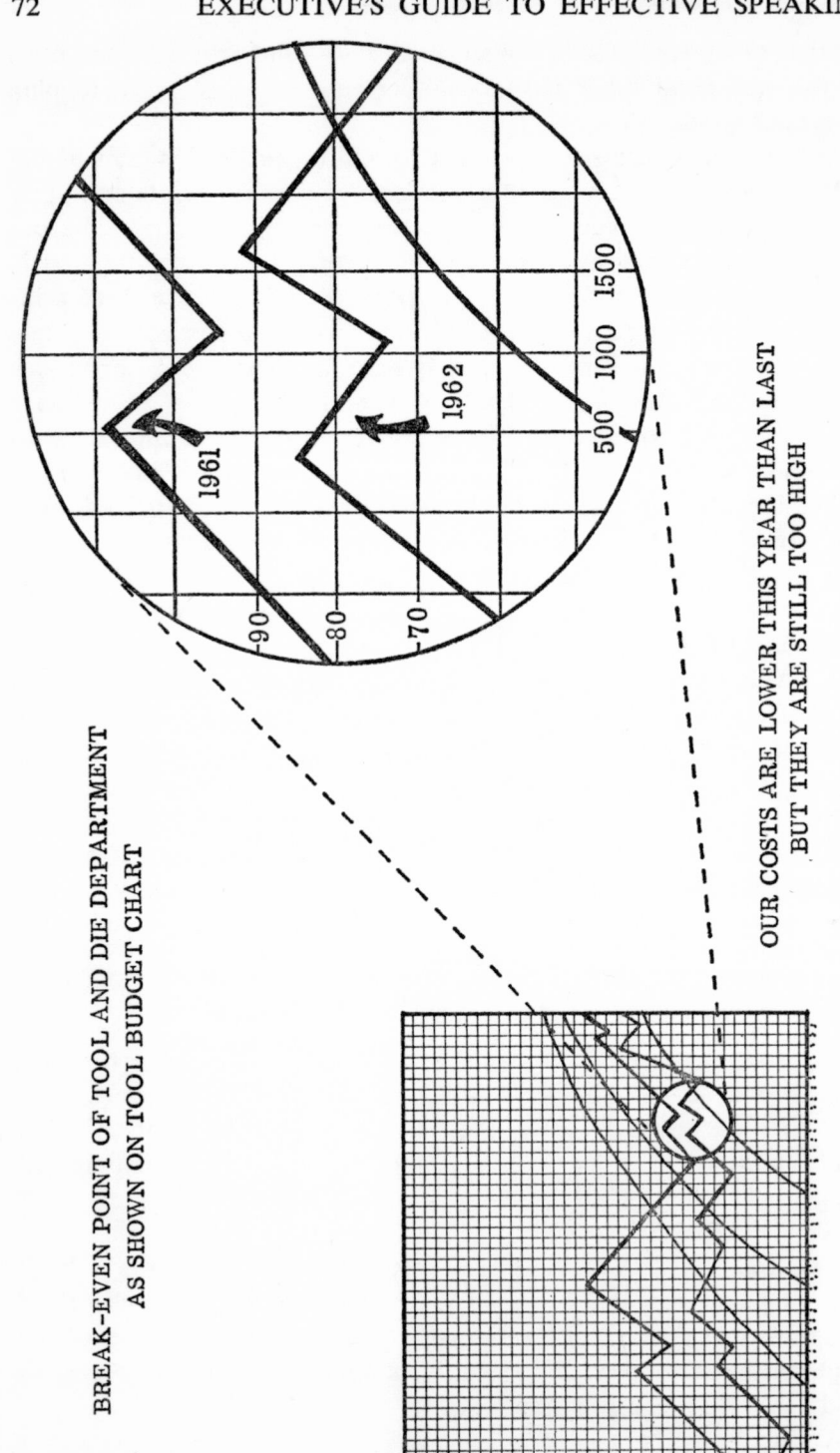

BREAK-EVEN POINT OF TOOL AND DIE DEPARTMENT
AS SHOWN ON TOOL BUDGET CHART

OUR COSTS ARE LOWER THIS YEAR THAN LAST
BUT THEY ARE STILL TOO HIGH

Converting a small technical chart for use as a larger presentation chart.

Four Rules for Writing Presentation Chart Captions

The following rules will help you make your presentation chart clear and interesting to an audience:

1. The main heading should be at the top of the chart in large print and it should be a simple declarative sentence. That is, the heading should tell what the chart aims to show. For example: OUR SALES HAVE INCREASED 30% IN THE LAST TWO YEARS. Or, THOUGH COSTS HAVE GONE DOWN, PROFITS HAVE NOT INCREASED.

2. Detailed explanations, numbers, and grid lines should be left off a presentation chart. The less wordage on the chart the better. However, any wordage on the chart should be complete and grammatical. Scales on the sides, bottom, and top are not needed, and usually should be left off.

3. Legends and pointers should be near the items to which they call attention.

4. When a lot of wordage is required in the captions and legends, you probably ought to have an additional chart or charts. It is better to use three simple charts and three simple statements rather than to try to crowd onto one chart and into one caption all three ideas and all three statements. Look at the figures on pages 68, 69, and 72, and note the use of captions, legends, and pointers as well as the directness and simplicity of the message.

EFFECTIVE USE OF OTHER AIDS

Films, Tapes, Chalkboards, and Other Devices

When the time comes to use a movie projector or tape recorder or prepare a transparency for an overhead projector, you will have to obtain instruction in the operation of the equipment.[6] However, one common theme runs through the employment of all aids: the aid should contribute towards putting the message across to the audience. Obvious? Yes, but a large number of speakers become so engrossed in the mechanics, or so fascinated with "exploiting the possibilities" of their artists or gadget makers that they put the *aid* before the *message*!

Accordingly, the following principles are listed as guides for obtaining the maximum message-imparting effect with the aid in question.

1. *Films and Tapes*

a. Always preview or prehear the film or tape and prepare a list of the key points in it.

---

[6] See *Putting Yourself Over in Business* (previously cited), for tips on the use of various aids.

b. Prepare the room properly so all can see or hear. Arrange for good ventilation, even if it means a little too much light.

c. Introduce the film or tape. Tell the audience why they should see it or hear it. Psychologists have reported that an audience will remember three times as much of a film or tape if they have been prepared for what to watch for or listen to.

d. Stay with the audience no matter how many times you have sat through the film or tape recording. If you walk out, the audience will lose some of their interest and respect for the film or tape.

e. After the film or tape has run, hold a discussion on the key points, and sum up what the audience has seen or heard.

2. *Graphic Aids*

Graphic aids are charts, posters, and diagrams.

a. Keep them covered or out of sight until needed; otherwise, the audience will be looking at the aid and wondering about it, instead of paying full attention to you.

b. Stand to one side and face the audience. *Repeat*: face the audience! Don't keep glancing at a chart that has one word, or one picture on it. This is a difficult thing for many speakers to avoid; when there is a blackboard or an easel near them their eyes are drawn toward it like to a magnet. Instead of maintaining eye contact with the audience they continually turn to the chart as though they expected it to tell them something. Remember, the chart is supposed to tell the audience something, not the speaker.

c. Plan the use of the chart in advance. Know when it should be shown, and how long you will expose it and discuss it. Don't let it "surprise you" or stay around longer than needed.

3. *Chalkboard (Blackboard)*

Blackboards are now called chalkboards because they come in other colors than black. We are so familiar with chalkboards that we can fail to use one to full advantage. Instead of taking the next chalkboard for granted, try to apply the following rules as you make use of it.

a. Plan your illustrations in advance. Think about what parts could be improved by marking them with colored chalk.

b. Remember to stand to one side; to write large and high up; and to touch the board when pointing to an item, with the back of your fingers so that you don't leave fingermarks.

c. Draw complicated drawings or complex figures on the board in advance in pencil (which cannot be seen except from close up).

During your talk, you can chalk over the lines rapidly and accurately. Or, prepare the drawing in advance and cover it with a sheet of paper until you are ready to refer to it.

d. Write clearly and in large firm hand—the audience would rather wait a little and be able to read your writing, than have you hastily scribble chicken tracks they cannot decipher.

4. *Models, Devices, Equipment*

Often you can use the actual part, assembly, equipment, or books and forms you are talking about. As with the other aids, remember the following rules.

a. Don't show it until you are ready to use it.

b. Don't talk at the same time the model or paper is being passed around or examined.

c. Provide an orderly method of passing the item around, or of having the members of the audience examine it. Don't let people crowd so that some cannot see.

d. Plan for when, how, and how long you will make use of the item in your talk. If necessary, bring or appoint an assistant to help expedite passing the item to the audience and away from the audience.

SUMMING UP THIS CHAPTER

The modern executive is faced with approving the use of aids in presentations for which he is responsible. Some men want no aids because they are unfamiliar with them or because their minds tend toward prose rather than toward charts, models, mock-ups, films, and recordings. Other men go overboard in favor of having an aid to do the job for them. The executive should study the message and the audience and pick the means which best carry the message to the audience. In some instances, he should encourage men to use more aids; in other instances, he will insist on fewer or less expensive ones.

A presentation chart should carry one main idea with a minimum of detail and distracting additions to an audience It should be designed for one minute or less viewing time and it should focus on a *relationship* of importance to the audience. A series of charts should have variety but be within a general "family style." Technical charts can be converted to presentation charts by highlighting ("blowing-up") the item of importance.

Any aid before being displayed should be previewed so the speaker can select the key points to emphasize in his introduction and in his closing remarks. He should keep the aid out of the way until needed and he should be careful to keep it from distracting, instead of helping, the audience.

Above all, the aid should be designed and employed to help the audience hear, see, and understand the message. It should carry the point to the audience, not just serve as a memory-jogger or stage prop for the speaker. In short, the presentation aid should aid, not the presenter, but the audience.

9

LONG-RANGE EFFECTIVE CONFERENCE LEADERSHIP

Hidden Agendas vs. Open Agendas

In Chapter Four we pointed out that a presentation can have a hidden purpose as well as an announced purpose. Similarly, a conference of 9 to 90 people can have 9 to 90 hidden purposes as well as the ones for which the conference was called.

The success of a conference can hinge on identifying and handling the hidden issues as well as the open issues.

The first step is to identify your own overt and covert desires—and get a good grip on them. You may not state your secret objective to the group, but at least state it clearly to yourself. That way you will gain better control over it, and you will be more alert to spot the people who will have the same or opposing objectives. And, you will be better able to detect when they guess your real aims!

Can hidden agendas be kept secret? Probably not, because if they are to be put across, then the other people present must undergo some change of knowledge or attitude, and most people can feel when such a thing happens to them.

Let's see how you can protect yourself from your own subconscious urges as well as from the secret or blind desires of others present at a conference.

Protecting Yourself from Conference "Sells"

In the long run, the surest way to avoid mistakes in a conference is to prepare your scale of values beforehand.

During the conference, when the participants appear to be turning away from what you think is right, you should get them to list their

own scales of values. Once they get their "values" in the open, pref-
ably on a board or chart, the right course of action will show no
matter who opposes it.

What is a scale of values? Let's begin with the personal values
of interest to everyone—and in about the following order:

General	Special Examples
Religion	Safety and health of persons
Personal integrity	Integrity of product
Self-respect	Protection of customer
Family	Care of equipment
Nation	Care of building
Local organizations	Care of grounds
Profession or job	Etc.
Company as a whole	
Immediate department or division	
Etc.	

Which do you put first? Suppose you had to trade your family for
your job? Your children for your homeland? Your self-respect and
integrity for your job? The good of your department at the expense
of the business as a whole?

In any conference take the matter at issue and see how each proposed course of action checks out against your scale of values.

Six Types of Questions That Clarify Values for a Group

The problem, of course, will be to get others to consider their scales
of values. This is done best by asking, not telling, them. The following questions—or variations of them—will keep any but the most
recalcitrant and selfish persons on the right tracks:

1. *What will be the effect* of the proposal on the whole company? This
   year? Next year? Five years from now?
2. *Who will profit* most from the proposal? How can we be sure the
   benefit will be a good one? At whose expense will he or they profit?
3. *Who stands to lose* because of the proposed course of action or inaction? How can the loss be minimized? Is the sacrifice really worthwhile? If so, how can the losers be recompensed?
4. *What will the consequences be?* As seen by the stockholders? As
   seen by the employees? As seen by customers? As seen by suppliers? As seen by the public?
5. *Will we be proud of the action—or inaction—*after the "heat" is off
   us for a decision? Can we live with our consciences? Will we will-
   ingly explain our decisions to our families? To our subordinates?
   To our professional peers?

6. *Are we trading a short-term gain for a long-term gain?* Are we compromising a "higher" value for the sake of one "lower" on our scale of values?

When a group is composed of competent, honorable men who are genuinely seeking the best solutions for the business as a whole, a brief run-through of a few of the foregoing questions will be enough to help them focus on the essentials in a situation.

However, when a selfish or obstinately blind person is present and tries to force a decision to his benefit, you may have to work for a long time on clarifying the scale of values inherent in the problem under discussion. Assuming you are the leader—or can take charge of the discussion—your best approach will be two-fold:

(1) Keep the difficult person explaining what will happen after his proposal is adopted. Keep boring into him with: "Then what will happen?" And, "How will that be done?" And, "Who will really gain by that?" Unless he has an unbeatable case, he will finally talk himself around into disproving his own arguments.

(2) Let others in the group "crack down on him." As long as they are arguing against him and refusing to buy his arguments, you can save your own objections. However, if he makes a statement that no one challenges, you should (a) first call on the others for any objections; and (b) state your own objections—preferably, if possible, in the form of more questions to him and to others in the group.

The Two Basic Secrets of Handling Conferences

1. The first and main secret of successfully handling conferences is to recognize what type of conference you are in. Don't, for example, try to run a "brainstorm" like an "expository" conference or vice versa. Don't invite people to a "problem-solving" conference and let it turn into a "pretended" conference. The chart on the following pages explains the 14 most common types of conferences and gives the key to their successful conduct.

2. The second basic secret is to make sure that the other persons in the conference also understand what sort of conference is going on. Give them a roadmap; e.g.: "Today we are going to have a problem-solving conference to figure out a way to reduce the costs of our in-house engineering research. Now the steps of the problem-solving conference, as I see them, are . . ."

Suppose the group strays from the path and veers into another type of conference; what should you do? Simply catch their attention by standing up, or by raising your hand, and say, "It seems to me this has turned into a brainstorm (or free discussion, etc.). For the past five minutes we have been doing such and such instead of such and such. Now, shall we pursue this technique further—say for another ten minutes—or shall we go back to the point we were on?"

In other words, don't be slow to explain to the others—straightforwardly and naturally—what you have observed about their conference behavior and the results of the meeting so far. As soon as they "see themselves," they can more easily decide what type conference will be most profitable.

There is nothing wrong with switching from one type of conference to another; indeed it is often a good practice. Don't let it happen with bewildering rapidity; but do make sure that everyone present knows the type of meeting to which you have shifted.

14 TYPES OF CONFERENCES OR DISCUSSIONS[1]

(The following are arranged in alphabetical order; the problem solving, staff, check-out, and training conferences are probably the more common and the more important.)

1. TYPE OF MEETING: BRAINSTORMING

What Happens:

Members "pop off" with any ideas that come to them (no holds barred); later you screen the ideas for the useful ones. Brainstorming is a form of creative conference.

Tips Toward Success

Expect to get about 5 useful ideas for every 50-100 suggested; don't be afraid of zany ones; saying them helps limber your creative cells. Try to get a homogeneous group, all of whom should know about the subject and what is needed. Have a shorthand expert take down the ideas.

2. TYPE OF MEETING: CHECK-OUT

What Happens:

Someone, usually the boss, presents his plan, and, in essence, asks, "Any comments or objections before I go ahead?" See *Staff* and *Yes-Man* below.

Tips Toward Success

Stick to facts; if you don't have a *fact* that supports the plan or that threatens the success of the plan, then you might as well keep quiet ... or go get the facts to support your "hunches," "doubts," and "feelings."

3. TYPE OF MEETING: COMPROMISE/IRONING-OUT

What Happens:

The problem is one of dividing or apportioning jobs, tasks,

Tips Toward Success

State the problem clearly on a chalkboard and tabulate under it the benefits and costs;

---

[1] What one man calls a "conference" another calls a "discussions"; the terms seminar, symposium, and meeting also vary in meaning. For the different uses of conferences, and how to handle yourself and others in conferences and discussions, see Chapter 12 "How to Use the Basic Types of Conferences," and Chapter 13 "How to Run a Conference Successfully," in *Putting Yourself Over in Business,* by Dyer, Evans, and Lovell.

money, benefits, annoyances, etc., and there isn't time for, or the occasion is not suitable for, new ideas or alternative courses. E.g., Half the parking area is torn up and half the employees will lose their parking spaces for a week—now who gets stuck?

then chart how they are to be applied or distributed. Each man present can see how his rights and the rights of others are affected. Make sure the problem is one of compromise or ironing out; keep reminding the members to seek the good of the whole organization; and keep them bargaining as pleasantly but as steadily as possible.

4. TYPE OF MEETING: CREATIVE

What Happens:
Group seeks a wholly new or original solution; or it seeks to dream up a new product, program, etc. May use brainstorming as method or starter.

Tips Toward Success
While change does not always mean progress, *progress always includes change.* And change usually seems unattractive at first. So don't fight the appearance of new ideas and don't try to dominate or speed up a creative conference. The purpose should be to help each member develop or contribute to a new idea; each member should be treated respectfully, and given time to get his germination process going.

5. TYPE OF MEETING: DISCUSSION

What Happens:
Group is not seeking a specific solution or decision but rather to improve their understanding of the subject matter and their responsibilities. A discussion may grow into a conference and vice versa; the trick is to be alert to which is the more desirable at the moment.

Tips Toward Success
Keep the discussion around the main topic by means of questions rather than by statements. Don't be "shocked" by what some members may say they think or feel; let others answer them; or keep them explaining what they mean by series of questions until they talk themselves out of their extreme positions. A good discussion takes time and performs the vital function of helping people *think*, as they may never have thought before, about a subject.

6. TYPE OF MEETING: EXPOSITORY CONFERENCE

What Happens:
A form of training conference which, in essence, is really a lecture or demonstration given the title "Conference" to avoid telling grown-ups they are going to "school" or to "class." "Conferees" has a more prestigious sound than "students."

Tips Toward Success
Ask plenty of questions and give experts in the audience a chance to answer or comment on topics in their specialties. For the rest, you are actually holding class or are in a class, regardless of the euphemistic title given it, and you might as well admit the fact and follow the TOMIPASTA or SPAIBASCATH outline given in Chapters 2 through 5 of this book.

7. TYPE OF MEETING: MANIPULATED

What Happens:

A pressure group holds the "conference" in order to give a "popular" or "democratic" appeal to a plan they want to put across.

Tips Toward Success

Do you want to accept the plan or to fight it? If you want to accept it, you have no problem, except to listen patiently to any objections raised or hinted by others—there might be real flaws in the plan. If you want to fight it, then keep bringing up the *facts* and *consequences* that the pressure group wants to overlook. Get the chairman to list all the consequences to the various departments of the business, and keep asking to be shown how the proposed plan will benefit the business *as a whole.*

8. TYPE OF MEETING: PRETENDED CONFERENCE

What Happens:

Group called together to provide an audience to listen to one man brag, shift blame, complain, or otherwise enjoy himself.

Tips Toward Success

Try to turn it into a real conference or discussion—that is, try to ask questions which will start the others and eventually maybe even the egoist thinking: ". . . and what can we do that will advance the aims and operations of this business as a whole?"

9. TYPE OF MEETING: PROBLEM-SOLVING

What Happens:

Group called to solve a specific problem or plan a course of action. Chairman should run it on a somewhat formal basis, calling on each person first for facts, then for solutions, then opinions or agreement. He should try to stay neutral (until the end); and concentrate on helping group clarify the problem and the solution.

Tips Toward Success

The recommended six steps of the problem-solving conference are:

(1) Collect the facts.
(2) Evaluate the facts.
(3) Propose possible steps to take.
(4) Test or explore the consequences of each of the alternatives.
(5) Decide on the solution or steps to take.
(6) Consider how the problem arose in the first place—to avoid getting caught the same way again.

10. TYPE OF MEETING: SEMINAR

What Happens:

Technically, a seminar is a meeting of advanced students with a professor in charge. In business it can mean the equivalent—that is, already qualified men exploring together, under an expert's

Tips Toward Success

If you are the leader, do plenty of advance preparation, and hold "skull sessions" with yourself and any available experts before and after each session. Decide on the important points to cover and, as long as you hit these points, don't be afraid of apparent guidance, a certain area of importance to them. Or it can be a nice title for a series of training conferences (or even lectures).

digressions and gamblings. The participants have to have time to think and to phrase things—if the material isn't new to them, why should they be at the seminar? If you are a participant, remember you have come to *learn*, not to impress your ideas or personality on the others—even if they (at first) seem backward and blind to your bright ideas.

11. TYPE OF MEETING: STAFF

What Happens:

A staff conference or meeting may be any or all of the other types of conferences. It may be a weekly meeting of independently powerful department heads who, in essence, report what they are doing just to let the others know. Or it may be a problem-solving session led by their boss. Or it may simply be a get-together at which the boss lays down the law for the coming period.

Tips Toward Success

Decide what type of conference is being held and be alert to any changes. If possible, help the others by frankly pointing out—and not accusingly—what sort of meeting is being held; e.g.: "Seems to me we aren't just reporting the week's doings as usual but are facing up to a new problem. Joe here appears to want to brainstorm it. Shall we do so for the next 10 minutes?" And so forth.

12. TYPE OF MEETING: SYMPOSIUM

What Happens:

Technically a symposium is a meeting of experts who present papers on the subject; or it is the collection of such papers. (When an outfit has used up the titles "conference" and "seminar" for what are really mixed groups of people in "classrooms," they sometimes use "symposium" to dignify a meeting of higher ranking personnel.)

Tips Toward Success

The idea of a symposium, a true symposium, is to bring the top men together and see what they have to say. Later you summarize, synthesize, conclude—and argue. If you really want a symposium, then don't try to run it like another type of conference: treat it as a series of independent reports. If it was not intended to be a real symposium, then decide what type of conference was really wanted, and behave accordingly.

13. TYPE OF MEETING: TRAINING OR WORKSHOP

What Happens:

Normally, a session to impart plainly labeled skills and knowledges. Differs from an expository conference in the greater

Tips Toward Success

If you are the leader, be frank and clear about the aims of the meeting and what the members are to learn and do. If you are a participant, try to cooperate and learn—

13. TYPE OF MEETING: TRAINING OR WORKSHOP:

What Happens: (*continued*)
emphasis on participation and in the effort to have each member learn that skill or knowledge "by doing." In the workshop all the emphasis is on the "doing," with the leader standing by to help, hint, criticize, or judge the work being done.

Tips Toward Success (*continued*)
later you can protest or argue about the things you disapprove of.[2]

14. TYPE OF MEETING: YES-MAN

What Happens:
The boss has the answer all worked out and states it as though any doubts would be impossible or foolish. Either he uses the occasion to bask in the limelight; or to appear "decisive"; or he kids himself that he is being "democratic" and is letting the "troops" participate.

Tips Toward Success
When he is the boss, then it's your decision about how much you *yes* him—maybe his solution is the best; or maybe you have the duty to raise important objections. If he is not the boss, ask for a listing of the advantages and *disadvantages* connected with his proposal.

FOUR LAYERS THAT OFTEN NEED TO BE UNPEELED

Suppose you have conducted the conference properly and have gone through all the problem-solving steps and have obtained an agreement on a solution. Yet you don't feel right about it. You aren't satisfied, and some of the men you most respect do not appear fully satisfied. Should you shrug your shoulders and say, "Well, we did our best. Now we'll try to live with our decision"? Or, can you take a more deeply probing look at your conference and find the trouble? Yes, there is a way of looking past the mechanics of conference organization, and even past the niceties of human relations techniques.[3]

---

[2] Suppose Mr. A says a thing will work, and Mr. B says it will not. Mr. A has actually tried the idea, and Mr. B has not. Doesn't the weight of the proof lie on Mr. A's side—and shouldn't Mr. B try the idea before he repeats his objection? Similarly, in a seminar or workshop the evidence at the start is in favor of the leader or expert who has conducted the program before. A newcomer should not begin by throwing all sorts of objections and complaints—which he may later have to swallow. Rather, he should cooperate for at least the first third of the program. The odds are that the sponsors of the program have already considered his objections and know it will be taken care of later. (This seems an obvious point; but just listen to the objections and "rationalizings" at the start of any training conference or seminar!)

[3] I am indebted to Lieutenant Commander John J. O'Connor, Chaplain, U. S. Navy, for this section. Father O'Connor, to the best of my knowledge, has been the

Individuals and groups have four layers—or reactions—through which they may go when confronted by a problem, situation, or difficulty. These "solutions" are related to:

1. Expediency—the quick, easy-appearing, answer.
2. Legalistic Compliance—follow "the book."
3. Social Adjustment—do what "everybody else does."
4. Moral Basis—what ought to be done.

Not everyone goes through each of these phases every time he faces a problem; and sometimes a group will jump ahead to the sound moral decision. But most people, and practically all groups, will be tempted to accept the expedient, social, or simply legal solution unless they take the time to think all the way through a problem.

1. *The Expedient.* The expedient solution may also be the right solution and the honest solution—and again it may not. In our terminology it means the "first easy way out that appears." For example, a plant manager has a shortage of a special steel and is faced with shutting down an operation. Someone suggests, "Let's just substitute some of the iron left from last month's job, and paint a new label on it." You can usually recognize the purely expedient reaction by the phrases "A man has to be *practical*..." "We've got to get the work out..." "Get the job done, and done fast, that's what counts..."

The trouble, of course, is that one can get an immediate job done, but at the cost of future efficiency, future production, or future good will. More importantly, even if the falsely expedient solution does not backfire, you have set an example or established a pattern which eventually you must regret. If you take the easy way out, those who follow you—and upon whom you must depend—will also take the easy way out.

When someone comes up with a purely expedient solution, ask him or the others, "Is that the best answer from a long-range point of view?" Or, ask the group, "Does that satisfy everyone, or are there other ideas?" The others will soon poke holes in the expedient solution, and will begin to turn up new ideas among which you will find a better course of action.

2. *The Legalistic.* The "book" is the refuge of the bureaucrats, of the narrow-minded, and of the rigid-minded. They look to see

---

leader in developing this important area of group dynamics and executive decision making. For further information see *Principles and Problems of Naval Leadership,* NavPers 15924, and *Moral Leadership,* NavPers 15890, both of which owe their authorship to Father O'Connor. They are available from the Superintendent of Documents, U. S. Government Printing Office, Washington 25, D. C.

what the company policy is, and blindly adhere to whatever they can justify by citing a "regulation" or "standard." The framers of a nation's laws or the devisers of a corporation's procedures manual would be amazed if they could see all the stupidities perpetrated by men and women who insist on (or hide behind) the letter of the law! When Pearl Harbor was bombed, the sergeant in charge of an ammunition storeroom refused to unlock it, because no one had brought the right requisition form! The soldiers had to break it open over his protests. All too many times a customer is told, "Sorry, we can't handle your order in that way because our policy is . . ." And the customer goes away thinking to himself, "If you have to do it your way, I'll take my business elsewhere."

An expert on the laws and regulations is a good man to have around, but don't let him cramp you within an unnecessarily legalistic view of a situation. Ask him: "Does that regulation really apply here? Is there another rule which supersedes or over-rides the rule you mentioned? Do you think the board of directors had this situation in mind when they wrote the policy? How can we do the right thing without upsetting the system which has been devised to take care of every situation but this one? What suggestions can we make for changing the rules so that they make more sense?"

3. *Social Adjustment.* All of us are powerfully affected by the social pressures around us. The appeal, "Aw, come on, everybody is doing it," has incited an incalculable amount of pilferage, "goofing off," embezzlement, faking of records, excess drinking, and other forms of foolish or criminal behavior. Just as in social life, so in business circles, the "custom of the trade," or the "normal practice" can be guides both to good and bad conduct. You must look closely at "what everybody does," to see if you really ought to do it. Few companies have gotten rich, and many have gone broke, because they did what their competitors did. When someone says, "Everybody does it," or "The people expect it of us," ask the group, "But should we do it in this case? Perhaps someone has an idea about another way which will be even more effective?"

4. *The Moral Basis—the Long-Range View.* None of us knows what the future will bring, and none of us can foresee the exact consequences of our acts and decisions. The management practice that works in one situation may not work in another; the human relations technique that soothes and inspires the men today may disgust and annoy them tomorrow. The purely expedient decision may blow up in our faces. The course of action taken to "please everybody" or to "fit the book" may turn out to do neither. Our only sure guide to the

future is to base our decisions and actions on sound moral principles. Then we can be sure that, having done what we ought to do, the consequences in the long run will be for the best. The management practice, the human relations technique, the legalistic, the expedient, and the social-pressure decision—all must be synthesized into courses of action of which we can be proud. But first we must take the trouble to check their level of morality before we embark on them.

Often the four factors—expediency, legality, social pressure, and moral judgment—converge on the same answer. This can be expected because in the long run the action that is practical, socially acceptable, legal, and moral, is also the most successful one. But make sure first!

Let's return to the example of the man who suggested the substitution of iron in a job that called for a special steel. He could justify it on the basis that: "Other shops do it when they get caught short," or, because: "We gotta get the work out"; and he might claim "There's no rule against it in the company's book." But after you have peeled off these layers—and it can take some patient discussion, you will meet the fact that the substitution violates three basic moral principles: (1) you lie to the customer; (2) you steal from the customer; and (3) you endanger his life and limb in the event of the material's failure. By holding firm to these moral principles you may lose an immediate advantage, but you can gain a hundred more, and you certainly avoid a thousand disadvantages—beginning with loss of your self-respect and the respect of the men around you.

SUMMING UP THIS CHAPTER

Most conferences are complicated to some extent by the presence of hidden agendas, whether conscious or subconscious, malicious or benign. The best way to direct or redirect these covert motives is to establish a scale of generally agreed-upon values. If necessary, put the scale on a chalkboard or sheet of paper and ask the members to compare their proposed courses of action against the agreed-upon order of values. This should be done in a calm objective fashion and mostly by means of questions asked of the others—not by challenging assertions or demands from you.

Probably the greatest cause of confusion and delays in conferences is the failure on the part of one or more of the members to realize what type of conference is required, or what type of conference actually is going on around them. The listing of the "14 Types of Conferences or Discussions" on pages 80-84 describes the key characteristics of the meetings you can expect to attend, and it suggests the best ways of handling them.

Often the failure to come up with truly satisfactory solutions or recommendations is caused by the natural propensity of men to accept too quickly, or to be too obtuse or selfish to think past the purely expedient, legalistic, or social-pressure solutions. The answer, of course, lies in keeping them thinking until they discern the truly sound solution, which will in the long run be the most satisfactory.

But not every one in every meeting will be willing to go along with your best efforts to make it a success. Accordingly, the next chapter will tell you how to handle hecklers as well as honest questioners.

10

HOW TO HANDLE QUESTIONERS AND HECKLERS

You Can Expect to Face More Question Periods

In Chapter Five, under Audience Action, we quoted Clayton Fritchey's statement: "The Q and A, once merely a nonfunctional appendage, is rapidly becoming as large as, or larger than, the body of the speech." Mr. Fritchey also said:

The speech with a long tail, so to speak, seems to be growing in popularity not only with audiences but with the speakers themselves. . . . The most powerful men in the world, up to and including Khrushchev, shape their speeches to fit the protocol of the National Press Club, the protocol being that the tail shall wag the torso. It is understood that the formal part of the speech shall be subordinate to the prolonged, frank, and sometimes rude question period that follows. . . .

The popularity of this technique with audiences is quite evident. . . . The public may wonder why the principal is willing to volunteer for the witness stand, but the fact is that he likes it, too. . . .

Real cross-examination on a real witness stand can be a fearsome experience, for a determined lawyer can pursue a line of questioning until the witness is truly at bay. Actually, the experienced politician has little to fear from the kind of "grilling" that he gets. . . . He soon discovers that the questions nearly always follow a familiar pattern, and he long ago has memorized the best way of dealing with them, no matter how original and embarrassing they may sound to the audience. . . .[1]

[1] "Now, If Ever, We Need the Stirring Word," *The New York Times Magazine*, March 6, 1960, p. 13.

Mr. Fritchey makes three points which are as applicable to business presentations as to political speeches. These are: (1) the question periods are getting longer and more frequent; (2) the speaker who is willing to try them will learn to enjoy them; and (3) with a little experience and preparation one can be ready to "field even the hottest appearing wild balls."

Three Opportunities and Two Dangers

Standing up to answer questions before a group provides three opportunities and two dangers. If you keep them in mind, you can obtain more profit from the opportunities and avoid or minimize the dangers.

The opportunities are:

1. Audience participation—audiences like to hear their own voices and to express themselves; and, as pointed out in Chapter Five, participation can entertain and involve the members of a group as perhaps no other known method. Moreover, you require no aids and no detailed memorizing of speeches.

2. Demonstration of your ability to think on your feet, to field questions, to handle people, and to display your knowledge of the subject under discussion.

3. The chance to find out what is bothering members of the group or what they particularly want to know.

The dangers are:

1. The questions may show up your areas of ignorance or incompetency.

2. Another person may use the question period to take the meeting away from you—to fluster, confuse, and upset you.

The dangers are as real as the opportunities; however, the tendency toward the question period is so great, and the probable advantages so outweigh the disadvantages, that you must expect to encounter more, not fewer, Q and A sessions. The man who does not seek them may well have them forced on him by his superiors—or by the audiences.

Two Basic Secrets of Fielding Questions or Hecklings

The two basic secrets of fielding questions successfully are: (1) Be prepared for them—plan for them, and (2) keep control of yourself in order to keep control of the audience.

1. *Plan for the questions.* "Suppose," someone always asks, "your

audience asks a lot of questions. Is that a good or bad sign?" The answer, of course, is, "It depends on the type of questions." Questions which involve the audience, or which show audience interest, or which help relate the points of the presentation to their specific needs —all such questions are good questions. But questions that ask you to repeat something, to define something, or to explain a fundamental point of your presentation, all such questions show that the audience missed your main points or that they are confused about what you meant to say. They signal that your presentation needs improvement. You might, for example, have purposely left out some incidental information or conclusions, or topics of interest to only a few persons in the audience. If such "pre-planned" questions are not asked, the audience misses nothing important. You should consciously decide what to take care of the presentation and what to leave until the question-and-answer or participation period.

2. *Keep control of yourself.* Even when you have prepared yourself to answer every imaginable question, someone in the audience may come up with a new one. Or, someone may express his question in a highly emotional way. Therefore, resolve from the outset that you are going to keep control of yourself—no matter what type of question is asked or how it is snarled at you. However well or poorly you may be able to answer to questions, remember to do so with dignity and courtesy. Let's look at how President Kennedy handles questioners and then the dangers of the "self-fulfilling prophecy" before we discuss the Q and A situations you can expect to face.

President Kennedy's Way of Handling Questioners

Mr. Charles Cooke, in an article on the Presidential press conferences,[2] described President Kennedy's handling of the newsmen's questions thus:

He, Mr. Kennedy, nodded gravely at the questioners as they questioned, and this, I thought, was with a double purpose: to indicate that he understood the sometimes complex questions; and to encourage and put at ease the questioners in case they were nervous. It was reassuring, the essence of courtesy, and exceedingly pleasant to watch.

And he nodded his head gently as he gave his answers. These nods seemed to say: "I am answering you to the best of my ability, on the basis of my present knowledge. I shall be pleased if time proves my answer to have been the right and best one, but in any case, I am pleased that we are all in direct communication with each other."

2 "The Weekly Ritual News Dance," *The Sunday Star*, Washington, D.C. April 16, 1961, p. D-3.

Note that the President did not try to make himself look good at the expense of his "nervous" questioners. Note, too, that his behavior could be characterized by the terms "patience and courtesy." Keep those words—patience and courtesy—in the forefront of your mind rather than "chip on the shoulder" as some Q and A leaders do.

The Self-Fulfilling Prophecy Effect

A self-fulfilling prophecy works thus: A man predicts there will be a depression, and begins to retrench. He warns his friends and acquaintances and they stop buying goods; they lay off workers; they quit making new investments; and they counsel others to do the same. At the end of the year there is a depression—depression caused by the prophecy.

Similarly, suppose a man tells himself: "I'll bet these people will be after my scalp. There's no use trying to make a good impression on them, because I can't do it." What will happen when he starts answering their questions? He will have such a stack of chips on his shoulder and he will be so quick to take offense that his prophecy will come true: The people and he will have a scrimmage.

On the other hand, when you predict success for yourself, and when you say, "I'm sure these people are sincerely trying to do a good job and will welcome what I have to say," you can cause the self-fulfilling process to work for, rather than against, you.

Three Occasions That Put You on the Q and A Spot

Three occasions that usually result in a question period are: (1) a call to the front office; (2) facing a wholly new group; and (3) an impromptu appearance before a known group.

1. *A call to the front office.* Mr. Marten in the executive suite tells his secretary, "Ask Mr. Jones to step in a minute." The secretary phones Mr. Jones' secretary and says, "Mr. Marten wants to see Mr. Jones right away." As Mr. Jones walks toward the front office he wonders "What's up?" He half hopes the boss wants to congratulate him on his successful projects; he half fears the boss wants to reprimand him for some projects behind schedule.

As he enters the inner sanctum, he says, "You wanted to see me, Mr. Marten?" Mr. Marten replies, "Yes, Jones, I'd like to review the Montgomery contract." Mr. Jones, while inwardly heaving a sigh of relief, says, "Yes, sir, let me send for the file and while my secretary is getting it, I'll fill you in on the general situation." Jones also thinks to himself, "Why didn't I bring it with me—or why didn't he let me know what he wanted so I could have brought it with me?"

Obviously, a man ought to be told why he is being called to the front office or to any meeting so that he can prepare his thoughts on the way. For example, Mr. Marten might have told his secretary: "Ask Mr. Jones to step around. Tell him it is about the Montgomery contract."

When Mr. Jones returns to his own office, how does he summon his assistants? Ten to one he does exactly what his boss did or even more peremptorily. When Mr. Jones says, "Send for Mr. Smith," or "Tell Miss Williams to come in here," or "Call the branch heads for a staff meeting at 2 P.M. this afternoon," does he give them a hint about the subject matter so that they can be prepared to expedite the business by having their facts and ideas ready? All too rarely! Whatever your level, you should always add a sentence to a summons to apprise the other person of what will be expected of him.

Another practice to make automatic is that of adding an acknowledgment to a summons, perhaps a phrase like: "Yes, sir, I'll be right there; can you tell me what it is about so I can bring the right information?" On half the occasions you will be replying to the boss himself, or to one of your peers, and he will readily answer, "Sure, it's about the XYZ matter. I need the latest figures." Keep asking, and after a few times the other person will learn to add to his summons or invitation the reason for the meeting. The other half of the time the call will be from his secretary to your secretary or to you. You, or your secretary, can still ask the question. Most of the time the other man's secretary will have an inkling of the topic and can say so, or with some encouragement may learn to add, "I think it is about such and such a matter." Or, she may learn to ask her boss, "Shall I tell Mr. Jones what you want to see him about?"

These practices can reduce the number of times you will be called wholly unprepared to a meeting. However, no warning does not mean no preparation. As you walk toward the meeting, and as soon as you see who is there, you can mentally list the items high on the company's priority lists and guess pretty shrewdly what the topic is going to be.

Winston Churchill is said to have spent a lifetime preparing for impromptu remarks!

2. *Facing a wholly new group.* When you face a wholly new group your preparation can only be general in scope. You can mentally outline what sort of things are most likely to be of interest to the average person. However, you need not stop with your own estimates; you can ask the members of the group what they want

to hear. This practice of frankly asking an audience what they already know about the subject, what they would like to hear, or what has been bothering them about the subject, can be most effective.

In three or four minutes you can arouse a group's interest and involve them from the outset in what you are to say by *asking them questions before they get a chance to ask you.* Here are some opening questions for a speaker who faces a host of new faces:

How many here have heard me speak on this topic before?

How many here have (worked in) (studied) (heard about) the area to be discussed?

When you were (invited) (directed to come) to this meeting what did you expect to hear?

What (element) (aspect) of the subject has most interested you or bothered you in the past?

The answers to these questions will reveal the audience's level of knowledge, their prejudices and misconceptions, and also their probable level of intelligence, skill, and managerial rank. Most importantly you will have shown them that you mean to *slant your talk to them,* an effort they will greatly appreciate.

But, avoid spending too much time on one question. At one meeting, the speaker started off by asking, "Are you all up to date on the status of the XYZ Program?" One of the group immediately asked a question which revealed he was unfamiliar with the whole program. The speaker took 20 minutes to review the past events.

After the meeting I asked him, "Why did you take so long on the one question? It cut down your time for the important new things you were to tell us." He replied, "The audience was so unfamiliar with what had been going on that I thought I had to bring them up to date before explaining anything new. Wasn't I right to do so?"

I had to reply, "No, because the audience was familiar with the program. That one man had been out of town last month and missed the earlier meetings. You should have collected some more questions before you dedicated yourself to just one."

In other words, when starting "cold," follow the parliamentary procedure of requiring a "seconder" for any topic. This is not hard to do and it is important, because in an audience of 30 people, you cannot assume that what bothers one man, also bothers the other 29. Therefore, after a man asks a question, you might say, "That's a good point"; then look to the other side of the room and ask, "How many more are interested in that aspect? Or, do you have other questions like it?" Or, you can say frankly, "I'd like to collect a few more questions before answering the first one. I may be able to answer several at the same time. Now, who will second that first question— or add another of his own?"

As you look at their faces you can detect how much interest others have in the question. And, usually one or two persons will say, "I second it," or "I'd rather hear about the Y part of the XYZ Program."

After you have collected three to five questions you can often summarize the answers to them, or you can explain that you will answer them in the course of your presentation. You should also promise to give the group another chance to ask the same or other questions. People will listen better to *your* message when they know that you are willing to listen to *theirs*.

3. *Impromptu appearances before a known group.* Suppose someone urges: "Let's hear from Mr. Jones on the subject." And you are Mr. Jones.

You should not be completely unprepared; otherwise, why are you at the meeting? You must have come because you had some interest in the subject, or your operations will be affected by what the group decides. If you are caught completely off guard, simply say, "Give me a few minutes to formulate my thoughts. Meanwhile, please continue the discussion." It is better to admit frankly that you need time to think than to stand up and fumble for words. Or, while you collect your own thoughts you can lead a question-and-answer discussion of your own. For example, you can say, "Before I present my own ideas, I'd like to get a clearer idea of your needs and desires."

While saying this, be sure to look around the group to signify that you are referring to all of them, not just to the person who asked for your opinion. Then you can begin with your own questions; for example, "How many here feel we have taken everything important into account?" Or, "Does anyone know of a factor that hasn't been mentioned?" And so on.

No one can reasonably object to—and most will appreciate—your efforts to discover what the audience knows or wants to know before you present your own ideas.

HOW TO HANDLE HECKLERS

When do thoughtful, challenging questions turn into hecklings? A man who is sensitive to any criticism may consider the mildest inquiry to constitute criminal heckling. A man who is sure of himself, who knows his stuff and is thick-skinned may welcome a free-for-all of accusations and counter-accusations. For our purpose let's consider heckling to occur when the purpose of the query or comment is no longer to advance the business at hand or to help clarify issues, but to annoy, discomfit, or "show up" the speaker.

The Unintentional Heckler

We must also distinguish between *unintentional* and *intentional* heckling. The unintentional heckler really wants to get information or to clarify an issue, but he happens to possess a cantankerous personality or a pugnacious manner.

Handling the unintentional heckler is not difficult. In most instances, you simply pause for a moment and then give your answer in a slow, dignified fashion. If this doesn't give the excited questioner the time—and the hint—to cool down, you can say, politely, but firmly, "You sound quite disturbed over this issue. I hope to answer your question to the best of my ability, but I'm not sure what answer you are seeking. Are you angry or critical of the facts and conditions of this matter, or are you upset about my way of presenting them?"

At this point an unintentional heckler will assure you that he is worried about the facts of the matter, that he holds nothing personal against you, and so forth.

The intentional heckler, however, is not after the facts, he is against you—or against the group you represent. Handling him, if indeed that can be done, is another matter.

The Intentional Heckler

Except for the businessmen who get into politics or who take positions in civic, or social, or labor-management problems, or in annual meetings of stockholders, the average executive does not have to fear the rabble-rousing type of heckler. But the subtle antagonists he does face can be dangerous to his peace of mind and even to his success as an executive.

In business meetings you can encounter three types of hecklers: (1) those junior to you; (2) those equal to you; and (3) those superior to you. Let's see what can be done in each case.

1. Junior hecklers. Obviously a heckler junior to you will be working for another executive or will be working for another division of the corporation. Such a heckler has been put up to it by his seniors—or thinks he has his boss's approval. Before you attack them—indeed, before you attack any heckler—think first to yourself: Will what I say or do make me look good or bad to the others present? And will it just vent my annoyances or will it advance the business at hand?

You can take any of three courses of action with junior hecklers:

a. Face them frankly and say something like: "Your last questions (or remarks) sound like you are trying to be rude rather than helpful. Why don't you be a good sport and wait until I am through. Then you can present your case." This will make all but the most reckless hecklers shut up—no one likes to appear a poor sport.

b. Face them and say, "So that we don't lose time now, why don't you take up those questions with your boss, Mr. Black? He can give you the answers or explain how the matter relates to your areas of responsibilities." This points up the fact that they should look to their own bosses for guidance. Then if they keep pestering you, they will make their bosses look weak and make themselves appear ignorant and unruly.

c. Face their boss and say, "Perhaps, Mr. Black, you can explain the details to your people later. If I try to answer all their special purpose or private vendetta questions now, we'll all lose a lot of time." This puts their boss on the spot to keep order among them. If he tries to shrug it off with a remark like, "Oh, let the young fellows speak up. We need to hear their ideas, too," then you can turn it back on him by saying, "Well, if you insist on taking the time, we had better poll the others present. If everyone feels it would be worthwhile to keep talking on one subject, perhaps you can explain the details to your people." What else can he say but: "Oh, no, this is your show. You go ahead, and we'll take up the unanswered questions later."

2. *Equal-rank hecklers.* Intentional hecklers of rank equal to you will be persons who oppose you and your progress for personal reasons, or who hope to gain an advantage by "cutting you down." You can't, as the saying goes, win in a spraying contest with a skunk. Answer their first two or three questions or nasty remarks with polite, friendly, factual answers. Then, if they keep attacking you, bring the issue into the open with a statement like: "Perhaps you don't intend it, but your manner seems unnecessarily bitter and suspicious (or sarcastic) to me. What is you are trying to prove? I am trying to present some facts and arguments to help advance the business at hand. What are *you* trying to do?" This puts them on the defensive and as soon as they answer or if they remain silent, ask them: "Just why was that so important that you had to interrupt me? How about being a good sport and let me finish? If what I say can help the

business we are all ahead. If not, then I can't fool anybody—and you'll have your chance to do a hatchet-job on me." After you have made that statement loudly and clearly, the heckler cannot continue without appearing to put his personal feelings ahead of business. Your goal, of course, is to make the hecklers and the audience realize the distinction between the effort to embarrass you and the effort to advance the business at hand.

3. Superior-rank hecklers. When your own boss or his boss starts to heckle you, then you have probably had it! You are probably being forced to seek a job elsewhere. If so, you can decide whether you want to subside gracefully, or bring the matter to a head. That's your problem. In any event, you should look him or them firmly in the eye and say, "I understood that I was to prepare this presentation and I believe this information is of value to the business. If someone is changing the rules in midcourse, let me know about it. Meanwhile, neither you nor I gain anything by being rude."

If they are stabbing at you for personal reasons, you can make your appeal over their heads to the most senior man present. For example, you might address the president, Mr. Blue, thus, "Mr. Blue, we seem to have differences of opinion here. Would you like me to continue, or would you rather Mr. Jones or Mr. Black took over?" The odds are he will say, "Go ahead. After we've heard from you we'll give the others a chance." Then you will be operating under his protection, and the others will be interrupting *his* speaker when they interrupt *you*. If he has joined the cabal against you, you never had or have a chance. Yet, if you can keep making the distinction between the attack on you and the attack on the information, data, and plans which you are propounding, the majority of people in the audience will eventually be on your side. Your immediate boss—or some other antagonistic boss—may hold out against you, but in the long run you will have gained the reputation of being a man who worked for the good of the business and not just for himself.

That is the sort of reputation that leads a man on to better jobs— even after he has been forced out of his present one.

SUMMING UP THIS CHAPTER

Nowadays, people expect to participate in discussion periods and Q and A periods. Most speakers learn to enjoy such periods. To make sure you handle questions well, be sure to:

1. Plan for the questions in advance; figure out what they will probably be, and have your answers ready.

2. Keep control of yourself; think of the importance of the subject and of the consequences of proposals and recommendations, not of your hurt or challenged feelings.

3. Follow Mr. Kennedy's example of patience and courtesy toward all questioners.

4. Make the self-fulfilling prophecy work for you rather than against you.

5. Visualize and prepare for the situations that most frequently require you to answer questions—a call to the front office; a talk before a strange group; a talk before a known group.

6. Avoid spending too much time on one question—ask for "seconds" or for related questions.

7. Warn the other person in advance of the type of information you will be asking of him.

When you face hecklers, build your offense-defense on the two solid bases:

1. Don't heckle back—maintain your dignity and good appearance.

2. Keep pointing out the distinction between advancing the business at hand, and attacking a person for personal reasons.

PART II

EFFECTIVE WRITING FOR EXECUTIVES

FOREWORD

Part I of this book was reserved for the chapters on how to improve your presentations or public speaking for three reasons:

1. Most men in supervisory positions already write well enough to hold their jobs, and they are producing memoranda, letters, and reports every day. But standing up to face an audience is something that occurs less often. Also, when they do speak in public, they feel their success or failure immediately and acutely—much more so than when they dictate a letter, sign it, and toss it into the outgoing mail basket.

2. The problems of public speaking require one to work towards writing improvement. When you start with writing, the reader rarely looks ahead to the possibility that he might have to change his public speaking in order to write better! But when you start with the speaking problems, the reader quickly realizes that he cannot improve his public speaking without improving his organization of words on paper. Most of what was said about the development of a speech, and about humor, visual aids, and the trends in modern presentations, applies to the practice of writing. You can apply the SPAIBASCATH approach when putting together a report, article, or chapter of a manual. You can use TOMIPASTA as a guide when you prepare a training publication for a group of employees.

3. Most people will accept hints about improving their public speaking ability even when they are not willing to accept criticisms of their writing practices—which hurt their "pride of authorship." Also, it is easier to observe mistakes in one's spoken words and in one's gestures than it is to see them in one's written words and punctuation. Public speaking seems difficult for those who have not practiced it, yet it is far easier to succeed in than is the accomplishment of good writing. When you speak you have many more ways of getting your message across than when you write. Paper does not smile, nor does it frown, gesture, or catch the listener's eye with eyeball-to-eyeball contact. But because we have been "writing for years" we can fool ourselves into thinking we do it quite well—though

we have, in fact, for years inflicted bad writing on people without realizing it.

Writing precedes public speaking in time, because it is a help in formulating thoughts as well as a method of recording them. By scribbling his thoughts on paper a man can make the job of thinking and of organizing his thoughts easier. But he ought to remember to take the second step of making sure that what he sends to others on paper has been worded to fit their needs. *Writing*, because it expresses men's thoughts, has the strengths and weaknesses of their thoughts. When well organized and clearly phrased, it speeds operations and facilitates business; when poorly organized and confusingly presented, it causes confusions and delays.

In Chapter One, we mentioned how the development of accounting and statistical tools have helped men find better ways of handling business, industry, and government. Similarly, good writing can provide a "feedback" that will help the thinker plan and the doer act with greater precision and success. By placing his thoughts on paper a man can usually descry what terms ought to be rearranged for clarity or illustrated by pictures and tables. Action is the test of policies and methods; writing can be the test of the logic, the proper sequence, and cogency of one's thoughts. A thing that works in theory must also work in practice—or it did not really work in theory. Words that do not read clearly and convincingly on paper are signals that we must check the thought processes and the data on which they are based.

If what you write is not clear, the reader will not know what you want of him. If you are confused in your verbiage, the reader will lose time figuring out what you mean, or he will have to send back to you for clarification. Improving your writing can lead to improving your business; it will also enhance your reputation as a thinker and as a leader.

Writing is the expression of thinking—the practice of writing is the same as the practice of thinking. Perhaps that is why people do not like to write?

11

HOW TO MANAGE YOUR OWN WRITING

Preparing Yourself

We must begin with the two assumptions: (1) the readers of this book are managers, or executives, not full-time authors; and (2) most top executives can write well. The truth of the second assumption is supported by famous writers like Robert Graves and Alan Hodge, who have stated:

Where is good English to be found? Not among those who might be expected to write well professionally. Schoolmasters seldom write well: It is difficult for any teacher to avoid either pomposity or, in the effort not to be pompous, a jocular conversational looseness. The clergy suffer from much the same occupational disability: they can seldom decide whether to use "the language of the market-place" or Biblical rhetoric. Men of letters usually feel impelled to cultivate an individual style ... and nowadays an individual style usually means merely a range of inaccuracies, ambiguities, logical weaknesses, and stylistic extravagances. Trained journalists use a flat, over-simplified style, based on a study of what sells a paper and what does not. ...

As a rule, the best English is written by people without literary pretensions, who have responsible executive jobs in which the use of official language is not compulsory; and, as a rule, the better at their jobs they are, the better they write. ...

"The better at their jobs they are the better they write"—this statement and others like it have been borne out in my experience and in that of other writers and editors. J. P. Marquand, for example, after his experience with the generals and admirals of World War II remarked that he found that most of them wrote extremely well. But, of course, men in key positions are able to express themselves clearly and cogently, because men with such abilities are most likely to be promoted, or once promoted they quickly develop the communicative skills.

Perhaps one cannot "manage" the production of a great poem, novel, or dramatic work; but one can certainly achieve better letters, reports, and articles by performing better as a manager of the writing. This chapter and the next will discuss how to manage your own writing; the chapter after that will cover how to manage the writing of your subordinates so that your work and theirs is performed more efficiently, economically, and *pleasantly*.

Must You Be in the Mood?

Writing, like everything else, is easier to do if you are in the mood. But even poets, novelists, and advertising copywriters cannot wait idly for a flash of inspiration; they must plan ways of hastening a flash of inspiration. If you are interested in doing a lot of writing, see Larston Farrar's book *Successful Writers and How They Work*[1] for some of the ways professional writers use to force themselves into the mood for writing. Businessmen, however, write about practical matters which can be discussed in factual, ordinary language; and they must meet deadlines: a letter is due today, a report tomorrow. An executive cannot do as the poet Horace recommended: leave his manuscript buried in the ground for years before digging it up to polish it for publication.

The mood for writing is proportional to three things: (1) the writer's experience and background in the subject; (2) his previous practice in writing; (3) his general health, freshness, and well-being.

1. *There can be no substitute for experience and background.* It is difficult to write about something you know little about. Yet people regularly try to beat this obvious fact. Time and time again, I have been sitting next to a businessman when an assignment to prepare a letter, a report, or a speech comes along. He, the man of action, will stick to his chair scribbling reams of paper mostly about what he thinks he thinks on the subject, or what he remembers from chance encounters with the subject in the past. Naturally, he finds great difficulty in writing clearly, cogently, and in a well-organized fashion. So he decides he hates to write. On the other hand,

[1] New York: Hawthorn Books, Inc., 1959.

I, the writer, will first go around the place to locate data, information, opinions, and ideas on the subject. When I come back and sit down, my paper almost writes itself. I know what the background of the problem is; I have the latest data; I have found out who is for and who is against various facts; and I have already discussed the matter with the men who are concerned with it and who therefore will be the ones to comment on my final draft.

My friend at the other desk, however, has struggled over wording and re-wording of sentences which will never come out right because they do not include all the facts. The more he writes and polishes, the more he becomes emotionally committed to what he is saying. He develops a vested interest in his hard-won pages and he instinctively defends them from criticism. Eventually, when his writings are reviewed, they run into adverse comments and plenty of "constructive" and "destructive" criticisms, because he has not gotten all the information or allowed for all the attitudes bearing on the subject. So, he grumbles about the "nitpickers" and the "fussbudgets" who just don't understand the difficulty of writing a paper which can please everyone. Or, he turns to a writer like myself for help—and what do I do? I simply put into his paper the facts, the data, and the opinions he never left his desk to obtain.

Hence, if you "can't get in the mood to write," try running through what you know about the subject either mentally or by jotting down notes on a piece of paper. Next, try talking the matter over with someone else. If an expert on the subject is not available, talk to a friend, or a member of the staff of a trade association, professional society, or library. Even though you may not uncover new information, you will have started your mind producing words and ideas that you can change from conversation to writing after you put down the telephone or return to your own desk.

2. *Previous practice in writing on the subject.* A man who has never played golf will have trouble getting started. A man who has never taken accounting, will find the first problems difficult. Similarly, a man who has done little writing will have trouble starting a writing job and keeping at it. Moreover, even though one may be an expert sport story writer, he can have a hard time starting a technical manual. An engineering writer may have difficulty starting a news release about the company's ball team.

In other words, fear, hope, threats, or good or bad human relations techniques cannot change the basic fact that the human mind requires a certain amount of time to ingest information, to mull over ideas, and to regurgitate them onto paper. This process can be helped or hindered, made more pleasant or less pleasant, but it must take place. The greater the familiarity with the subject, with the practice of writing, and with the practice of writing about the subject, the more quickly you can succeed in writing *well* about it. (So why not look ahead to the types of writing required in the executive positions above you, and start practicing them now?)

3. *Health, freshness, and well-being.* Writing, and especially the thinking and the decision-making that go with it, constitute a tiring process. Just as good health is vital to any executive in any tough job, so it is vital to good writing. Authors are often thought of as fragile creatures, and perhaps some are. But there are a lot of he-men authors, men who have been soldiers, sailors, bullfighters, prize-fighters, explorers, executives, and so on. There have also been successful businessmen who have been sickly. As someone once said, *half the work of the world is done by people who aren't feeling well.* In general, however, the extra energy required for creative thinking and for good writing, also requires extra strength of mind and body. (Don't you find yourself able to write better when you are rested than when you are tired? Obviously, yes. Then why not plan your schedule so that your hardest writing is done when you are in the best condition, at whatever time of day that occurs?)

Dr. Henry Wriston, President Emeritus of Brown University and Chairman of President Eisenhower's National Goals Commission, in his book *Academic Procession, Reflections of a College President*,[2] explained his practice in these words:

I have never been a good sleeper, and in the wakeful still of the night ideas sometimes take shape and crystallize. . . .

On arrival at the office this was my first business—to round out and complete, if possible, what the night had begun. To let correspondence . . . break my train of thought proved foolish. . . . Therefore, I learned to postpone till later everything that was not both primary and urgent. The first business was to clear my own mind. . . .

Try "Cascading" Your Store of Energy

For myself, I have found a "cascade system" useful in applying my daily store of energy to writing and editing assignments. When I am fresh in the morning I jot down ideas for new chapters or articles, or study someone else's work that has to be considerably edited or rewritten. Later, when I've lost my first freshness, I turn to the easier tasks of finishing chapters already roughed out, putting the final polish on work submitted to me for review, and writing letters and

[2] New York: Columbia University Press, 1959.

memos on routine matters. Finally, I switch to finishing up odds and ends, checking references, making calls, and talking over assignments with various people.

A man can perform administrative jobs for 10, 12, and 14 hours a day because the *work comes to him*: people call him, write to him, visit him, and ask or tell him something. He has many legitimate interruptions of his work during the day. When people call him or bring him things, they chat with him. When he supervises or checks on a job he moves around, speaks to people, and obtains ideas from them. On the other hand, the writer and editor must create from within themselves; their work does not flow to them, they must generate it from inside. When the writer, editor, or copy reader looks up to rest his eyes, or speaks to a fellow worker, or gives his mind a "break" he appears to be loafing. Hence, a 10-hours-a-day managerial job can be less of a strain than a 2-hour writing job.

The moral is: If you are having trouble with a writing assignment, don't decide you cannot write. The odds are that a professional writer could not do the job either in the way you are going about it. You must expect to have trouble with any sort of writing beyond the routine filling of forms, if you violate any of the three conditions which we have been discussing: These are:

1. Have the facts, ideas, opinions, and information from the real world outside of you—not just those already in your head and your heart. "Look in your heart and write" may be good advice for a poet; but an executive should look outside his prejudices and beyond his old conceptions.

2. Have some practice in the type of writing required, or try to get some as quickly as you can. Meanwhile, expect to write slowly and painfully.

3. Be in good health and rested. Don't save your energy for the coffee klatch, the executive's lunch, the big party, or the daily mail; save your best energy for the new writing job, and give the leftover energy to the other jobs.

This chapter has emphasized the importance of treating yourself intelligently and foresightedly as a "writing machine" which needs oiling, maintenance, and "tender, loving care" if it is to produce thoughts which can be turned into writing for others to read.

The next chapter will tell you how to estimate the time to budget for a writing assignment, how to get started, keep going expeditiously, and how to cut off when you have said just enough.

12

MANAGING YOUR OWN WRITING

STARTING, EXPEDITING, STOPPING

Remember when you were in school how you waited until the last week to do the term paper which had been assigned you three months earlier? But now every business proposal, speech, report, letter, and article has to be done on a crash basis, so the days of stalling are gone forever.

But are they gone? Isn't it true that some of your letters, proposals, and reports are not well written because you don't start them soon enough? Are the "rush-rush" and the "crash" conditions always the real reasons for the "quick and dirty jobs"? Or, have you managed your timing so badly that you have never had enough time for the extra thought, polish, and editing, which some writings needed?

More importantly, have you allowed "term papers" to be forgotten because of the day-to-day assignments? That is, have you failed to write up your long-range plans or some thoughtful analyses of the problems of your organization?

Every man in an executive, managerial, or supervisory position has observations, ideas, criticisms, and recommendations, regarding what is going on around him. Too often he excuses his failures to write about these things by saying to himself, "If only I had time to do a real report—to write an article—to prepare the background presentation this matter requires." In most cases the real reasons why a man does not produce the report or article (which so often is needed and could make a name for him) are two-fold: (1) he thinks he

110

would have to take a week, or a month, or three months off his job in order to write; and (2) he thinks he needs two or three uninterrupted days during which he should "lock himself in a room to do the writing." So he lets the matter slide until the problem becomes a crisis or someone demands an answer; then he rushes to put his "term" report on paper!

In this chapter, we will discuss how to estimate the time required for writing letters, reports, manuals, and articles; how to get yourself started writing something that is more than just a form letter; how to expedite the writing process; and how to decide when you should stop.

How To Estimate a Writing Job

Let's assume, for the purposes of budgeting time and energy, that our common denominator is a page of typed material. Granted, one page is not like another, and one will be easier than another, but over the years they will average out. Let's further assume that the page is a standard 8½ by 11 inch sheet and has been typed on only one side with attractively wide margins and double-spaced lines. Each such page represents about 250 words of pica-size type, or 300 words of elite-size type. (Your secretary can show you the difference; she can also show you how other pages of single-spaced type, and varying margins, compare in wordage.)

Estimating speech lengths. Right off you have a ready guide for estimating the length of a speech. Most speakers average about 125 words a minute—a rate which balances the fast-spoken sections with the pauses and interruptions that usually occur. Thus, each page of the speech (typed as described above) is roughly equivalent to 2½ minutes of speaking time. A 5-minute speech requires two full sheets; a 20-minute speech requires eight to nine pages.

But how long will it take you to write those pages?

Estimating time for writing. As we have already pointed out, it may be easy to write quickly and well about familiar items. Thus, a man will be heard to say: "At my last job my boss never complained about my writing. But this new boss finds everything wrong." Another man says, "I can't understand why I'm having such trouble putting my report on paper." What these men have overlooked is the fact that they have not yet become familiar with their new situations.

There are reporters and fiction writers who can turn out 1,000,000 words a year—the equivalent of a 20-page report a day. But a news reporter who can write rapidly about what he has observed will sweat over an assignment which requires him to analyze the causes behind events and to "report in depth" about people and places unknown to him. Similarly, an author who can turn out 100 western stories a year will find his production slowed down when he tries to do a new biography and has to do research and think out new approaches.

Larston Farrar in his book *Successful Writers and How They Work,* which summarizes the experiences of 37 modern writers, corroborates the estimates which have been given by many other writers from Somerset Maugham to Thomas Mann, namely, that a writer averages from one to three hours of actual writing a day. Some men may write 10 hours a day for a week, but they usually pay for it by not writing for the next month. All in all, then, the average man can expect to average one to three hours of writing a day—at one stretch or spread over the whole day.

How much can you write in one to three hours?

Over the years, I have collected information about average rates of writing production from free-lance writers and technical writers, and from presentation and publishing companies. They pretty well agree on the estimate of "one book per man per year, and one book page per man per day." This estimate includes the time for research, rewriting, review, and final editing.

The manager of a large (over 100 people) technical writing department in a major corporation said, "We require our engineering writers to produce at least 3,000 words a week and we expect them to accomplish at least one page a day. The 'one page' includes the research, rough drafts, planning of illustrations, final drafts, and reading of galley and page proofs." Note that 3,000 words a week amounts to approximately 10 typewritten pages of "raw production"—which in turn might convert into perhaps five final book or report pages.

About 10 pages a week means only two typed pages a day *on the average*, or a production of 400 to 700 words a day; and these words will be written during the one to three hours of creativity available to the average man on an average day. In my experience, *creative editing*, and *creative reviewing* take almost the same amount of time and energy as creative writing. Thus, if you have a 30-page report to do, you can figure it will take you a month. If you want to do it more quickly, you should arrange for other writers to do sections of it and for an editor to be ready to work the whole thing over.

Writing always takes more time than you expect it to; it is not something you can perform on a sustained basis like stamping out doughnuts or signing form letters; and you must carefully budget the time available from the beginning.

The staff of a leading graduate school, where the "students" are all mature men in their forties, gives this advice: "Assume that it will take you two or three months to prepare any sort of an original, well-thought-out and presented report, study, or article. Assume that any paper which will run 8,000 to 12,000 words (20 to 40 typed double-spaced pages) will require at least two hours a day spread over a 2-month period, and arrange your schedules accordingly."

Again, we see the pattern emerge: A man can write for about two hours a day; he can produce at a rate of about a page a day of completed work.

Do these estimates fit letter writing? Perhaps you know of men who can spend whole days writing letters? Men who can dictate for three hours straight in the morning and again in the afternoon? Yes, but what kind of letters are they writing? If they are preparing new letters on new subjects, their production when converted to a 300-word page will average out to the same rate of a page a day. The other letters will be found to be routine replies to routine business.

The comparison will become clearer if you visualize each page in a report or book as a letter to the reader. (Indeed, your reports will be more interestingly written if you do think of each page as a personal message to each reader.) Because each page differs from the preceding page, you are, in essence, writing a letter *on a new subject* when you write a page of the report. Now, look at your letters again: which of them is simply the same page being repeated, and which of them constitutes a turn of the page to a new topic? Fatigue from writing routine letters is simply clerical-fatigue; fatigue from writing unusual, complex, or new-policy letters is the same as that caused by the effort to write a page of a new report or book.

The mechanics also take time. A national survey of secretaries some years ago revealed that their average production came to about three lines of typing a minute. Of course, a qualified typist can type many times faster than at that rate; but when allowances are made for inserting carbon paper, aligning the headings, making corrections, deciphering notes, and taking rest periods, the actual production comes to three lines a minute—about 10 minutes a page, or six pages an hour.

For a report you must also allow for duplicating, collating, and stapling or binding the pages. All these mechanical steps take time, and if rushed or done poorly, can reduce the effectiveness of your report. More than one man has "completed his report on time," only to find that a "week of frantic typing, proofreading, and printing" was required before he could place the finished report into the hands of the people who had expected it seven days earlier.

Getting Yourself Started

A blank white page can be a difficult hurdle for dynamic business-men, engineers, and government executives as well as for high school and college students. Even professional writers complain about their difficulty in getting started. Riley Hughes[1] says that the free-lance writer probably has the sharpest pencils and cleanest typewriter in existence, because he trims the pencils and cleans the keys when he is not staring out the window or making coffee during that painful period before the first words appear on the page. Henry Roberts[2] says that the worst three words for a speech writer are "Ladies and Gentlemen." The writer puts down those words and then stares at them, paralyzed by his desire to produce a great opening paragraph. Comedians, too, know the deadliness of having someone say, "I hear you are funny. Say or do something funny." Only the most practiced professional can overcome the wet-blanket effect of such a challenge. Thus, a writer who looks at the "blank white page" and thinks, "My style must be clear, concise, brief, logical, grammatical, brilliant, and correctly punctuated," is telling himself to have a "braincramp."

Brainstorm to break the braincramp. The experts of *creative thinking*[3] advise us to "turn on the green light" in our minds, "reject all negative criticism," and "let the mind range freely." During a brain-storm session one must not say, "It won't work," or, "It's not good." The brainstormers try to spout as many ideas as possible without censorship or criticism. After they have listed all the ideas they can, then, and then only (and several days later if possible), do they put on their critic's caps and dissect, choose, reject, and polish the ideas which have been collected.

A writer undergoes a similar experience. If you start with your critical faculties in the driver's seat, you will find that ideas and words come with difficulty—if at all. Therefore, to start writing, tell yourself: "I'm going to write something. Indeed, I've got to write something. I'll put down the words as fast as they come to me and in any order just to get the beginnings on paper. Later I'll worry about the grammar, syntax, punctuation, readability index and fog count."

This method, or some form of it, is used by all writers. It is par-ticularly needed by the "slow starters," because a great part of their

---

[1] Professor Riley Hughes, Georgetown University, Director of the Georgetown University Writers Conference, and author and editor of many books and articles.

[2] Professor Henry Roberts, speech and presentation consultant, Washington, D.C.

[3] For example, Alex Osborn, *Applied Imagination* (Scribners); Charles Clark, *Brainstorming* (Doubleday); Charles Whiting, *Creative Thinking* (Reinhold).

"braincramp" is almost always due to the psychological block which arises from the conflicting efforts to be creative and critical at the same time. In short, don't try to write perfect prose; just put words on paper. Later you can revamp, cull, cut, and reorganize.

Think and write, or write and think? Some people say that the best and easiest way to get into a writing project is first to think about the subject, study all the angles, do all the research and checking, and then sit down and spin the whole piece out of your head. If you are able to write that way, go ahead. Many writers, especially experienced ones, are able to accumulate all their material, mull over it, and finally, filled with ideas and words, they write easily and steadily.

But not all men have minds that work in such a logical manner. Some men cannot think a whole paper through and then write it down in one continuous effort. Others have too many additional problems and too many interruptions to be able to hold in memory all the details of a lengthy project. Others have learned that all too often something comes up to prevent that hoped-for day of steady writing. And many others have found (like myself) that the longer you can let the words mull, steep, and soak on *the paper* the better. Words have a way of sounding good in your mind, on your tongue, and even of appearing brilliant the first time they hit the paper. A few days, weeks, or months later (Horace, the famous Roman poet, suggested seven years!), the words appear a lot differently. They have the mysterious capacity of rearranging themselves to lose their brilliance; while you are not watching they even creep into patterns of downright nonsense!

A good practice is to write sections and subsections as they come to your mind. Whether you brainstorm or think logically, putting jottings on paper has the advantage of allowing more time for reviewing and editing your work. It also has the important advantage of providing you with part of your work already on paper in the event of a last-minute emergency or delay.

Four Tips for Getting Started

In short, to expedite getting started, try the following practices:

1. Don't try to be "great"; just put something on paper—"brainstorm" the beginning on paper.

2. Rough out any and all sections that are easy to write or which you can write, and let them sit on paper for awhile.

3. Allow as much time as possible between your creative writing and your critical review and editing.

4. Give yourself a series of deadlines. Remember the "term" paper: you finished it when you knew it had to be done without further delay. Remember how people on one occasion can take a whole day to do something, but on another occasion, finish the same job in an hour when told they must, or else. Assign yourself a series of deadlines for each section of the writing project and let these little deadlines serve as goads to keep you accomplishing a paragraph an hour, a page a day, or a table of data a week. When the big deadline comes, you will be ready, because you will be the victor of many small, and therefore, easier starts—not the exhausted, frantic, last-minute sprinter with most of the whole track yet to run.

Six Tips for Expediting Your Writing

1. *Should you use an outline?* Yes and no. Outlines can be convenient, useful tools particularly for those men and women who think easily in terms of outlines. However, many people have difficulty generating the beautifully clear, logical outlines so highly admired by school teachers and lecturers on research methods, and so rarely developed by professional writers or practicing scientists. The trouble with an insistent demand for an outline is that it can cause "brain-cramp"—thinking through a long outline in precise detail can be as difficult as writing the whole paper.

Jotting down a series of notes and arranging them into a rough outline can help you remember and organize them. But laboring over an outline that lists everything in a complex numbered system can be a waste of time and effort. People who want to "have the whole outline before beginning to write" just don't understand how the human mind jumps about, and how at one stage a man is ready to outline or write on one section, and at another time wants to focus on another topic.

Thus, some writers will finish a rough draft of any part of the project when they can take advantage of a sudden gush of words. After their wells of inspiration have gone dry, they examine what they have written and outline it. They use this outline to help check the organization of the material, to locate gaps or ramblings, and to see where to put the titles and headings. In short, they avoid an outline at the beginning, because it might delay their creative flow of ideas. After they have written something, they employ an outline as a device to help them criticize and edit what they have written.

The point is: Don't delay over the mechanics of an outline. **Put** some ideas on paper or on cards or notepaper and juggle them around until a workable outline appears. If a formal outline is needed for a proposal or for briefing, it can be typed from the notes on the cards or pieces of paper.

2. *Don't delay over the preface.* Many writers have the tendency to spend too much of their available time on prefaces, forewords, and introductions. The experienced writer learns to write the prefatory material last. He may start with a rough draft in order to have a general idea how his paper will begin, but he saves the final polishing until he has everything else ready. He does this because: (1) in the course of writing the paper he may run into new ideas on evidence which will mean a change in the prefatory material; and (2) the longer he waits to do the preface or introduction the more his mind has had time to "steep" in the materials, and the more likely he is to produce an effective, well-written preface.

Of course, a good opening is important to arouse the interest of the reader, and to tell him what to expect and why he should read the paper. But to write a good preface, you need to know, and know well, what you are going to say in the rest of the paper.

3. *Don't start over—cut and paste or staple.* Some writers scribble on half a page and then tear it up. (This is a way to look busy, but it wastes time and paper.) A better way is to keep going and simply cross out the section you reject (you might want to look at them again). Similarly, when typing, don't pull out a page because of a few "goofs," just xxx-out and keep going on the same page. Later, you can cut out the parts you want and staple or paste them where they fit in best. Also, as you pile up pages for a report, put the last written on top; you will be able to check back through them more quickly and easily than if you keep stacking the pages with the last written on the bottom.

4. *The paper costs less than its handling.* The sheets of paper cost far less than your time and the time of a typist. So don't crowd a lot of words on a page. Leave plenty of margin, and when working on a difficult or doubtful passage, half a page is not too much to leave unused. Normally, too, it is better to use standard-sized sheets of paper, even if with only a few sentences on them, than to use small or odd-sized bits of paper. The full-size sheets are easier to handle, type on, file, collate, or work with when editing and polishing the sentences.

5. *Delegate minor editing as well as the mechanics.* Some authors hold their work close to their chests until they are satisfied that it is perfect to the last comma and the gerund. This practice relegates

the secretary or typist—or wife—to the bare mechanics of straight copying. People who can read and type can also make corrections in spelling and run-of-the-mill grammatical errors. Few writers, if any, can go from their first *rough* rough draft directly to a final manuscript. By giving your rough work to the typist and telling her "clean it up as best you can," you expend a bit more clerical effort in exchange for the much more important savings in your own writing and editing time.

6. *Use a reader over your shoulder*. Some writers are like the woman who, after being defrauded of her life savings by a confidence man, went to the Better Business Bureau. The manager of the BBB asked her, "Since you already knew about us, why didn't you come to us before you invested your money?"

"I was afraid," she replied, "that you would try to persuade me not to make the investment."

Similarly, many writers avoid showing their work to anyone for fear another person might find an error, and they would have to do some rewriting. As though not seeing an error will make it go away!

Other writers are "loners" and clutch their work until they are positive it is ready for the eyes of others. They want to hear only praise, never criticism. Others have a mistaken notion of what constitutes "completed staff work". (See Chapter Thirteen about this.) Whatever the reason, writers who wait too long to have their work reviewed by a superior, colleague, wife, friend, or hired consultant, lose the opportunity for two important advantages: (1) early discovery of errors, with more time, therefore, to find out the true information; (2) having a friend catch one's "goofs" before an outsider or opponent does.

How to Keep From Rambling

One piece of advice, undoubtedly given by every teacher of writing, is: "Write till you reach the end, then stop."

But when do you reach the end? Some writers, once started, have difficulty deciding where to stop. They feel that each statement requires further clarification and qualification. Some elongate the introduction as they warm up and warm up and warm up to the subject. Others reach the end of the conclusion and summary and then think of another bright idea, an additional quotation, another authority to quote, and so on.

Here are three things to do when you have drafted a sizable part of your paper and are looking at it to see whether you should bring it to a stop or continue it for a few more pages.

1. Look at each paragraph, at each topic and item, and ask yourself: "Can it be left out?" The odds are your impulse will be to decide to keep the thing in—no father, mother, or author can be expected to discard his own child. If you do decide the item is important, interesting, and sparklingly well-written, ask yourself the second question, "But does the reader really need this paragraph? Granted the point is interesting and deserves to be expressed, should it be expressed in *this* paper? Obviously it is something *I want to say*; but does the intended *reader want to read it or does he need to read it?*" In other words, don't fight the issue with yourself over whether or not the item is worth saying; instead make it a question of whether to state the item or to save it for another occasion.

2. Make an outline of the paper—if you have not done so—and examine it with these questions in mind: "Is the introduction too long? Are there things in the summary or conclusion that belong in the main discussion? Which topic appears too often? Which seems out of order?" An outline before or after the rough draft has been made can help you visualize the whole paper and thereby see what looms too large and where you repeat too much.

3. Show your outline and draft to another person, preferably to the person who will receive and approve your final version. In most instances another person can quickly tell you, "That part is enough. That's too much. That needs amplifying." And so on.

SUMMING UP THIS CHAPTER

This chapter has made the following points:

1. Writing always takes longer than expected. Allow *extra* time for research, study, rough drafts, final drafts, reviews, typing, duplicating, and distribution. The average writer can "create" for two or three hours a day, and he can average two pages or 400 to 700 words a day.

2. Writing is creative thinking, so use brainstorm techniques to break the starting barrier. Get something, however clumsy, on paper as quickly as you can. Later you can criticize, outline, rearrange, and polish.

3. Use an outline as an aid, not as something sacred or foreordained. If an outline springs into your mind, jot it down; if sections of the writing come first to mind, jot them down. Later you can build material around the outline, or you can outline the already written materials.

4. Give yourself several deadlines so that you are goaded to do

a part of the project every hour, or every day, or every week. A page a day does not sound like much, but it adds up to a 20-page report in a month, or a 200-page book in a year.

5. Don't delay over the preface or introduction; get the whole piece written and then you will see what you should say at its beginning.

6. Delegate the editing and "cleanup" as much as you can; show your work to others as you go along, and welcome criticism early in the game.

7. When you get to the end, stop. You can locate the end by checking an outline of your paper and seeing if all the topics have been included and given a fair share of attention. To pinpoint the end, ask yourself: "Have I given the *reader what he wants or needs?* I have certainly delivered myself of what I wanted to say; but what part of it answers the desires of the reader?" Your paper should end at the point where the reader, not you, would want it to end.

13

HOW TO BE A GOOD MANAGER OF OTHER PEOPLE'S WRITING

CREATIVE EDITING VS "NITPICKING"

Management of Writing Functions

Reviewing written materials is a managerial function. Every executive at some time or other must prevail—by inspiration or force—on his subordinates to produce letters, reports, speeches, articles, and even books.

What was said in Chapter Twelve about managing your own writing function goes double, of course, where others are concerned. They will encounter the same difficulties and problems you have experienced. As their boss you should not only sympathize with them, but be able to guide them intelligently and effectively.

"What's the use of learning to write better," someone always asks, "when the boss will nitpick your writing to death anyway? Why improve, when we have to write according to the boss's whims of steel?"

The answer, of course, is: "Seek improvement now so that when you become the boss you will not perpetuate the unnecessary or annoying 'nitpicking' to which you object. If you learn to write better, chances are that more and more of your writings will please the boss." Moreover, many of the men and women who are most vociferous in their complaints about the "nitpicking" of their bosses, later come to the recognition that much of their work did require correction. They end by admitting: "To be honest, I now see that a lot of my writing deserved criticisms. Since I've improved, my boss doesn't have to chop my stuff."

The Human Relations of Writing Management

The manager of a large office said: "The junior supervisors write some clumsy letters and some reports and memos that can stand

121

ıt. But unless the writings could cause error, or create
nding, I let them pass. The young fellows obtain a great
sfaction out of seeing their letters go unchanged out of
ıent to carry on the business. Moreover, they learn to take
responsibility for what they say. Most of the time I don't have to
point out their awkward spots, much less their errors, because they
usually detect their own errors when they review their correspondence
files, and most of them are their own best teachers. Of course, if a
man's letters, etc., don't show improvement, I hold a few training
sessions with him on how to follow company policy, address customers correctly, and so forth."

Isn't that a good practice to follow? When next you are tempted
to blue-pencil a piece of writing, ask yourself: "Who will get this letter? How will he react? Can it do any harm if it is less than perfect?
Is the change worth the retyping?" And, most importantly, "How
will the effort to correct it affect the originator?"

As the policeman said to the priest, "Father, if the world were
to reform completely, you and I would be out of jobs." So, if subordinates could do perfect work, the executives and managers would not
be needed. The big job of a boss is not to punish errors or pounce
on deficiencies, but to take every opportunity that arises to show his
people how they can more effectively organize and perform their
work. This responsibility includes improvements in how they express
their thoughts, their judgments, and their information about the
business at hand.

Many executives have an all too-strong tendency to become angry
with clumsy wording, awkward phrasing, and confusing statements.
Misspellings and grammar lapses drive them to apoplexy. But the
boss who slashes viciously with his blue pencil or makes sarcastic
notes in the margins of the letter, gains nothing, beyond the venting
of his spleen, from such bullying. People try to write well; their
trouble often is that they are trying too hard to produce "good
English." They have great "pride of authorship" in what they have
put down on paper, and their feelings can be deeply hurt—even
though they may appear to take the criticisms calmly. If you don't
believe this, note your own reactions when someone "chops" your
epistolary or literary masterpieces! (For more about the management of creative people, see the *Executive's Guide to Handling
People*.)[1]

Criticizing a man's writing implies criticism of his intelligence, of
his judgment, of his education, and of his upbringing. Unfortunately,

[1] F. C. Dyer (Englewood Cliffs, N.J.: Prentice-Hall, Inc., 1958).

there is a lot of snobbery connected with writing, and to some people a slip in grammar is as serious as wearing the wrong clothes to a social function.

Stern discipline and brusque reprimands may be necessary to keep a man alert on a watchman's job, to make sure an inspector doesn't let defective parts slip by him, or to ensure that an otherwise careless workman will attend to his dials and gauges. Perhaps a "tough, carping" boss can keep clerks mindful of their p's and q's, and frighten them into doing perfect copywork of form letters. But good writing requires more than fear to stimulate it; particularly if the writing is to be characterized by imagination and enthusiasm. A manager or an editor will get better results if he sticks to constructive criticisms and keeps free of personal animus.

Constructive Criticism or a Mask for Meddling?

Sometimes even constructive criticisms can mask what Edwin Laird Cady calls *meddling,* in his book *Developing Executive Capacity.*[2] He writes:

Meddlers are frustrators. . . . Here's how to know when you are meddling. There is placed before you, let's say, an advertisement or some other written words that will be printed in behalf of your company. You read it. You feel resentment within yourself. Although you never admit this to yourself, the resentment is caused by the fact that the writing is so good.

Then you feel a "flash of inspiration." You see a way to "improve" the copy, or, to use an outdated phrase, to "polish" it. This is the danger sign.

A wave of exultation comes over you. You make the changes, or else you prepare to demand that they be made. Within yourself you feel that the man who wrote the copy has become an enemy who must be conquered.

You go into conference with him. All your innate honesty flies out of the window. "Our advertisements are written for our customers," you say. "The nature of our customers is such that they will be interested only if my changes are made in this copy." The original writer argues with you. You duck, sidestep, slip out of his every argument, by simply changing the nature of the customers to fit whatever will support your demands for your changes.

Your exultation grows, and with it your stubbornness. In conferences, meddlers have been seen to become intoxicated with their own exultations.

[2] Englewood Cliffs, N. J.: Prentice-Hall, Inc., 1952, p. 42f.

When you are not meddling, but are demanding needed changes, then you won't feel resentment, you won't exult, and you won't shift ground in order to find support for your arguments. The man with whom you must work will seem a cooperator, and not a combatant.

"Amen" to the foregoing and let's add that another test of meddling and "nitpicking" is a feeling of righteousness and a relish for the chance to find something wrong. The man's meaning may be clear and his writing will do the job, but the meddler feels better after he has found a semicolon out of place or a split infinitive.

Help Your Subordinates "Capture Your Style"

The burden of conforming to standards of writing falls, of course, on the writer, on the subordinate. First, because the reader is the customer of the writer, and the salesman has to please the customer, not vice versa. Second, because the boss is responsible for the style and tone of the letters and reports released by his "shop," office, section, group, or unit. Creative reviewing, like creative leadership, does not require an executive to permit inadequate performance. Far from it! The purpose of the executive's review is to make subordinates write better, not help them find excuses!

The boss must also decide the *tone*—an elusive, hard-to-define quality—in which his office will speak to the public. The tone of a senior executive is different from that of a branch manager; the tone of an older man is different from that of a younger man; and the style of the sales manager rarely resembles the style of the manager of engineering, accounting, or production. Few writers can fully "capture the style" of another person. Hence, even the most expert writer must expect his bosses to make changes that will better "express their personalities."

Confusion and ill feelings arise when the boss does not explain clearly what tone he desires, or when a subordinate is too obtuse to see what is wanted. For example, one man likes to use the words "advert," "contemplate," and "adumbrate"; the other prefers "turn to," "think about," and "foreshadow." In one office a man wrote: "This will keep the matter from bothering us again"; his boss changed the phrase to read "This will preclude an unfortunate reoccurrence." When asked why, the boss replied, "Frankly, it's just because my mind thinks with words like 'preclude.'"

In one company, correspondence originators had their letters regularly returned for rewriting until they realized that the top man had a fixation against certain practices, notably using the word "however" in the middle of a sentence, or splitting an infinitive. Another executive did not like letters to have less than two paragraphs, so he always rewrote short letters just to stretch them longer.

Sometimes these quirks of a boss are based on sound reasons: he knows what words and phrases will do the job best. In other instances, the man is blindly applying ideas of grammar which he picked up 30 years ago in school, and which are no longer taken seriously by professional writers. In either case, the *managerial error* consists in not letting subordinates know one's rules or whims. Too often a subordinate is heard to complain: "When we get a new boss, we need months to learn how to write to please him."

Amazingly enough, the average boss, and the average subordinate rarely do the obvious thing which is to make up a list of the pet peeves and preferred word usages. If a manager will circulate and post a list of his policies and idiosyncracies, his writers will suddenly be easier to manage. Moreover when a man writes down his policies and preferences (and maybe baseless prejudices) he may realize how outmoded or how unnecessary are some of his notions about good writing practices.

Reviewing and editing are managerial functions; an executive should provide organized, not hit-or-miss, editorial guidance to his subordinates.

Completed Staff Work for Getting Things Written

"Completed staff work" means that you do as much of a job by yourself as you reasonably can. You consult with everyone who might be involved; you include a solution to every difficulty; and you are able to say: "Mr. Top Executive, I would sign this paper if I were in your place, and I'll stake my reputation on its worth."

On the other hand, an exaggerated "completeness" of staff work can cause additional work. A disillusioned executive once said, "The doctrine of completed staff work has cost business and government millions of dollars." Here are some real-life examples of the costs of exaggerated staff work.

The assistant to the vice-president of a large corporation was assigned the task of finding answers to a series of complex problems. During a six-month period he attended committee meetings, read an immense amount of data, and visited many field activities. As he got deeper in the subject he found that many basic preconceptions had to be changed. His report, therefore, included a large number of findings and recommendations which surprised his boss, the vice-president. The boss would not "buy the report" and, grumbling about its "poor writing," assigned another man to "rewrite it and tighten it up."

The writing, as a matter of fact, had been fine; the error lay in trying for too-completed staff work. The assistant had too nobly carried out the mission too much by himself. He should have given his boss's mind a chance to follow the developments. A man working on a long study should report at least once a week informally about his progress, and give special emphasis to anything new he has uncovered. For example, "About the personnel staffing study: I've gotten the reports from the home office and from the major field offices. The ratio of the home office looks better than that of the field offices which is the opposite of what we expected. After I get the remaining data and double check it, I'll give you an advance tentative report. But if the trend keeps up, we'll have to tell the executive committee that the overhead fat is in the field offices, not at headquarters—which is a surprise to me and I suspect will be a surprise to others." By such interim reports, the staff man can keep his boss up to date with the implications of the data he is compiling.

A bright new assistant sales manager had the job of preparing a "round-robin" letter containing paragraphs on everything from new products and prices to social notes about the VIP's to go to the hundreds of field sales offices. Wanting to make a good impression, he had the first draft typed in the smooth along with six carbon copies. The treasurer was one of the first officials to read the 12-page draft. "Nice job," he remarked, "but the figures in several places have to be changed. Too bad, it will mean messing up your neat pages and copies."

"Not at all, sir," replied the eager young man, "there are five more reviewers to go, and I'm sure they'll make changes in addition to yours."

"Why didn't you bring me a rough draft so that I could make changes in it?" the treasurer asked in surprise.

"Sir!" exclaimed the young man, "That would not be completed staff action! I try to make a job perfectly complete at every stage in its accomplishment."

We don't know what the treasurer may have muttered under his breath, but he said out loud:

"Completed staff work or not, it would save a lot of paper and typing time if you incorporate the changes into the rough draft rather than into a series of smooth copies. Henceforth, just bring me a legible, rough draft—and skip the carbon copies until you are ready to have the final version typed."

A Navy commander, newly assigned to the staff of an admiral, worked a week preparing a report which he thought would bring him many commendations. Instead the admiral said, "Commander, you could have saved yourself a lot of work if you had come to me sooner and gotten an idea of what I wanted. I don't need half of this report, and in regard to three of your recommendations, my policy on them was established last year and won't be changed. Henceforth, don't try to be so d--- complete with your staff work. Give me or one of my aides a chance to crank in my ideas before you file your report as a completed project."

The doctrine of completed staff work is a good one in the sense that the writer does not run back to the boss for the answer to things he can and should find out for himself. But to say, as some writers have, that you should never refer to the boss until the report is ready to "sign, seal, and deliver," is to say too much. In the first place, the boss's mind has to have some inklings as you go along; otherwise, the report can come as too great a shock to him. The report should be about something important, something challenging—otherwise, why go to the trouble of making the staff study?—and, therefore, will turn up new evidence, ideas, and proposals. In the second place, the boss probably has background knowledge and ideas which only he can possess, and which should be taken into account. Why shouldn't his ideas be included as you go along?

Effective Staff Action

Following is a chart of how-to-get effective staff action—the efficient, businesslike preparation of written materials, letters, memos, reports, etc., for approval or signature by a higher level.

EFFICIENT STAFF ACTION

Effective Action: the Boss Should Do the Following	Effective Action: the Assistant Should Do the Following
1. Mark out the problem in enough detail for someone (*outside* your mind) to know what you want.	1. Study, write, restudy, and rewrite.
2. Assign one person the responsibility for pulling the answers together and getting the final paper written.	2. Check all the data, information, and persons that *oppose* your ideas, as well as those that support your preferences.
3. Let the staff man know your experience, ideas, biases, and hopes in regard to the problem.	3. Work out the details completely; have the answers ready to objections; and in doubtful areas have at least two answers

EFFICIENT STAFF ACTION (*Continued*)

	ready; (a) what further research or study appears required for a final answer, how much will it cost, and how long will it take; and (b) what degree of probability is connected with each doubtful alternative.
4. Authorize him to check back with you and to call on others for help.	4. Present a positive, organized solution with the proposed courses of action spelled out. There is no use praising a course of action that would cost too much later on. Don't shilly-shally; advise your boss what he should do.
5. Set a time limit; or let him pick the completion date; and set the frequency of interim reports.	5. Look at your paper and ask yourself: If I were the boss would I sign this paper, staking my reputation on it?
6. Put yourself in his place: if you were he, would *you* understand what is wanted? Would *you* consider the help and guidance sufficient?	

If you must answer "No" to the final questions in either of the columns in the foregoing chart, then go back and start over: either give more guidance to the assistant, or seek for more accuracy and completeness in the paper on which you are working.

The late Charles E. Wilson, who went from President of General Motors to Secretary of Defense, during his first days in the Pentagon had to be briefed on the background of each issue which came to him. According to the oft-told story, the briefings went as follows. The military or civilian expert man came into Mr. Wilson's office, and raising his right arm would begin: "Mr. Secretary, the main points are:" and then tick off the five or ten points in favor of the proposal.

"Fine," Mr. Wilson said, "I'll sign it."

"But wait," the briefer would cry: "On the other hand, there are the following points." And raising his left arm, he would tick off the five or ten points in opposition.

After several days of such presentations, Mr. Wilson is reputed to have said, "What the Pentagon needs is more one-armed briefers."

The logical course, but so often not followed, is that of presenting the issues on one side with one arm, the issues on the other side with the other arm, and then taking the proposed solution in both hands and holding it forth clearly and forcefully for the boss to see.

HOW TO REVIEW A WRITTEN DOCUMENT
LETTER, REPORT, ARTICLE, MEMORANDUM, BRIEFING, OR BOOK

Anyone who has done much writing will have had both the following frustrating experiences.

You prepare a paper carefully and, because it involves a number of processes, functions, and policies, you route it to all the departments. The Head of the Procurement Department returns it with the notation "Full of errors. Needs complete rewriting." You march off to his department, puzzled over what the errors can be. Naturally, you have expected him to focus on the details that might affect Procurement. Instead you find that he is a meticulous grammarian and an authority on what he believes is "company policy and public relations."

He lectures you on some misspellings, a typographical error, a few misplaced commas, and then lingers over the five places in which you haven't used the "right nuance of tone" or in which you have failed to "gain proper emphasis on the exact company policy." Some of his points are well taken and you can be grateful for the extra editing he has added on to his review, but most of the points are outside his purview—and would have been caught by someone else anyway. He may think he has been helpful, but he has wasted his time and your time. When you ask him, "How about the section on Procurement? Are there many errors in it?" he replies, "No, you did a good job there. I added the latest cost figures and changed a word here and there, but have no objections to it at all." In short, he had been asked for a *substantive review*—to check for accuracy of content—of his area but he gave you a literary or *editorial* review of the whole paper.

Conversely, a reviewer who has been asked to check a manuscript for editorial niceties, but who becomes a technical expert, can be equally frustrating. You pass a paper to Mr. Brown, the office manager, to check the typography, spelling, and grammar. He grandly and benignly overlooks the errors you hoped he would pick out, and confines himself to some generalities on the need to recheck your formulae or your accounting data.

Perhaps you have given an author a hard time over some substantive and editorial items, which in fact were "none of your d—— business"? How can you distinguish in one review between the writing style of a paper and the accuracy of the facts and the logic of thoughts presented in it? The following suggestions drawn from the experiences of the U. S. Naval War College and the General Motors Institute can be most helpful in this regard.

Criteria for Reviewing

The U.S. Naval War College, in its *Guide for Use in the Preparation of Term Papers,* suggests the following questions to ask when reviewing a term paper. These same questions also can serve as criteria when evaluating any letter or report, and even an article written in a popular style.

1. *Purpose*: Has the purpose been stated? If so, has the purpose been attained through a logical development of the subject?

2. *Assumptions*: If stated, do they appear to be reasonable? Are the assumptions true assumptions and not confused with facts? If not stated, are they apparent in the presentation and does the thesis stand or fall on the validity of these hidden assumptions?

3. *Clarity of Reasoning*: Is the line of reasoning clear; is it developed in an orderly fashion?

4. *Objectiveness*: In presenting material, are all issues explored with reasonable impartiality or are some weighted unduly to support the thesis? Is there an objective appraisal of alternatives, and does it result in a reasoned choice?

5. *Credibility*: Are the arguments substantiated by facts? Are the facts interpreted in a well-reasoned manner? Are the conclusions drawn from arguments presented in the body of the paper?

6. *Breadth of Vision*: Is the subject treated in proper perspective, or is it treated in a vacuum, though it is an integral part of a many-sided problem? (Have you projected your study and conclusions into the future?)

The author should further criticize his paper, using the following checks:

- Check paper as a whole: the plan, the proportioning of parts.
- Check agreement of title, table of contents, and introduction.
- Check agreement of summary and the introduction.
- Check agreement of headings with table of contents.
- Check proportion of unit parts.
- Check details of text: transition from topic to topic, part to part, sentence structure, and wording.
- As a final test, get someone, preferably with a critical mind, to read your paper—and then be willing to accept the criticisms gratefully.

Technical Evaluation and Editorial Evaluation

Mr. Charles L. Tutt, Jr., of the General Motors Institute, has attempted to overcome the confusion between the *technical* evaluation and the *report* evaluation by devising a form which treats separately the technical and editorial elements. The following chart has been developed in imitation of Mr. Tutt's ideas, but has been modified to make it applicable to other types of writing than reports. Use it the next time you review a paper and you will be able to distinguish the *technical* or *substantive,* elements, from the *literary* or *editorial* style.

QUESTIONS TO ASK ABOUT A PAPER

TECHNICAL	EDITORIAL
1. Does it fulfil objectives and cover essential points?	1. Is the arrangement and order of presentation well-balanced and pleasing?
2. Does the preface or introduction explain what is to come and in what order?	2. Is there a suitable title page, table of contents, list of illustrations?
3. Are the proper acknowledgments and assumptions included?	3. Is the writing clear, unambiguous, precise, and readable?
4. Is the information exact and accurate? Are specific sources given?	4. Are the sections and subsections identified with accurate and interesting headings?
5. Are the conclusions or recommendations significant, pertinent, and valid?	5. Are the typographical errors corrected or marked for correction?
6. Are the findings supported by data presented in the report?	6. Is the typing clean enough for the purpose for which the document is to be used?
7. Does the main discussion or body describe the data, tests, procedures, etc., with completeness and accuracy?	7. Are the illustrations, charts, and tables numbered for identification? Are they near the data they support? Are they referenced in the sections they support?
8. Could the reader use the main discussion as a guide to a similar problem? Could he repeat the operations described?	8. Is the level of language appropriate to the readers? Is it too technical, too bureaucratic, too loose and flip, too much jargon?

QUESTIONS TO ASK ABOUT A PAPER   *(continued)*

TECHNICAL *(Continued)*	EDITORIAL *(Continued)*
9. Are the illustrations necessary, valid, and apt?	9. Are abbreviations and new terms explained?
10. Does the appendix contain all the materials referred to, or required to support or explain the arguments?	

Why Did the Writer Say That?

Above all, when evaluating a report or other piece of writing with which you do not agree, or about which you have doubts, try to discover why the writer wrote what he did. Too many reviewers react in terms of their personal prejudices and biases. They flare up with demands like: "How dare he say that? Who does he think he is?"

The crucial question is "*Why* did he say that? What information, what data, what reasoning processes led him to such conclusions?"

If there are no surprises, no challenges, no "disturbing" news in a report, it probably was not needed. The man with a new idea—be he a scientist, artist, politician, military man, businessman, or writer—has a hard time with the initial selling or presentation. The boss or the editor will automatically refer the idea to an expert; but the expert is committed to the theory, attitude, or practice with regard to which he is an authority and will react against the new idea—be it a new drug, cosmic theory, book, or new process—and will recommend against it.

One must be careful, therefore, not to turn down a paper just because it sounds "too different." It ought to sound different, or it probably is not worth much. Nor should the adverse criticism of an expert or great authority be accepted too quickly. His disagreement may only prove that the idea is new to him. Instead one should look at the facts, the data, and the chain of reasoning which the author followed. Again and again, men have argued strenuously over the "writing" of a paper, when the argument should have been over the facts and information on which the paper was based. This sounds obvious; yet you will find that most review and editorial problems will be caused by or complicated by the tendency to argue about the "right way to say something," when the argument should be about the "evidence that caused the people to speak the way they did."

The burden is on the writer—as on the salesman—to tailor his presentation to fit the desires and needs of the reader, the customer. However, the writer in order to have written about a subject must have studied and thought about it; assuming he has normal intelligence and integrity, his statements should be taken seriously until one has clear proof to the contrary.

Hence, the management of writers and of writing functions is complicated and difficult. In essence, it is the management of thinking, and thinking is the most difficult, obscure, emotional, and surprising thing that we do. The good writer expresses his thoughts after several rewrites on paper in terms which are less obscure, less emotional, and more logical. The good manager helps and guides the writer in accomplishing this important task.

SUMMING UP THIS CHAPTER

This chapter has focused on the problems of managing the writings of other people. Perhaps no amount of executive skill can provide the magic spark of creative imaginative literary ability, but certainly one can go a long way toward making the best of whatever spark is present and toward avoiding the harassment of others by unnecessary nitpicking.

Writing is the expression of thinking; it is also a process for facilitating the job of thinking. When you manage people's writing, you are managing their thinking—a task calling for good human relations technique, as well as for technical and editorial know-how.

The manager ought to distinguish between idiosyncrasies and modern literary conventions, between substantive content and editorial presentation. He should spell out his preferences for the sake of his subordinates and he should ask his seniors for a listing of their preferences.

Completed staff work is an ideal goal, but the completeness must not be over-emphasized lest the staff man "spin his wheels" too long or get too far ahead of the people to whom he must sell his final report.

Above all, the manager should remember that he, too, is a writer and his writing is managed by those above him. Let him, therefore, remember the golden rule of management: Treat the letters and reports of others as he would have his own treated—but lean over a long way in being more objective and more critical of his own "masterpieces." He who would successfully edit the work of others, must learn to accept editings of his own.

14

ORGANIZING REPORTS AND STAFF STUDIES — FOR THE READER

A Report Is Its Own Kind of Beast

Professor Paul Douglass (*Communication Through Reports*)[1] says that to make a report means "to find out the facts and come back and tell what they mean."

Messrs. Gaum, Graves, and Hoffman in *Report Writing*[2] say that a report "is a communication of information to clients, superiors, or employers. Its essential ingredient is fact, new information."

The definition of a report may not be important, but everyone involved in the writing situation ought to know exactly what is needed. All too frequently a man will confuse an article with a report, a letter with a staff study—and vice versa.

For example, the manager of an engineering department complained that his professional engineers never gave him the reports he wanted. At the same time the reports he sent to top management kept running into criticism. A brief investigation revealed that half the engineers conceived a "report" to be a scientific monograph of the type they saw in learned journals. The others thought a "report" meant a thick pile of laboratory data sheets and reference materials. Thus, his "scientists" and "engineers" were viewing with contempt the "management" type reports he was trying to write. Conversely,

[1] Englewood Cliffs, N. J.: Prentice-Hall, Inc., 1960
[2] Englewood Cliffs, N. J.: Prentice-Hall, Inc., 1961.

because he was an engineer at heart himself, he had loaded his reports to top managment with engineering details. Top management wanted only to know: "Will the thing work? How much will it cost? How long will it take to build it?"

Once he and his people recognized the situation, the answer was easy: each man wrote his "paper," "report," or "experiment record" the way he wanted to. Then they got together and rewrote it for the purposes of top management. The scientists could submit their versions to learned journals, the engineers could put their detailed reports in the library for purposes of record, and the manager could send to his superiors the information they wanted.

Similarly, accountants, budgeteers, and production managers tend to view reports as "factual presentations of important information"— by which they often mean that it should show only "the information that makes them look good." The public relations manager, however, wants to see a short, snappy article full of eye-catching color pictures and memorable phrases—a piece of writing that could be placed in a trade magazine or newspaper.

In this chapter we will assume that a report is a well-written document that is intended for a special audience, but from which articles, letters, or popular expositions might be drawn. It is an answer, *a direct answer*, to an expressed or unexpressed question. The reader is asking (otherwise why read the report?) questions like:

How are we doing?	How much effort should we expend?
What plans can we make?	How much will the proposal cost?
Where can we get help?	What do the customers think of it?
Are we ahead or behind?	What are the problems ahead of us?

Focus on the Results, Not on Past History

Too many report writers feel that the reader should retrace the whole process that went into preparing the report. They expect him to read it like a novel, keeping the ending in suspense. But the man who wanted the report already knows a lot about the subject and he is interested in the findings and recommendations. Sometimes the reader may want to know how the findings and recommendations were obtained; if so, a few words about methods and sources can appear in the introduction; but, normally, one should save the details for the *body* or the *appendix* of the report.

Most executives have learned to skip all the palaver; they turn directly to the conclusions or recommendations whether at the beginning or end of the report. A busy executive is annoyed when he has to search for the findings and conclusions because they are hidden among long sections of windy theorizing or scattered in different places in the report. An experienced executive usually skims a report to make sure the right bases were touched; then he focuses on the findings and recommendations. If he agrees with them, he has nothing more to read. If he disagrees, then he will turn to the body of the report to see the proofs and arguments for the items in question.

Therefore, you might as well list the conclusions and recommendations at the beginning.

If the reader wants to know more, then, and only then, need he dig further. The purpose of a *report* is not to provide entertainment, study material, or something to read on a long rainy afternoon. Its job is to provide information for decisions.

Four Short-Form Report Formats

The core of a report consists in the *findings*, the *conclusions*, and the *recommendations*. Next in importance is the *discussion* or *body*, in which you justify the findings, conclusions, and recommendations. Ancillary, but most helpful, are the *introduction* and the *appendix*. The introduction states the problem, defines the subject, and explains the purpose and scope of the report—and, when advisable, indicates how you went about preparing the report. The appendix supplies the details, the documentation, and the data and statistics which back up the discussion or body of the report.

Accordingly, a modern *short-form* report will appear in one of the following or variations of the following four formats:

1	*2*	*3*	*4*
Introduction	Introduction	Introduction	Introduction
Findings	Summary	Recommendations	Abstract
Discussion	Procedures	Discussion	Body
Details	Results	Appendix	Conclusions
			Recommendations

In report No. *1*, only information—findings—was called for, and therefore no recommendations appear. No. *2* would be used for a report of an experimental study. No. *3* would apply when the boss asked for recommendations and the facts were well known or unquestioned. No. *4* would fit a report which was to be distributed to a large number of people, among whom were persons unfamiliar with the subject matter and who therefore needed to read the body of the report before they could understand the conclusions and recommendations. The *abstract* (see Chapter 19) serves a double purpose: (1)

to enable an experienced person to see at a glance what parts of the report he should read; and (2) to enable any one who picked up the report to see what relevance it had for him.

Barring special circumstances, the best rule to follow is: Put the recommendations as near the front of the report as you can; they are what the other person wants to read.

The Complete or Long-form for Reports

You ought to know about the long form because: (1) you may have to produce one in connection with a major problem or proposal; (2) by going through the long form you can better understand the variations in the short forms; and (3) as an executive you will have to study many reports—commercial, engineering, scientific, industrial, personnel—and recommend approval or disapproval of their contents. The following guide will serve you when you prepare a report; it will also help you when you read and evaluate reports by others.

The Long Form For Reports

1. Cover 2. Title Page	The Cover and Title Page state the subject of the report, its origin or reason for existence, the organization or person for whom it was prepared, and other identifying codes, numbers, or names.
3. Table of Contents	The Contents should be on a separate page and should be written so the reader can see what is in the report and where. Major and minor sections, illustrations, and charts should be keyed to their page numbers.

4. Prefatory Material
 	
    Foreword
 	
    Abstainer
 	
    Transmittal Information
 	
    Acknowledgments
	Prefatory Material is not always required, and when required can often be lumped in a single Preface. The Foreword can precede the Contents. An Abstainer or Disclaimer is a statement like: "Views expressed are not necessarily those of the organization"; or "For internal use only, not to be released to the public." Transmittal Information includes letters or statements of authorization, acceptance, submittal, and approval.

The Long Form For Reports (*Continued*)

5. Introduction	The Introduction can stand by itself or it can be an opening chapter, or a Section 1. Or, it may be left out if enough introductory material has been included in the title, prefatory materials, and summary of findings.
6. Summary	The Summary can follow the Introduction or it can take the place of a formal Introduction.
Purpose of Report	The Purpose is a brief reminder of the purpose, scope, and agreed method of approach.
Abstract or Concise Statement of Findings	The Abstract, Summary, and Recommendations should have identifying numbers or other references to the
Summary of Information or Conclusions	parts of the report which support them or which have the details so the reader who wants to check can turn directly
Recommendations	to the page on which its background and details are developed.
7. Body of the Report	The Body contains the description of the problem, necessary history of it, why the report was requested, definition of terms, methods of obtaining the data, equipment, and facilities used, coordination and review steps, development of information and arguments, and so on.
8. Findings in Full	The Findings are facts learned or established by the report.
Findings	The Conclusions relate to the significance of the findings—their evaluation
Conclusions	cance of the findings—their evaluation and pertinency.
Recommendations	The Recommendations are the proposals for action which have been derived from the conclusions.
Concluding Remarks	The Concluding Remarks include the critique, evaluation, or after-thoughts; for example, after the called-for report has been made according to specifications, the author adds his personal findings or some unexpected additional

information. Perhaps he found some things which would be worth further study. Perhaps he has doubts about some of the data which were supplied him. Perhaps he wants to say, "This is what you asked for, but I think you ought to have asked for it in a different form."

9. Appendix

The Appendix contains useful and pertinent materials (not padding!) which did not have to be read by a person in order to understand or use the report.

Notes

Footnotes and references or citations appear under Notes (unless they appeared earlier).

Exhibits

Tables, photographs, drawings, and other materials which were not required earlier, appear as Exhibits.

Bibliography

The Bibliography contains publications useful for the reader or which contain the back-up proof or explanations for parts of the report. (What the reader may need, not what the writer thinks will look impressive)

10. Index

Unless the report is extremely long—book size—an Index is not needed If the Table of Contents is complete, and if the report is well organized, a reader can find the sections he wants without an index If used, the Index should contain the items the reader will want to locate or refer to as he uses the report.

Remember the reader's sequence: Whether you use a long form or a short form for a report, remember that the reader's sequence differs from your writer's sequence. As the writer, you tend to follow this sequence:

1. State the purpose of the report.
2. Obtain the information you need.
3. Analyze the information and think about it.
4. Make your conclusions and recommendations.

That job may have been long, arduous, and painful. However, there is no law that the reader must repeat your sweat and tears. He has paid you to do that for him. He wants to receive the message without having to carry the mailbag to himself. So the sequence of *presentation* should be:

1. State the purpose, what the reader will get.
2. Present the conclusions or recommendations.
3. Discuss and prove your findings.
4. Give the details.

Staff Studies in Civilian Life

The study expected of you in a civilian situation will probably not be called a "staff study" as it would in the Armed Forces, but it may be just that. Many top jobs are held by ex-Generals and ex-Admirals, and every year since 1942 the military services have "graduated" more men than all the colleges and universities combined. Hence, the military type of staff study will be "in the bones" of many people and they will follow its style or expect it of you. Moreover, the staff study has its own intrinsic merit and can be used in touchy areas to provide a more complete and objective approach.

Essence of the Staff Study

In essence, a staff study is a formal paper that presents in a prescribed form an analysis of and a recommended solution to a problem. It also provides for the required implementing action. When well done it protects the boss from half-baked ideas, confusing memoranda, and partially thought-out proposals. It does this by providing him with answers, not with more questions. When badly done, it adds to the amount of paperwork and can even "snow" the boss into making the wrong decision or into avoiding a decision. The test, therefore, of a good staff study is that it should provide facts and recommendations accurately, quickly, and directly.

The Basic Elements and Form of a Staff Study

The basic elements and basic form for a military staff study are:

Basic Elements	Basic Form
1. Problem	1. Headquarters (Originating office)
2. Discussion	2. Place
3. Action Recommended	3. Date
	4. Classification (Secret, etc.)
	5. Subject
	6. *Problem*
	7. *Assumptions*

8. *Facts bearing on problem.*
9. *Discussion*
10. *Conclusions*
11. *Action recommended*
12. Signature of initiator
13. Enclosures or annexes
14. *Concurrences*
15. *Nonconcurrences*
16. Answers to nonconcurrences
17. Action by approving authority

All the items from 1 through 17 are self-explanatory; however, the important italicized ones—Problem, Assumptions, Facts, Discussion, Conclusions, Action Recommended, Concurrences and Nonconcurrences—are often misunderstood, so let's say a few words about them.

The Problem. There should be one problem to a study and it should be clearly stated to avoid digression and confused presentation. The problem should be a statement of what is to be accomplished, the difficulty to be solved, or the information to be found. It should not be *worded as a question*, but in the form of an objective. Don't write: "How much will we have to spend to launch Product B?" *But*: "To determine the cost of launching Product B."

Assumptions. Three common faults made with regard to the assumptions are:

1. Putting down too many of them—the writer goes back to the assumptions on the existence of the world, the laws of nature, and the U. S. Constitution.

2. Confusing the assumptions with the facts bearing on the problem.

3. Trying to use assumptions as crutches or short-cuts. The writer tries to "assume his way to a foregone conclusion" and what he can't find out or prove, he sticks in among the assumptions.

Five rules for making good assumptions are:

1. Make assumptions only when necessary—make an assumption only when there is no way of establishing the point.

2. Keep the assumptions realistic and not mere wishful thinking or platitudes. An assumption that "most people are honest" or the assumption that the weather will be good on such and such a day does not supply much, if anything, to a study.

3. State the assumption in positive terms, use the verb "will" with it. For example: "The Federal Reserve will continue to take anti-

inflationary actions for the next two years." Or, "Our competitors will not make a substantial change in their models during the next nine months."

4. See if any of your conclusions would be valid if one of the assumptions did not hold. If it would, then you can discard the assumption because it is not a requirement that must be met.

5. Check your assumptions with your boss or with the agency requesting the study. Unless he agrees with the assumptions on which you will be working, there is no use going further. Get his agreement or guidance before you continue.

Facts Bearing on the Problem. The world is full of "facts"; your aim is to identify and list those which bear on the problem at hand. The facts should be real ones, not just opinions, speculations, and probabilities. However, you can state the fact that something has been said or believed to be true by such and such a person or agency. Two common errors are: (1) to include among the facts a statement that is actually a conclusion, or (2) to word the statement so that the matter becomes an assumption or a conclusion rather than a statement of fact.

If the list of facts is very brief, a separate paragraph is not needed; the facts can be included in the discussion. If the list is very long, it should be summarized in a paragraph, and the details placed in an enclosure (or annex). The facts section can include necessary definitions as well as references to sources of facts. Finally, the facts should be arranged in a sequence that is related to the discussion so that the reader can find his way along a logical path through the study.

The Discussion. The discussion is an analysis of the facts as they have been found to exist. Opinions, if any, should be plainly labeled as opinions. If the study is long and complex, the discussion should be condensed for presentation in one or two paragraphs and the details placed in an enclosure.

Conclusions. Your conclusions ought to follow from the assumptions, facts, and discussion—no more, no less. Any implementing ideas or measures, should be transferred to the Recommendations; indeed, in many studies you can eliminate a conclusions paragraph and go directly to the recommendations.

A common mistake in presenting the conclusions is to include with them justifying statements or new materials which were not in the facts, assumptions, facts, or discussions. Therefore: after you have stated your conclusions, check back to make sure your discussion does substantiate them.

Actions Recommended. The action recommended should meet the tests of *suitability, feasibility,* and *acceptability.* You recommend not just what you would like to see happen, but what the boss can and ought to do. The recommendations should be clear, positive statements, worded so that the boss need only approve them in order to get the ball rolling. For example, a recommendation might read like this:

It is recommended that:

(a) The letter (Enclosure A) be sent to the Board of Directors with the plan for the new building (Enclosure B) as its enclosure.

(b) Upon approval by the Board, the request (Enclosure C) for bids for construction of the building should be mailed to the list of approved contractors (Enclosure D).

(c) And so forth.

Concurrences and Nonconcurrences. A wry comment often heard in the Pentagon is that congressmen, judges, and supreme court justices consider and deliberate and dissent, but military chiefs and business leaders wrangle and bicker. In complicated matters you cannot expect complete agreement. The concurrences show the boss who has lined up on your side and will support your conclusions and recommendations; the nonconcurrences show him who the people are whom you failed to convince. Nonconcurrences, no matter by whom or how strong, do not mean you must compromise. But there is no use trying to hide them. Simply state them with sufficient explanation to show their reasons for disagreeing. You can add your answers to the objections, or perhaps add alternative proposals in the event the boss decides in favor of one or more of the objections.

BASIC FORMAT FOR THE STAFF STUDY[2]

Issuing Office:
Place of issue:
Date   :
File number :

SUBJECT:

1. PROBLEM: concise statement

2. ASSUMPTIONS: necessary for logical discussion of problems which cannot be accepted or considered as facts

3. FACTS BEARING ON THE PROBLEM: essential facts stated in logical sequence

[2] Reprinted from *Communication Through Reports* by Paul Douglass (Englewood Cliffs, N. J.: Prentice-Hall, Inc., 1960), p. 306.

4. DISCUSSION: careful analysis of essential facts, inventory of pros and cons, logical deductions

5. CONCLUSIONS: statement of results of inquiry based on reasoned judgment of effects and implications of essential facts, any alternate lines of action being excluded from report

6. ACTION RECOMMENDED: concise, unambiguous statement of proposed action permitting simple approval or disapproval

_____
Signature Initiating Officer

ANNEXES: number and list annexes accompanying study, including implementing directives

CONCURRENCES: have officers concerned indicate concurrences by initials followed by name, rank, official position title, and telephone number

NONCONCURRENCES: have staff officers indicate nonconcurrence by initials followed by name, rank, official position title, telephone and brief reasons for nonconcurrence stated on separate memoranda attached as additional annexes

CONSIDERATION OF NONCONCURRENCES: attached initialed statement of staff study author showing result of his consideration of nonconcurrences with reasons why, if any, nonconcurrences cannot be supported

ANNEXES ADDED: list annexes containing nonconcurrences attached

ACTION BY APPROVING AUTHORITY:

Approved (including)

Disapproved (excluding) exception

_____
Signature of Executive

SUMMING UP THIS CHAPTER

The purpose of a report is to present recommendations or a "package" of information to the man who wants them. Therefore it should be oriented to the reader's needs; it should answer his problems, not those of the writer. Its purpose is *not* to show that its author is a great scholar or researcher, *nor* should it include the writer's troubles, desires, and hopes.

After you have roughed out a report, look at it from the eyes of the future readers, and arrange and edit your final version accordingly.

The purpose of a staff study is to present the assumptions, facts, conclusions, recommendations, and concurrences or nonconcurrences related to a problem bothering the top men. It is a good tool because it makes you take into account all the key elements and to touch base with all the interested parties. Reports usually put the recommendations at or near the beginning, the staff study builds towards them.

Here again we see the working out of the principle explained in Chapter 1, namely: To write a good report or study you have to follow good management practices; to follow good management practices, you need well-written reports and studies.

It is also well to keep the distinctions between an article and a report or study in mind because the reader who expects an article will be bored by report; a man asking for a report will be frustrated by an article. In the next chapter, we will discuss the organization of articles and letters so that the distinctions will become clearer and more useful to you.

15

HOW TO ORGANIZE LETTERS AND PROFESSIONAL ARTICLES

HOW TO ORGANIZE LETTERS

As one goes up the business ladder one finds—sometimes suddenly —that letters with which one is familiar are no longer good guides for the bewildering variety of executive correspondence. Perhaps a man has become expert in the sales letter—the reply to a complaint—the credit letter—the purchasing request—the production control or quality memorandum—the personnel inquiry; but now he becomes responsible for all types of letters.

Or, he may have been a foreman, an engineer, an accountant, or a salesman who wrote no letters.

Whatever the background, whatever the reason, the fact is that many top executives complain that their middle managers and junior executives write "confused and rambling letters."

Therefore, the first part of this chapter will focus on the essentials of good organization in a letter. For further information about, and examples of letters from sales to inquiry, from dunning to complimentary, you can refer to any of the many good texts on the subject. Two excellent ones are:

> *How to Write Successful Business Letters in 15 Days* by John P. Riebel. (Englewood Cliffs, N. J.: Prentice-Hall, Inc., 1953)
>
> *Business Executive's Handbook* by S. M. Brown and L. Doris, contains in Section 1—Successful Selling by Direct Mail, and in Section 5—How to Write Effective Business Letters, a total of 282 pages on the subject of business letters. (Fourth Edition, Englewood Cliffs, N. J.: Prentice-Hall, Inc.)

In addition, *The Direct Mail Newsletter* (Garden City, N. Y.) and *Better Letters* (Economics Press, Montclair, N. J.), and the materials

146

produced by the Direct Mail Association provide continuing up-to-date advice about business letter writing. Here we will discuss the basic organization of an executive letter and of a general business letter.

Basic Organization of an Executive Letter

The organization of an executive letter is essentially simple: the first paragraph should tell the reader what the letter is about; the next paragraph or paragraphs should explain the circumstances and state the action; that is, give orders, make requests, give consent, refuse permission, approve or disapprove.

The common causes for confusion and rambling in a letter are:

1. Failure to follow the basic pattern—purpose, circumstances, action.

2. Including more than a single idea in a sentences, more than a central thought in a paragraph, and more than a single subject in a letter.

3. Failure to consider what the reader needs or wants.

1. *Basic Pattern*. Each of the steps—the "why" of the letter, the reasons or circumstances, the action to be taken or not taken—can be brief and simple. Follow the famous rule: "Never underestimate the intelligence of your reader, but never overestimate his knowledge about a matter."

2. *Single Subject*. Sticking to a single subject in a letter sounds easy but many writers fail to do so. They accumulate a deskful of problems, comments, inquiries, and requests and then unload them in one long letter. What happens at the other end? The receiver has to untangle the separate subjects and work out a complicated routing for the letter or for copies of its parts among all the people responsible for the answers or action.

Suppose a manager of a branch office writes a letter with three different topics in it. One subject can be answered in a day or so, the second will require a week, and the third must be routed to several offices and perhaps even referred to other branches for comment. At each of these stages people who have no interest in the other parts of the letter must wade through them.

Paper is cheap in comparison to the costs of human handling, of human reading and thinking time. Three practical checks on the possible "multiple-subject" letters originating from your office are:

a. See if the letter could be logically broken into two or more shorter letters by simply using the phrase: "the . . . (facets, factors, implication) of the . . . matter will be covered in a separate letter." If so, do so.

b. See how often other offices when replying to your letters use a similar phrase, e.g.: "The matter of . . . in your letter of . . . will be answered by separate correspondence." Why did they have to split up your letter? Too many subjects in it?

c. Visualize who must answer each item in a sample of your letters, and how long each answer will take to prepare. If you can visualize a lot of hurly-burly and scurrying around in the other office while they dig up the answers to your chockful letters, don't smile at their possible discomfiture. Rewrite your letters so that each covers only one subject.

3. *Consider the Reader.* Many managers stay immersed in their own affairs and don't consider the other fellow. They know their department's problem—and all its urgencies, delicacies, and ramifications. But does the reader? Should he?

After you have written a letter, *particularly one on a matter of intense interest to you,* sit back and try to see it with the next man's eyes. Put yourself in his place and ask yourself how you would understand it and go about answering it if you were he. Try to become the other man, and edit your letter accordingly.

Organization of Business Letters in General

A successful business letter, says Mr. Riebel (*How to Write Successful Business Letters in 15 Days*), must have a beginning, a middle, and an ending. The *beginning* should gain the reader's attention and arouse his interest; the *middle* should convince him of, or arouse his desire for the *action* which is called for in the *ending*. The following discussion is based in large part on Mr. Riebel's instructions for the "Fourth Day" of his *15-day* course in successful business letter writing.

A letter is either (a) the *start* of a hoped-for correspondence or (b) it is in *answer* to a letter. Its *beginning, middle,* and *ending* should be structured accordingly. Let's see what happens first with an initiating letter and then with an answering letter.

Organization of an Initiating Letter

Beginning. In the first sentence or paragraph you should do one or more of the following:

(1) Tell who you are.   (I am the new representative assigned to handle your account. My name is . . . .)

(2) Tell why you are writing. (Your firm has long been noted for the quality of its meters. My firm would like to know if . . . .)

(3) Tell who told you to write. (Mr. Robert Merryam has written me that you are interested in relocating in our area . . . .)

(4) Tell what kind of letter you are writing. (I have a complaint to make about the squeaks in . . . .)

(5) Get right to the point. (The money you asked for is on the way.

(6) Put a "hooker" into the reader to hold his interest. (Would you like to double your earnings but without doubling your efforts or investment?)

Middle. In the middle, or body, or main part of your letter, you should do one or more of the following:

(1) Present your main point if you have not done so in the opening. Sell the reader with the strongest appeal so he will keep on reading. Catch his eye with the best argument before he has time to drop the letter in the wastebasket.

(2) Give your second, third, and so forth points in succeeding *separate* paragraphs. If you have many main points, number or label them.

Ending. Your ending may be a paragraph—preferably short—or a sentence. You should, according to Mr. Riebel, strive to be all the following:

(1) *Clear*—let the reader know what you want him to do and where, when, and how. (I will meet you in Conference Room B at 9 A.M. sharp on February 15.)

(2) *Courteous*—ask nicely, say or imply "please," and be complimentary. (Thank you again for sending me the order. It was thoughtful and neighborly of you. Please let me know when I can stop by to explain how the gadget works.)

(3) *Concise*—be brief, but not curt, friendly but not effusive. Few readers want a long drawn-out ending; but no one wants to be cut off with a terse "that's it, bud" type of closing.

(4) *Complete*—don't leave reader wondering if you have finished or if there was another page you forgot to include. Don't be vague or general, be specific.

(5) *Modern*—avoid the old-fashioned phrases like "we beg to remain your obedient servants."

Organization of an Answering Letter

Beginning. When answering a letter, your opening sentence or sentences should do one or more of the following:

(1) Refer to the letter you are answering.	(Your letter of May 10 asked for . . . .)
(2) Tell why you are writing the answer.	(Mr. Adams will be out of town all week, so he asked me to write you . . . .)
(3) Plunge right into the business, if you are sure the reader cannot mistake what you are talking about.	(Your order was shipped last night, and here is the invoice . . . .)

(Note: Some instructors of letter writing have gone too far in criticizing the use of a "reference" or of phrases like "In reply to your letter of. . . ." One of them has said, "Why tell the correspondent about his letter? He knows what he wrote you." Such advice might be good if all letter writers were solitary citizens, very small businessmen, or independent small farmers—people who write one letter a month and can remember it. But a large corporation or government agency will receive and send thousands of letters a day on all sorts of subjects. Therefore, because of the shortness of men's memories and the turnover of personnel, it is good practice to make some sort of identifying reference in all letters.)

Middle. In the answering as in the initiating type of letter, the main body of your letter should present your main point, beginning with the more important ones—that is, more important to your readers. Each main point should be in a separate paragraph.

Ending. As in the initiating type of letter, your ending should be clear, courteous, concise, complete, and modern.

HOW TO ORGANIZE A BUSINESS OR PROFESSIONAL ARTICLE

"What, Me Write An Article?"

There are hundreds of business and professional publications, and thousands of house organs and trade journals. All these print an immense number of articles, many of which are written either by an executive or professional person, or by a writer working under their direction.

"But I'm not an author! I can't write an article." Perhaps you can't write for a magazine like the *Saturday Evening Post,* or *Reader's Digest.* But you can write for your fellow businessmen, fellow engineers, fellow employees, or potential customers and suppliers. From the standpoint of professional prestige and development, an engineer would prefer to have an article in an engineering journal than in a popular magazine. Similarly, it can mean more to a manager to have an article in *Advanced Management, Supervision,* or one of the periodicals of the American Management Association.

You know your job; you know things about running your business, handling your subordinates and customers, and operating equipment, processes, and facilities. People will read what you have to say about subjects within your area of expertness—in some instances, it may be only a paragraph in a house organ; in other instances, it may be a long article in a professional journal.

Five Reasons for Writing Business and Professional Articles

There may be more, but there certainly are at least the following five advantages to writing an article, or articles. Publication of an article with your name on it will:

(1) Increase the prestige of your department and provide good publicity for the business.

(2) Enhance your personal prestige. When your superiors and colleagues see your name in print you go up in their estimation.

(3) Enable the company or division to obtain desirable personnel. Many business and professional people—particularly engineers— view a company in terms of the "image" it has in the trade and professional journals.

(4) Promote an interchange of ideas. Other people with similar interests—or disagreements—will write you or speak to you at conventions and meetings about your article.

(5) Give you valuable experience. Most important of all, even if your article is never printed, you will have the practice of focusing and packaging your information, ideas, and judgment. Most successful writers, speakers, executives, and professional men owe their visible accomplishments to their preliminary attempts. You never lose when you try to write an interesting, coherent article. If the piece succeeds, you gain recognition and prestige. If the piece is not accepted, you can gain a valuable editorial lesson. To paraphrase Thomas Edison: You have learned what does not work, a valuable thing to know. Finally, when the occasion comes—as it inevitably does—for you to discuss the subject, you will have the advantage of having already made the effort to present it in an organized and interesting fashion.

Professor's Campbell's Four-Step Plan for an Article

As with reports, letters, and presentations, the average non-professional writer usually finds his greatest difficulty in getting his thoughts and words organized. He knows what he wants to say, but he has trouble untangling the jumble of ideas that rush through his mind.

Some years ago, Professor Walter S. Campbell, at the University of Oklahoma, proposed four steps to an article, labeling them as follows: *Hey, You, See,* and *So.*

1. Hey. That is, "Look at me! I've got something interesting to say." This "hooker" to catch the reader's eye, can usually be a direct statement about the new product, development, or idea you are going to describe. Or, it can be a promise that what you are writing will make the reader wiser, richer, or healthier, or protect him from something unpleasant.

2. You. That is, how does the article relate to the reader's interests —life, pocketbook, job, family, etc.

3. See. That is, the message of the article—this and this is what you have to tell the reader.

4. So. And therefore, you summarize, conclude, and recommend the points you have been making.

Note how closely this formula follows that of Richard Borden in his *Public Speaking—As Listeners Like It!* Remember, his formula is: (1) Ho hum! (2) Why bring that up? (3) For instance! (4) So what? (See Chapter Three.)

When using Campbell's formula try these two techniques:

1. Work on the *See* and *So* parts of the article; then develop the *You* emphasis; and finally think about the *Hey* opening.

2. Start with four separate sheets of paper, one for each step— Hey, You, See, So—and label them accordingly. Jot your ideas down on these sheets of paper, adding to them, and polishing them as time permits—or the mood impels you. After awhile you will have each section done and you will have only to merge them together with perhaps a few words of transition so that the one slides smoothly into the other.

SUMMING UP THIS CHAPTER

A business *letter* organized to please the reader has the following characteristics:

1. It is about one subject.
2. The opening tells the recipient why he should read the letter.
3. The contents are "reader oriented" not "author oriented."
4. The action desired is clearly and courteously stated.

A business *article* organized to please a reader has the following characteristics:

1. It opens with a reason why the reader should read it.

2. It explains simply, quickly, and clearly a new product, idea, or development. (A *business* article is not an essay on the belles artes, or a story, or a complaint or exhortation, though it can and should be written with some drama and excitement.)[1]

3. It ends with a brief summary which restates the main theme, conclusions, or actions.

[1] For information and advice with regard to better writing see Chapters 21 and 22, and the references in Appendix B.

16

USE OF VISUAL AIDS IN WRITTEN MATERIALS

What the Executive Needs to Know

An executive is not expected to be an artist or a printing expert. However, he operates in a world filled with "visualizations."

Mr. J. Donald Adams, in his column in *The New York Times Book Review*,[1] wrote:

> We cannot realize the enormous change that has taken place in the use of the picture unless we remind ourselves that it was once used merely as a supplement to the text.... This use is still made of the picture, to be sure, but the change is evident in the increasing number of books in which the text is definitely subordinated to the layout ... one more indication of the current emphasis on visual approach.

What we need are some general principles for the use of illustrations in a publication and for dealing with the people responsible for preparing those illustrations.

Distinction Between Presentation Art and Publication Art

What was said in Chapter Eight on the use of charts in a presentation is applicable to the contents of this chapter; *but bear in mind the crucial distinction*: *A presentation chart is spoken about; a publication illustration must be read about.*

The speaker can control the timing of exposure of the chart to the audience; he can watch faces; he can ask questions; and he can vary

[1] December 5, 1954

154

what he says about the chart. Moreover, the chart will be shown in large-size to a group of people at the same time and place.

An illustration in a text, however, has no one standing by to explain it. The reader finds out about it, looks at it, understands it, only when he takes the trouble to do so or its interest to him impels him to look at it.

Presentation and publication charts are not interchangeable. When they are about the same subject, there is a good chance that they can be adapted to both uses; however, do not blindly try to do so. A chart that makes an excellent appearance when blown up to size 6 feet by 8 feet may seem picayune in a 6 by 8-inch pamphlet. Paper does not smile, frown, pause, or raise or lower its voice, or handle a pointer. Conversely, a man in an audience cannot turn back the pages to re-read a point he missed nor can a speaker avoid showing a chart too slowly for some people and too quickly for others.

In any event, you can always ask if a presentation illustration could serve as a *springboard* for a new idea that could be used in a publication, or vice versa.

Do You Intend to Instruct, Amuse, or Distract the Reader?

"Let's brighten up this report so people will want to read it," is some frequently given advice. When the speaker means to make the material easier to read, as well as more eye-catching, the advice is good. But when he means, as too many do, that a report should look like a popular illustrated magazine, he may be way off base.

During World War II the military service used cartoons to teach various subjects. Perhaps the cartoons helped to hold the men's attention and to reinforce some of the messages, but quite often the men smiled at the cartoons and that was all they did. As one educational expert put it: "When you treat a subject in a light casual manner, the student treats it in the same way." Another training consultant reported that a series of cartoons about a "fouled-up" aviation cadet named "Dilbert" had actually back-fired. The cadets instead of being warned away from stupid or reckless stunts by "Dilbert" actually tried to imitate his "dillies!"

Many of the novels published in the 1920's included photographic "stills" from the silent films which had been based on the novel. These pictures were frequently placed in another part of the text from where the action was described; sometimes they showed scenes and characters that had appeared in the film versions, but not in the book.

We smile at the ways in which the old stills were stuck in the books, but if we look at a number of modern corporation reports, studies, handouts, and other publications, we can find examples of pictures used in an equally haphazard fashion. At best they simply take up expensive space which might have been filled with something more to the point; at worst, they lower the reader's faith in the company. He wonders, for example, why the booklet shows a picture of the West Coast plant when the text is about East Coast operations.

Types of Visual Aids in Publications

There are six types of visual aids commonly used in publications. These are:

Photographs	Decorative designs
Drawings	Charts and Tables
Cartoons	Printing devices

1. *Photographs* are often called halftones, because of the process used to reproduce them. In theory they have the advantage of being easy-to-take, *accurate* views (the camera can't lie). In practice, however, a good picture requires an experienced photographer and can cost a lot of money. The event you see with your eyes, and the one that comes out on the developed film are often quite different, especially when perspective is involved. Your eyes may see the clouds on the horizon clearly; but the little 4-by 4-inch photograph shows a smudge. You see the new mammoth machine clearly when you stand in front of it; the picture of it however shows a looming bulk of black and gray blocks and bulges. Also, people are so used to glancing at photographs while turning the page, that it is hard to predict the impact a photograph will have on a reader.

In general, the following rules apply:

a. Use photographs to show people. "Names make news" and pictures of people make interesting viewings. Here is where many business writings could use more photographs to good advantage; when an employee or customer or supplier is mentioned, why not show his picture?

b. Use photographs for close-ups. Any book on the subject, any picture editor can show you how "cropping" will help a picture. For example, the amateur photographer takes a picture of the whole baseball park. The editor "crops" away all the picture except the small area showing the runner sliding into base, and then enlarges that part of the picture. The professional photographer would have focused his whole film on the key point of action or interest, thus saving much of the cropping and enlarging.

c. Start with a large picture and reduce. When you enlarge a picture, you lose sharpness of detail; the picture becomes "grainy"—just as on a TV screen. In the example of the baseball scene, enlarging a small section would probably result in a fuzzy picture; but starting with a large picture of a small scene, one could either leave it the same size, or reduce it, and gain apparent sharpness. Even if a picture in report, pamphlet, or book, is to be the size of a small postage stamp, shoot the photograph and develop the film to provide a size 8 by 10 "glossy" print.

d. When you use a photograph to show a landscape, plant layout, machine installation, or type of product, study it carefully to make sure it shows, not what you are familiar with, but what the *reader* ought to see. If necessary, show the same scene twice, once in a general view, or "establishing shot" and then in a close-up of the key point or points.

e. Let the professionals edit the photographs for you. They understand the requirements of layout and of the various printing processes and can take pictures which will do the job and will also be easier to edit and print.

2. *Drawings,* often called *line-cuts* because of the reproduction process used with them, require an artist to prepare, and may take more time and cost more than a photograph. In general, line drawings are used when:

a. The item or process cannot be photographed.

b. You want to highlight certain elements.

c. You want to show "depth" or perspective so the reader can see how one part works against another.

As you might expect, technical publications and how-to--do-it manuals are the prime users of drawings.

3. *Cartoons* are types of photographs and drawings which can vary from touched-up photographs to abstract creations. They also range from sober, serious pictographs, noble-appearing faces and stately figures, to caricatures and boisterous "comics." Like all forms of art they are only as good as the artist who prepared them, and there will always be a measure of subconscious skill or "luck" with them. A touch of the pen, a change of mood, or an unpredictable reaction, and one man's "humor" turns into another man's "satire"; one man's effort to "lighten a heavy text" becames another man's conviction that the company has degraded itself by frivolous illustrations. When deciding on the use of cartoons, consider the following factors:

a. The availability of an artist who has proven success with the subject matter and with the type of audience you have in mind.

b. The effect you desire on the reader. The cartoons ought to entice him to read, not distract him from the intended message.

c. If the message is so unimportant to the reader that we must trick him into reading it by cartoons, why try to reach him at all?

d. After the reader has laughed and enjoyed the cartoon, what will he think or feel?

Cartoons are best suited for the following situations:

a. The subject is important to you, but dull or disliked by the probable readers.

b. The subject is a light one—the directions to the annual picnic, for example—which can be portrayed by cartoons and offend no one, while making you or the company appear to be a good-humored sort of person or corporation.

c. The message or report is an old topic which has been made in the same way for so long that no one reads it any more. By adding cartoons, you hope people will look at it again.

4. *Charts and Tables*. Tables are not actually artwork or illustrations, but let's include them with charts because: (1) they break up the pages of text and provide variety as do illustrations; (2) they can substitute for long sections of narrative or explanative writing, like a good chart does; and (3) the process of designing them and locating them in the text is similar to that for charts and illustrations.[1]

When deciding on the use of a table or chart, keep the following in mind:

a. Does the table or chart belong in the text or in the appendix? That is, does the reader need it as he goes along or can it be placed in the appendix to be referred to only by readers interested in the data or curious how a conclusion or fact was derived?

b. Tables can show non-statistical data; this use is often overlooked. For example, SPAIBASCATH on pages 8-9 shows how non-digit information can be presented in tabular form.

c. The table or the chart should serve the reader, not the writer. The reader has not done all the work you have; he has not struggled with the data and finally gotten them charted on the paper. Don't expect him to read the chart with your eyes. Step back and try to

---

[1] For explanation and demonstration of the different types of charts and tables and for more about their use, see *Communication Through Reports* by Paul Douglass and *Putting Yourself Over in Business* by Dyer, Evans, and Lovell. Both books are published by Prentice-Hall, Englewood Cliffs, N. J.

visualize it through his eyes: does it tell him plainly, quickly, and easily what he needs to know at this point in the text?

d.   A reader can refer to the same chart many times; hence a publication chart or table can contain more information and be more complex than one used in a spoken presentation. *But*: if it contains more than three curves, or if the columns of figures get too small for the "bifocal-age" group, you had better show the information in two or more charts or tables.

5.   *Decorative Designs and Printing Devices* can be quite abstract (pure "frou-frou") or they can be swatches of photographs, charts, and tables, used not to carry meaning, but to decorate the text. The main questions to ask about them are:

a.   Does the text really need such "fancying up"—will the effect on the reader (the real reader, not imaginary ones) be worth the cost?

b.   Will the decoration enhance the message or detract from it?

c.   Are the decorations—the vignettes of the plan and products, the glimpses of charts and tables—intended simply to "set a mood" or to carry a real message? If they are just to decorate, you must be sure they inspire the proper mood. If they are to carry a message, then don't kid yourself that the reader will get it subliminally, or through the back door of his mind. Most readers have been conditioned to the "borders" of a publication and they do not notice anything unless it is of direct interest or profit to them. The average man already has too much paper crossing his desk; therefore, if you have something to say to him, do so quickly and directly; don't try to slip him hints on the side.

Of course, you should give a professional, well-done appearance to anything you write or publish, but don't count on an "impression" to carry a message.

Five Tips for Obtaining An Attractive Text Appearance

1.   Don't crowd the page. Don't try to save paper by packing each page full of words. Leave wide margins at top and bottom, and double space between paragraphs. Artists call this "providing plenty of light and air" and they recommend an "airy" page in preference to a heavy, crowded page.

2.   Don't use long lines. Studies have shown that columns from about 2½ inches to about 4½ inches are easiest to read. Note the width of the columns in a newspaper or in a magazine like *Reader's Digest*. If you are using wide pages, try to run two or three columns

down the page—but with plenty of "air" between them. If you are using typed material, forget the margins recommended by the company correspondence manual (by all means ignore the Government manuals!) and use a 5- or 6-inch wide line. The human eye—particularly when trained in the new rapid-reading methods—prefers to scan a line that can be taken in one or two glances. When you have to make three or four eye-fixations a line, the reading becomes onerous. (You have to watch out for this practice yourself, because many, if not most, typists and printers will automatically run the material all the way across the page. Even when there are only a few lines, some copy setters will spread it into a wide rectangle at the top of the page, rather than center it in a more easily read, narrower column.)

3. When using tables, charts, and pictures, remember to:

a. Place them near their references in the text, and make sure they are clearly numbered and labeled.

b. Vary them from place to place, don't run them all at the tops of pages or all at the bottoms of pages, but do try to insert some text between them. A continued series of tables or charts, and even of pictures, can be confusing and can cause the individual ones to lose their impact. Avoid filling a whole page with two charts or tables. Place at least a fifth of a page of text between them, or move one to another page. (When in doubt, choose a blank or nearly empty page in preference to an overcrowded one.)

4. Do use some variety in type: CAPS, SMALL CAPS, *italic*, **bold-face**, and some underscores—but not all on the same page! You want the change in type to emphasize an important point, not make the page look junky.

5. People read from left to right, and from the top down; therefore, the place on a page which catches the reader's eye is the upper left quadrant. If you want to make sure he sees something on a page, place it above and to the left of the center of the page.

6. Best of all, find and use a good layout editor and a good printer.

HOW TO GET GOOD ARTWORK

Types of Artists

In Chapters 11, 12, and 13 we discussed directly or by implication the matter of getting along well with writers and editors—sometimes you are the writer, sometimes you are the editor as you labor to get the right words on paper. When you include illustrations—artwork—and printing designs and layout, you must deal with the functions of the artist. An impressive, four-color, original creation for the cover of an annual report can require a professional artist whose fees run in the thousands of dollars. On the other hand, a few simple organization charts, or a sprinkling of pictographs can be produced by a junior draftsman working for $3 or $4 an hour.

A less obvious but, from the standpoint of the business executive, a more important distinction is that between the artist who can create an illustration, and the artist who at best can copy or develop an idea given him by someone else.

Artists by nature and training are different from executives and from writers and editors. There are a few "triple-threat" men in the world—men who can manage, write, and illustrate—but they are very rare. (In fact, they are running their own enterprises and are wistfully searching for good writers and artists to help them!) The writer cannot understand how the editor can be so ornery and blind about good writing; the editor, on the other hand, shakes his head sadly over the drivel, the clumsy sentences, and the confused outpourings he encounters from the writers. But both writers and editors agree that the artist rarely grasps what is wanted, rarely meets deadlines, and rarely draws what he was asked to draw. In turn, the artist has learned that writers and editors are people who mess up pages with words about some uninteresting matters of their own, instead of giving him the space—and all the time he needs—for a really good visual presentation.

Hence, if you, as a business or professional man, encounter confusion and difficulty when dealing with artists, do not be surprised. Other people do, too. Artists—and ultimately this fact is a fortunate one—think differently than executives; they have been trained differently; they have different goals, concepts, and techniques. If you have not learned to paint a picture, neither have they studied balance sheets, business indexes, or production control data.

In general, you will find three main categories of commercial or presentation artists. At the bottom (for business purposes) is the draftsman who at best can make a clear drawing from a rough sketch provided him. In the middle, is the all-around artist who can create an illustration. At the top (and very rare) is the man who can read your material or talk to your people, then orginate a comprehensive plan for the illustrations, the over-all design of the publication, and even find and supervise the artists and draftsmen who execute the design. These top men are the art directors of large corporations and large advertising agencies, or they are making from $20,000 to $100,000 a year as heads of their own agencies.

The following five principles will help you avoid many difficulties when obtaining artwork—and will help you obtain the best service from the artists.

Five Principles for Dealing with Artists

1. If the artist is just a draftsman, or a beginner, or inexperienced in anything but "pure" art, you cannot expect him or her to analyze your material and come up with the charts, pictures, and captions. You will have to decide what you want and draw a rough sketch for him to develop and polish.

2. On the other hand, when working with an experienced artist, remember that his job should be to provide material that *pleases the intended audience*, not just you, his boss or client. Sometimes an artist will compromise his own ideas too soon—or too cynically— and just "give the boss what he wants." But if the artist is a good one and has had experience with the type of audience you have in mind (which you can find out by checking his past work), he should be listened to in regard to how the illustrations should look and where they should be placed.

3. Be sure the artist understands: (a) what you want, (b) when you want it, and (c) how it will be used. When you are dealing with a contractor or art director, you can hound him, and he will hound his artists. When you are dealing directly with the artist, whether an "in-house" or "out-house" one, remember he will probably be more interested in how well he draws or paints than in how soon you need the artwork. Keep after him. Ask to see his rough sketches so that you can request or demand changes early in the game. Be sure he is not planning artwork that is too large or too small, or in colors that will not reproduce.

4. State clearly what you like or don't like about an illustration. Bill Blasingame, the commercial artist (you can see the "William E. Blasingame" signature on billboards and brochures all over the country), says that an artist wants a client to be definite and specific. "I prefer him to say, 'It stinks,' or 'I like it' to a vague, 'I don't know,'" says Bill, "because then I know where I stand."

"I make several rough sketches," explains Bill, "but I show only one to the client. To show several at a time can confuse him, or he may want a piece of this one and a piece of that one and the result can be a hodge-podge. If he likes the drawing I've shown him, I can make changes to it and modify it to suit his requests without messing up its composition. On the other hand, if he definitely doesn't like the concept, then I show him another one. The important thing is that he lets me know what he likes or doesn't like. You don't hurt a professional's feelings by being definite; he appreciates it." (Of course, being definite does not mean to be rude or insulting.)

5. Be sure there is supporting materials for the proposed illustrations. Bill Blasingame explains this rule as follows: "Sometimes an artist or client will plan to use a picture of such and such a piece of equipment, and then find out too late that the picture or the model to base it on is unavailable. Hence, I never present a layout or proposed illustration until I have the supporting materials."

Bill means: Don't plan to use a picture of nuclear reactor here, or a picture of an Iroquois chieftain there, unless you have the picture in question. Too often you will find the information required for the object cannot be released, or the museum does not have a picture to copy. Then you are stuck with a plan that has to be jiggled around to cover up the missing key elements. The point is: Don't accept or approve plans for an illustration unless the information or materials to support it are guaranteed to be available.

SUMMING UP THIS CHAPTER

1. Do not presume that a presentation chart and a publication chart will be interchangeable; usually a special effort must be made to adapt one for use as the other.

2. Be sure that an illustration or piece of artwork does what you actually intend it to do—whether it be to amuse, distract, or instruct the reader. You don't want to pay for his instruction and get instead his amusement.

3. Use photographs for showing people; line drawings for showing equipment, machinery, and processes; cartoons for light subjects or for changes in pace; charts and tables for "packaging" masses of data; decorative designs for eye appeal and general appearance of artistic competence—and obtain professional advice and help for all of them.

4. When planning the layout or format of a typed or printed report, keep the following guidelines in mind:

a. Don't crowd the page.

b. Don't use long lines; do use columns from 2½ to 6 inches wide.

c. Place illustrations near the place where they are mentioned;

label them clearly; reference them clearly; and separate one from the other by at least a few lines of text.

d. Do use a variety of type, but don't overdo the italics, capital letters, and underscored words.

5. Remember that not everyone who says he is an artist can originate and carry out a master plan of visualization for a complex subject. If he is inexperienced, you must provide him with a rough sketch; if he is a qualified artist, let him do it his way. In any event, be clear, definite, and specific about what you like or dislike in the plans he shows you.

6. Be sure the supporting materials for any proposed illustrations will be available when needed.

17

PUNCTUATION AND GRAMMAR FROM THE EXECUTIVE'S VIEWPOINT

Rules Are For Clarity, Not Snobbery

Unfortunately, the subjects of grammar, syntax (word order), and punctuation are tied up in many people's minds with the painful struggle they had in grade school to distinguish adverbs from adjectives. Many also worry about something called "good English" which reputedly separates the cultured from the uncultured. Often the person who frets the most over grammar does so because he is not sure of himself. Others, who cannot contribute anything constructive, make a big to-do over catching "terrible errors" like "ill-advised capitalization and unorthodox division of words."

The real purpose of grammar and punctuation, of course, is to provide a set of "playing rules" to make it easier for the reader, the observer, to understand what he is supposed to understand. Rules of grammar and punctuation provide guidelines which the writer follows so that the reader can see more quickly and more clearly the "game" which the writer is describing. To mix these rules up with social position adds more emotion and less understanding to the situation. To consider grammar and punctuation things to take out or put into a piece of writing is nonsene. We do not write in order to achieve good grammar; rather we use grammar to achieve clear-to-the-reader writing. If the writing is clear, the grammar will be good. This chapter and the next will look at the matter from the standpoint of what the executive needs to know in order to follow the modern rules of grammar, punctuation, and more importantly the attitudes he should have in order to avoid quibbles while encouraging his subordinates to produce better writing.

The Four Secrets of an Executive's Attitude Toward Questions of Grammar and Punctuation

In practice, there are only four main things the manager-as-writer-and-editor ought to keep in his mind with regard to questions of grammar and punctuation.

These four principles or executive attitudes are:

1. Problems of grammar or punctuation are signals of human relations problems or of thinking difficulties.

2. Don't enter into arguments over grammatical niceties.

3. Don't use a grammar or punctuation error as an excuse for a criticism or rejection of an idea.

4. In general, use less, not more, punctuation.

Let's see how these principles work out in practice.

1. *Points of grammar and punctuation are signals.* When a "big issue" or "puzzlement" arises over a point of grammar (to split or not to split an infinitive) or punctuation (should there be a colon or semi-colon?) look for either of two situations: (a) a human relations problem—one person is using a language nicety in order to throw his weight around, browbeat others, or take out his frustrations on others; or (b) the facts, the reasoning, or the statements are not clear—poor grammar or punctuation almost always signal a lack of clarity or definiteness in the thoughts behind the words.

The human relations aspects should be handled by human relations techniques, not by a course in grammar and punctuation or by appeals to the dictionary. Yet one sees grown men and women scrabbling through dictionaries to settle an argument about a word! (For ideas on how to handle the human side of management see our books, *Putting Yourself Over in Business* and *Executive's Guide to Handling People,* both published by Prentice-Hall, Inc., Englewood Cliffs, N. J.)

The lack of clarity as signaled by poor grammar or punctuation—indeed by any form of clumsy or awkward wording—can best be taken care of by rewriting the sentence. Don't waste time trying to prove the language is "grammatical" or "ungrammatical," just treat the point as a red or amber light on the road of communication and rethink what you are trying to say.

2. *Don't enter into arguments over details of grammar or punc-*

tuation. You should simply mark the spots on the page that seem unclear or awkward to you, and ask for "another way of stating the point." Or say, "I'd like you to put that in a different way." If you have an alternative ready, put it down, if not, return the paper. Let the other fellow look up the grammatical point, let your secretary work it out, but don't you, the executive, take time to search through dictionaries. And why try to keep in mind all the rules of spelling, punctuation, hyphenation, phrasing, paragraphing, and so forth? Proving the "correctness" of a phrase will not make the ultimate reader enjoy what is boringly written or confusingly thought out. So, when your secretary or assistants bring a grammar point to you for resolution, just smile and say: "Change it any way you think best, and if you are not sure, look it up in the dictionary."

3. *Don't use a point of grammar as an excuse, or red herring.* Above all, do not use a point of grammar as an excuse for turning down a page of writing. If the spelling and grammar are bad, your secretary or a good typist can straighten them out. Jumping on a person's grammar because you don't want to argue the facts or reasons of his case will solve nothing, and indeed will usually make him all the more angry and resentful. He will either realize subconsciously that you are sidestepping the issue, or he will be hurt because you have shown up his "lack of education and culture." So keep your arguments to the intended content of the writing and leave the format, grammar, and punctuation to be supplied by a person paid to do such things—an editor, technical writer, or professional secretary.

4. *Use less, not more, punctuation.* In general, the modern tendency is to use less not more punctuation, to use fewer not more capital letters, and to Americanize foreign words and phrases more quickly than was done in the past. Hence, when in doubt, leave the punctuation out; use a lower case (non-capital) letter; and don't italicize a foreign word (e.g. apropos not *a propos*). If the punctuation is needed to make the wording clear, use the punctuation; otherwise, follow the rule of using less, not more.

HOW TO PUNCTUATE IN THE MODERN MANNER

We are not going to repeat grade-school punctuation rules,[1] because you would not be reading this book if you were not already able

---

[1] The discussion in this chapter and in the next is based on: *The Reader Over Your Shoulder* by Graves and Hodge; *The Technical Report* edited by Weil; *Plain Words, Their ABC* by Gowers; *Communication Through Reports* by Douglass; *The Concise Use and Abusage* by Partridge; *Get It Right* by Opdyke; *Words Into Type* by Skillen and Gay; *Better English* by Vallins, *Guide for Air Force Writing* AF Manual 11-3, and *Writing Guide for Naval Officers*, NavPers 10009 (of which the author of this book was the editor and main compiler).

to read and write at a relatively advanced level. We will focus on the type of punctuation problems that are most likely to arise in business and professional situations.

Misconceptions About Punctuation

"There is a widespread ignorance among writers of English as to the use and usages of punctuation," says Graves and Hodge. "Many of them leave their commas, semi-colons, and the rest of the more difficult signs, to be corrected by their typists, or by the printers." Which, as I have said, is not a bad idea for an *executive* to do, because he ought to devote his time to more important things. However, when a businessman is called on to write or to approve a piece of writing, he does need a general idea of the standards of the art—and a place like this chapter to turn to for quick advice.

"The trouble is," Graves and Hodge continue, "that there are two conventions for English punctuation, which contradict each other. The older convention is that punctuation-marks denote duration of pause between parts of a sentence or paragraph. . . . The more sensible and more modern convention, which we recommend, is that all punctuation marks that do not (like the question and the exclamation mark) merely denote tone of voice, show in what relation to one another sentences, or parts of a sentence, are intended by the writer to stand."[2] In other words, modern writers do not write to be read out loud, so they punctuate to help the eye, not the voice or ear.

Another misconception is that punctuation is an art or a secret science known only to teachers of English, graduates of writing courses, and highly trained secretaries. Note that Graves and Hodge use the term "conventions" not "rules." Conventions change over the years, but their purpose remains the same: that is, to provide convenient signals to expedite business. As in driving a car, once you understand the occasion for which signals are required and the purpose of each signal, they are easy to remember. While you are driving properly and in the right direction you need few signals, but if you get yourself mixed up, you need a turn, stop, and go-ahead signal all at once. After such a tangle happens, you either pay more attention to your driving or you take a different route. Similarly, when you find yourself in a spot where you don't know which punctuation mark to use, take it as a signal to back out and untangle the thoughts and words that got you into the mess.

The following conventions for the use of punctuation will take care

[2] *The Reader Over Your Shoulder* (New York: Macmillan Company), pp. 162-63.

of you in all except the most esoteric situations. If an occasion arises when these guides are not enough, you can call on a professional editor for assistance—or just punctuate in the way that seems sensible to you. The average reader, being a lot like you, would probably have used the same punctuation, and therefore will understand what you meant.

The following signs are arranged alphabetically for ready reference and not in the order of their importance.

THE MODERN PUNCTUATION SIGNAL SYSTEM

1. *Asterisk* (*) The asterisk is used to signal a footnote: one asterisk means footnote Number 1; two asterisks mean footnote Number 2; and three asterisks mean footnote Number 3. Usually, you switch to the space sign (#) for footnote Number 4, and so on. Better yet, don't use so many footnotes.

A row of asterisks means an omission that cannot be avoided or is the sort of thing you would rather not put on paper. (See the *Dot* for the type of omission it stands for.)

Example 1: (Unavoidable Omission) The part of the company's record that was saved from destruction stated: "The company has agreed to p * * * and this sum sh * * * by the date set."

Example 2: (Deliberate Omission) The salesman, Mr. * * *, who had had too much to drink not only insulted his hosts but he suggested that the wife should * * * And that was that.

2. *Brackets* ([]) Brackets are a form of parenthesis used to show that the words have been added by the editor or publisher. They are usually critical or explanatory and are set off by brackets to indicate that they are not by the person who is presently speaking or writing.

Example: The president said that the Company's policy [which had been established in 1954] could not be changed and he directed the credit manager [who is Mr. Paul Brown] to refuse payment to the XYZ Company.

See Parenthesis for the use of the curved parentheses signs ( ) and for the use of a parenthetical remark within a parenthetical remark.

3. *Colon* (:) The colon can have some tricky uses in long sentences where semi-colons and commas complicate the structure. However, if you limit your use of the colon to the following five occasions you will do the right thing 95 times out of 100.

(1) After the salutation in a letter: Dear John:

(2) With "as follows" when introducing a list of series or enumeration of things. Example: Results were as follows: better public relations, better morale, more vacations, and less work.

(3) When *say* or the equivalent of *say* has been left out: The boss jumped on me: "Why did you lose that sale?" (With *say* or its equivalent present, use a comma not a colon: The boss jumped on me and demanded, "Why did you lose that sale?")

(4) In sentences where the parts are complete in themselves and you think you could use a period (full stop) or semi-colon or a colon, then use the colon if the succeeding part illustrates, restates, or depends on the first part. This sounds complicated, but it isn't. Just remember that where the sections of the sentence seems too long or too important to be set off by a comma, you use a semi-colon, *but,* if the second part explains or carries out the first part, then use a colon instead of the semicolon. For example:

Electric power requirements in the plant vary according to the time of year and time of day: in the summer less electric light is needed; at night only half the machines are operated and these draw proportionately less current.

See how the colon leads into the two explanatory statements which are themselves sentences, and, because they are equal, i.e. parallel, they are separated by a semi-colon.

(5) When enumerating, but not when the thought, i.e. the sentence, is continuing without interruption. Thus:

Right: Three cities were picked for the sales test: Dayton, St. Louis, and Pocatello.

Wrong: The three cities picked for the sales test were: Dayton, St. Louis, and Pocatello. (This sentence should read: The three cities picked for the sales test were Dayton, St. Louis, and Pocatello.)

4. *Comma* (,) There is a lot of clucking over "comma faults" in some of the books and courses on good English; and the rules for using a comma can run to 10 or 15 pages without covering all the possible applications. (If you are a *comma perfectionist,* or want to be an authority on the subject so that pretty young typists will admire your erudition, you can study more about the comma in the books listed in the footnote on page 167.)

The basic comma rule is: If putting a comma in a certain spot makes you feel better, do so. In other words, follow your subconscious mind and put commas where they look right to you.

Remember, too, the more general rule: the modern tendency is toward less punctuation. When you have only a faint desire to insert a comma, flip a coin and put the comma in or take it out—you can't lose much either way. When you have a moderate feeling or strong desire for a comma, add the comma and go on without a backward look.

The original meaning of *comma* was "cut-off," that is the part of a sentence which is cut off by the comma sign or signs. Note, that the cut-off part is still part of the sentence, and hence the commas are employed, as Graves and Hodge explain, to prevent "two or more parts from running together in a way that might disturb the sense." And that is a good clue to its use: a comma is needed if leaving it out will disturb the sense of the sentence.

The commonest comma pitfalls (I hate to say "faults" as the purists do) are those involving the word "because" and its equivalents "for" and "since"; those which involve parenthesis or opposition; and those where a semi-colon or full stop (period) ought to be used.

Example:

Because: I did not make the budget report, because the boss did not want me to. (This means you kept your mouth shut in obedience to your boss's wish.)
I did not make the budget report because the boss did not want me to. (You now are saying, whether you intend to or not, either of the following two statements:

(1) You made the report, but the reason you made it was not just to go against your boss's wishes; or:

(2) You failed to make the budget report but your reason was not because of your boss's objections.

When you see a "because," look to make sure what sense the sentence makes with or without a comma before "because."

Parenthetical matter: The salesman who had failed his quota five times was fired. (You are telling which salesman was fired—the quota failer.)
The salesman, who had failed his quota five times, was fired. (You are saying that there was only one salesman and he was fired.)

In the first of the foregoing examples, you are distinguishing which one of the salesmen was fired. In the second sentence, you imply that you have already identified the salesman as the discharged one and you are adding the information that he had failed his quota five times. A grammar or dictionary will explain these clauses and phrases under the terms "restrictive" and "nonrestrictive".

Apposition: Appositives are simply shortened clauses, and you apply the commas according to the sense you intend. Thus:

> The salesman, a five-time loser, was fired.
> (The salesman, who was a five-time loser, was fired.)

However, with proper names you usually don't use commas:

> My friend Wilbur stood by me.

But you watch their meaning, lest this happens:

Wrong: The industrial engineer, Frederick Taylor, recommended the use of time study. (This implies that there was or is only one industrial engineer.)

Right: The industrial engineer Frederick Taylor recommended the use of time study. (Now you know he was one among other industrial engineers, or that he was one whether or not others existed.)

In place of a semi-colon, colon, or period: This pitfall rarely occurs in short sentences, because there is a special rule that the comma can take the place of a semi-colon in short sentences; for example: I came, I saw, I conquered. But when you get into a long sentence look closely to see if it should be broken into two or more separate sentences or into clauses separated by a semi-colon. Thus:

Traffic requirements change with the season, in winter comes the Christmas rush, in the summer the longer vacations. (Doesn't that sentence cry out for a semi-colon after season?)

5. *Dash* (—) Don't use a dash because you are too lazy to finish your sentences or too timid to choose among commas, semi-colons, parentheses, or brackets. In fact, you should lean the other way and not use a dash when any other signal will suffice.

Use a dash on purpose, or not at all; that is, use a dash when you desire to show that someone is speaking hastily or confusedly, not because you are writing hastily and confusedly. Here are the four approved uses of the dash:

(1) Where a comma is not quite enough to mark the change of pace or thought or sudden switch; for example: The boss is going to fire Susie—no, he has changed his mind.

(2) Where commas are not enough to set off the parenthetical statement but for which parentheses or brackets are too much. (See parentheses for more about this distinction.)

Example: Of the five facets of business enterprise, only the three ancillary ones—accounting, statistics, and communications—were mentioned in this book.

(3) After a question mark or exclamation point if what comes next explains the question or exclamation; for example: How can you ask for a raise?—you haven't increased sales one dime!

(4) To separate a brief summarizing enumeration from the main statement:

Example: More money, more vacations, more fringe benefits, more say in management—these have been the goals of the average working man.

6. *Dots* (. . .) A dot by itself is used only at the end of abbreviated words, such as Mr., etc., and so forth. A row of dots shows that something has been left out because it is not needed or because it would take too much space. A row of *four* dots shows that the omitted part ended in a period (full stop), a row of *three* dots shows that the omitted part was within the same sentence.

Note the difference between a row of dots and a row of asterisks: the dots indicate that you omit on purpose in order to save space or time; the asterisks indicate that the omitted part is beyond your power to obtain, or that it is of such a nature that you should not print it.

One other use of dots is to show that a speaker is hesitating; for example: "I was about to . . . ah, hum . . . or . . . er, . . . say that dots show stammering."

7. *Exclamation Mark* (!) An exclamation mark may end a sentence, or it may be used within a sentence. For example: During April our sales jumped 200%—hurray!—but sagged for the rest of the year.

The main thing to remember about the exclamation mark is not to over-use it lest it lose force. Don't try to strengthen a weak phrase by putting an exclamation mark after it; save the exclamation sign for the words and phrases that cry out for it.

8. *Full-Stop or Period* (.) The full-stop or period ends a sentence. If the sentence has not actually ended at that point, other punctuation should be used. The end of a paragraph is signified by a full-stop with the rest of the line left blank. The next paragraph begins on a new line, and usually with an indentation.

9. *Hyphen* (-) The modern practice is to use fewer hyphens; when in doubt leave the hyphen out. However, when the reader might be confused by the words if left separated, they should be hyphenated. For example, if an engineer wrote: "The blue steel tool" would you be sure he meant that the tool was "blue-steel," or that the "steel tool was blue"? Word combinations which were hyphenated in the past—check-list, for example—are written as one word, checklist.

However, if putting the words together would pile up four consonants in a row, the practice is to hyphenate the words; for example, cleaning-brooms.

10. *Italics.* When typing you show italics by underlining. As with capitals and exclamation marks, the modern tendency is to go easy on the use of italics. Their use now is generally confined to the following four occasions:

(1) Show emphasis; for example: The new budget does not indicate a profit in the near future but a *probable loss.*

(2) Distinguish a letter, word, or phrase; for example: The term *presentation* has come to take the place of *talk* and *speech.*

(3) Point out a term used for the first time and defined; after the term has been defined, it need not appear in italics; for example: *Vu-graph* is the trade name for an overhead projector for transparencies used as visual aids in a presentation. The Vu-graph we have here has been equipped with a polaroid lens which can give the effect of overlays.

(4) Indicate quoted material—for the most part an infrequent use because italics type costs more than ordinary quotation marks.

11. *Parenthesis* ( ) Parentheses signs, like brackets, always come in pairs. According to Graves and Hodges, parentheses "denote an explanatory comment or aside of such a sort that, in speaking, one would naturally lower one's voice slightly to show that the comment was not part of the main argument of the sentence. Where the explanatory comment does not need this lowering of the voice, it is customarily put between long dashes."

If you have to put a parenthesis within a parenthesis, it is better to use long dashes for the inside parenthetical matter to avoid confusion.

Example: The XYZ Corporation (still a big company—remember when we worked there together?) has moved to St. Looey [sic], a town which long ago (and after plenty of hard work) enforced a strong anti-smoke control program.

Note, the use of [sic] in the foregoing example; it is a handy editorial device consisting of the Latin word *sic* which means *thus.* Sic indicates that the word, phrase, or sentence is to be left as it is, or that that is the way the person speaking or writing spelt or pronounced the word. Sic signals the reader, typist, or printer: "Yes, this looks funny or incorrect, but leave it so."

12. *Quotation Marks* (") Quotation marks are used to enclose quoted material, slang expressions, misnomers, or words used in a special way. Single quotation marks (') enclose a quotation within

a quotation. Commas and periods are always placed within quotation marks; other punctuation marks are placed within the quotation marks only when they are a part of the quoted material.

Example: The Boss, a "real guy," said, "Joe, I want you to put a 'hypo' into your sales drive, until your assistants say 'Ouch!' "

Quotation marks are always used in pairs (don't forget to close the quotes); however, if a quotation runs more than one paragraph, the quotation mark is repeated at the beginning of each paragraph, but not at the end of the first or succeeding paragraphs until the end of the last paragraph.

If you have a lot of material to quote, a good idea is to indent the material and type it single-spaced, or as printers say, *set solid*. See page 215 of this book for an example of indented quoted material. Note that if you indent the quotation, you do not set it off with quotation marks.

13. *Semi-colon* (;) When you have a sentence with parts that seem too closely connected to break apart with a period, and yet too independent to be held together by a comma, you probably need a semi-colon. To make sure, apply the following rules:

(1) Use a semi-colon to prevent confusion when there are a number of comma clauses or phrases.

Example: A modern corporation has several departments: the executive department, or "front office"; the production department, which includes manufacturing, inspection, and procurement; the marketing department, which, in addition to the sales division, may or may not include the advertising, public relations, and promotion divisions; and the financial department, which includes accounting and budgeting.

(2) Use the semi-colon when two clauses, both of which could stand as sentences (they possess subjects, verbs, and predicates), are *not* joined by a conjunction like *and* or *for*.

Example: The president visited the plant yesterday; he walked all over it and inspected every section; then he sat down; he was tired. (Put *and* in place of the semicolon after "yesterday" and after "section," and "for" or "because" after "down," and you will see that the semicolon is no longer needed.)

(3) Use the semicolon before such words as *however, therefore, as a result, consequently,* and *nevertheless,* when they connect two complete but related thoughts.

Example: Business is business; however, the rules of ethics and charity are still paramount.

TWELVE RULES FOR CAPITALIZING WORDS

In general, you should tend to under-capitalize, not over-capitalize. While there are certain conventions—twelve are listed below—which are generally accepted, the basic rule whether to capitalize or not is: What meaning do you intend? If you are singling out a word, capitalize it; if it is just another word being used with a common meaning, don't capitalize it.

Example: Under our constitution, the president is commander in chief of the armed forces. (Any president). *But:* Last year the President, using his powers under the U. S. Constitution, vetoed four bills sent him by the Congress.

When to Capitalize

Here are *six rules for when to capitalize* a word:

1. Capitalize the word that begins a sentence, or an incomplete sentence standing by itself, or the entries in column. For example, this incomplete sentence. For an example of capitalizing column enumerations, see page 8 of this book.

2. Capitalize proper names of persons, places, and organizations.
John Martin Dyer, Wilkes-Barre, Republican Party

3. Capitalize official titles when used as titles or when referring to an important person by his title.
General Washington; Vice-President Jones; the President of the XYZ Company said, "There are too many vice-presidents in this organization, get me the Vice-President in charge of management studies."

4. Capitalize trade names unless they have become so common that they are applied to types of articles rather than just the makes:
Ny-Gen, Esso, Pepsi-Cola, Nabisco
aspirin, cellophane, zipper, escalator

5. Capitalize a common noun if context or custom has singled it out as something special:
the Channel (English Channel; the Lake (Lake Michigan)
the Civil War (of 1861); the Great War (of 1918)

6. Capitalize words derived from proper names or from adjectives:
the study of English; the Patton tank

When Not to Capitalize

Here are six rules for when *not* to capitalize:

1. Don't capitalize titles when they do not refer to a specific person or are used with a proper name:

The organization included several managers, military representatives (a commander and a general), and even political and ecclesiastical representatives—a state governor, a U. S. senator, and a bishop and a cardinal.

2. Don't capitalize a part of a slogan or quotation if it was not capitalized in the full slogan or quotation:

You can too "sell iceboxes to Eskimos."

3. Don't capitalize the beginning of a sentence if it appears in parentheses or dashes within another sentence:

The XYZ factory was closed (this had been agreed upon earlier) and the employees were trained for new jobs.

4. Don't capitalize enumeration within a sentence (that is, not in a column):

Good communications in business include a knowledge of: (a) the modern state of the art of writing, speaking, and presenting; (b) where to find expert help—professional writers and editors; and (c) the basics of punctuation and grammar.

5. Don't capitalize the names of seasons of the year:

winter, spring, autumn, fall, summer

6. Don't capitalize directions or points of the compass unless they refer to specific sections:

The far west has a dryer climate than the northeast coast.

How to Write Numbers

The modern practice is to write out whole numbers *ten* and below; one, two, etc.; *but*: 1½, 5¼, etc. Above *ten* the numbers are written as numerals: 11, 20, 200, etc.

However, for the sake of clarity, to make a more pleasing appearance, or to keep a row of numbers in the same style, you can ignore the foregoing rule. For example: you would not write a hodge-podge like, "The children were aged five, 12, 8½, seven, 14, and three." You would write, "The children were aged 3, 5, 7, 8½, 12, 14."

The following numbers are usually written as figures:

Type of Number	*Example*
Age	She was 33 years, 6 months, and 13 days old.
Dates	The war lasted from April 8 to December 30, 1888.
Measurements	He stood 6 feet 3 inches in his size 12 shoes; his vision was 15/20, and he could run 100 yards in 11 seconds.
Unit Modifiers	The union wants a 38-hour, 5-day week. He ordered a 5-foot length of 2½-inch cable.

The following numbers are usually written out:

Type of Number	*Example*
Numbers beginning a sentence	Sixty-two men went on strike.
Indefinite or whole numbers	About five hundred men were required for the same job during the fifties.
Fractions standing alone	He went one third of the way with me.
Numbers less than 100 if before a compound modifier containing a figure	The job required three ¾-inch cables, 115 2-inch boards, and thirteen 5-inch bolts.
Numbers relating to serious and dignified subjects	The Thirteen Original States have been replaced by fifty States.

SUMMING UP THIS CHAPTER

This chapter has covered the following main points:

1. Rules of grammar and punctuation are signal systems to help a reader catch your message—in business you try to avoid the academic, social, snobbish and emotional overtones which unfortunately accompany all too often the use of the rules.

2. An executive should first look to the substance, to the meaning of the intended message. Thus, he should:

   a. Not treat points of grammar or punctuation as signals of poor learning or low culture, but as signals of difficulties in meaning.

   b. Not enter into arguments over niceties—let others decide, or tell them to rephrase the passage.

   c. Not use points of language as excuses or red herrings to escape the meaning of the written or spoken material.

3. However, an executive is responsible for the form, as well as the substance, of his writing and the writings of his subordinates. Accordingly, this chapter has listed the more important and most-often used conventions of punctuation, capitalization, and the writing of numbers.

The next chapter will discuss the words and phrases that often cause difficulties in meaning, and which account for the majority of grammar and syntax difficulties in business and technical writing.

18

TWENTY WORDS TO WATCH OUT FOR

Take Care of These 20 Words and the Rest Are Easy

The "Cool" Approach to Grammar

In the previous chapter we explained that if you check the punctuation where it seems a bit odd, and recheck what you are trying to say, you will automatically clear up most grammar and syntax errors—at least those likely to appear in a business letter, report, article, or speech.

A man does not have to know all 500-plus fields of higher mathematics in order to become a good accountant, budgeteer, industrial engineer, statistician, or operations research expert. The reason is simple: 99% of the time the abstruse problem does not arise. When it does, you have only three courses of action to decide among: (1) call in an expert; (2) restate the matter to avoid the abstruse element; or (3) ignore it, because the people you deal with know nothing about it!

Similarly, when you run into a point of grammar which you or your secretary cannot easily solve, you can (1) reword to avoid the issue (usually this is the best course); (2) take the choice that appeals to your instinct (most people will have the same sort of hunch and will see the point, the same way you do); or (3) ask the advice of a local editor, writing librarian, English teacher, or friendly expert.

Can the Wording Do Any Harm?

More importantly you should scrutinize a disputed statement, word, spelling, or idiom with these questions in mind: What harm can the wording do if it is misunderstood or sneered at? Who will be the reader? Is the piece of paper simply for the file, or will it only be seen by a clerk in passing? If so, who cares how correct the grammar is? Must you spend money retyping material because someone has a compulsion for grammatical perfection?

If the paper is to go to the public, to a customer, to a vendor, to a newspaper or magazine, then you must ask two more questions: (1) Can the wording be misunderstood so that you will lose money, good will, or a sale, or be forced into unwanted legal commitments? (2) Is the wording so clumsy that the average man will suspect you of being an ignorant, uneducated oaf?

These questions may appear obvious, but year after year millions of dollars are wasted in correcting the grammar on pieces of paper that have no importance; while at the same time an almost equal number of inadequate papers are sent into the world by impatient or conceited fellows who think that because they are in managerial and supervisory positions they automatically write with clarity and brilliance. If the over-fussy people waste money, the too careless and arrogant lose good-will and respect by their flabby, fatuous, or clumsy writings.

Fortunately for us we can invoke a principle analogous to that used by an executive when checking his bookkeepers and budgeteers for accuracy and reasonableness. He has learned what common errors to look for, he uses devices like "casting out nines," he tests balances, checks credits against debits, and rounds off numbers in order to make quick estimates of the validity of an estimate or account. Similarly we do not have to know all the 500,000 plus words in the English language or all the rules in all the dictionaries and grammar books, because for most business writers a few "danger signals" and "executive's rules" will suffice.

If you will study the usages involved in the following words, and remember in a general way the rules for punctuation given in Chapter 17, you can be sure that your American-English will be good for the purposes of modern business communications.

THE 20 WORDS TO WATCH

1. *As.* Avoid using *as* in the sense of "because." There are occasions when such use is permissible, but why bother making sure?— just substitute *because* for *as* and see the improvement.

Wrong: I stopped explaining the budget, as he kept interrupting.
Not wrong: As he kept interrupting, I stopped explaining the budget.

Much better: Because he kept interrupting, I stopped explaining the budget.

People when speaking use "as" for "because" quite often, but a lot of "as's" in a sentence or paragraph make the writing appear clumsier and muddier.

2. *As to.* As to the use of *as to,* this is the only safe place to use it: that is, to introduce a new subject or bring something into prominence at the beginning of a sentence or paragraph.

Right: As to the proper use of cost accounting in the factory, we will refer you to the shop production control office.

Otherwise avoid *as to* because it leads you into one or all of the following consequences: (1) use of the wrong preposition; (2) roundabout expression or elaborate circumlocution; (3) vagueness and incorrect grammar; or (4) unnecessary wordage.

Examples:

(1) Pushing aside the right preposition:

    Wrong: We gave instructions *as to* how the equipment should be operated.

    Right: We gave instructions *on* how the equipment should be operated.

(2) Causing roundabout writing:

    Wrong: The plant manager didn't have clear information *as to* what happened.

    Right: The plant manager didn't know what happened.

    Wrong: The budget-making process can be a strain *as to* its effects on clerks.

    Right: The effects of the budget-making process on clerks can be a strain.

(3) Causing vagueness and incorrect grammar:

    Wrong: Unless we are positive *as to* whom the property belongs, we cannot make payment.

    Right: Unless we are positive who owns the property, we cannot make payment.

(4) Causing unnecessary wordage (particularly before who, what, how, whether):

    Wrong: Your request *as to* whether the company will pay in advance has been referred to the treasurer.

    Right: Your request that the company should pay in advance has been referred to the treasurer.

3. *Actually. Actually, basically, fundamentally, in fact, in effect,* and *relatively* are almost always "stammering" words. That is, you speak or write one of them while trying to think of the next thing

to say. They are like the "uhs" and "ers"—the "whiskers" of speech, as the Toastmasters call them.

After you have written one of those words, look at it with a hard eye to see if it carried any real meaning.

Relatively is another "stammering" or "whisker" word, but it usually signals something more serious than just excess wordage. When a speaker or writer feels impelled to stick in "relatively" he frequently means, "I'm not really sure of this point, or I haven't thought through to see if there are other factors or ways of doing the thing, so I'll hedge by adding *relatively*." But the word *relatively* does not rescue him because: (1) if there is an error in his facts or reasoning, or if he has left something out, saying the word *relatively* will not solve the difficulty or correct error or take care of the omission; and (2) if there is nothing to hedge, then the word is excess verbiage and may create a doubt about your accuracy or make your writing appear vague. Therefore, after you have written *relatively*, look at it and ask yourself: "relative(ly) to what?"

4. *Aspect.* An *aspect* is the expression, mien, side, or view which you see of an object. It is not a *part* or *element*. You can look at several aspects of a matter, but you cannot deal with the "fundamental aspects," nor can aspects add up to anything or do anything. An aspect is a vision, not a thing. The trouble with using the word aspects, says Gowers, is that "it induces writers, through its vagueness, to prefer it to more precise words, and it lends itself to woolly circumlocution. . . . *Aspect* is one of the words that should not be used without deliberation, and it should be rejected if its only function is to make a clumsy paraphrase of an adverb." Gowers suggests similar caution with *point of view, viewpoint, standpoint, angle.*

One of the examples Gowers provides is: "From a cleaning point of view there are advantages in tables being of a uniform height." He notes that one should simply say, "For cleaning there are advantages in tables being of a uniform height." To this I add that one should similarly avoid the use of "-wise." (See *Wise,* page 189). Don't write, "Cleaningwise there are advantages in tables being of a uniform height." Or, after you have written it, go back later and try to find a better way of phrasing it.

5. *Basically.* See *Actually.*

6. *Because.* This is a good, strong word whose meaning is unmistakable. Use it for causality in preference to *since* or *as*. *Since* also refers to time, and *as* and *for* have several meanings, so a reader often

has to look twice or slow down when he hits a *since, as,* or *for* to see from the context what meaning is intended. Try putting *because* wherever it can replace *since, as,* or *for* and note how your statements will become clearer and more forceful.

7. *Case. Case* is a fine word but it is so handy that it is used too often as a substitute for the more exact word. Fowler (*A Dictionary of Modern English Usage*) gives the following good uses of the word:

A case of measles

A case of burglary—or murder

In case of need—or fire—or emergency

Circumstances alter cases.

You have no case.

A law case of any sort

But, as Gowers says (*Plain Words: Their ABC*), don't resort to the word as a trouble-saver and consequently end with flabby writing. Here are some examples based on those given by Gowers:

Resorting to "Case"	*Doing Better*
That is not the case.	That is not so.
It is not the case that I did not send a check.	I sent the check.
The cost of maintaining the new assembly line was higher than was the case with the old one.	The cost of maintaining the new assembly line was higher than that of the old one.
The personnel department is not so far behind in filing records as was formerly the case.	The personnel department is not so far behind in filing records as it used to be.
The union stewards in the case of each major grievance ask for special hearings.	The union stewards ask for special hearings for each major grievance.
Packages for export in many cases must be specially insured. (Here the reader can be confused by thinking, if only momentarily, of a *material case.*)	Packages for export in many instances (or, Packages in a certain class) must be specially insured.

8. *Concerned.* Gowers and others point out the phrase *as far as* (or *so far as*) ... *concerned* is generally a symptom of muddled thinking. It is legitimately used when you want to imply that you are thinking of one element of a matter, while others may be thinking

of other elements. For example, "So far as I am concerned, the investment in Amalgamated Onion is as good as any." That is your opinion; other people may have different opinions.

On the other hand, the usual practice is to drag the phrase in where it either confuses the issue or pads the statement.

The following examples are also based on Gowers:

With "concerned"	*Without "concerned"*
The panel members agreed that overtime pay should also be paid for extra work where women were concerned.	The panel members agreed that women should be paid overtime pay for extra work.
Guided missiles are a new development in the art of war so far as time is concerned.	Guided missiles are a new development in the art of war.
His possible retirement will affect our planning so far as the future is concerned.	His possible retirement will affect our planning.

9. *Etc.* (Abbreviation for Latin *et ceterae: and the rest.*) *Etc.* and *and so forth* often indicate fuzzy or incompleted thinking. When the writer is not sure what to say next, he sticks in "and so forth." The indiscriminate use of *etc.* and *and so forth* can lead to absurdities like the following:

This product should appeal to all customers—men, women, children, and so forth. (Who can the *and so forth* be? Martians?)
We must check our costs of bulk transportation—air, rail, sea, truck, etc., —and see which is cheapest. (What are the *etc.*? Pony express? Rickshaw?)

When you are writing or speaking hurriedly—trying to get your thoughts out as quickly as possible—go ahead and say "etc." or write "and so forth." Later, when you review your material, treat the "etc.'s" and "and so forth's" as flags for the places where you probably failed, or were too busy, to think through to all the consequences. In other words, treat an *etc.* or *and so forth* as a memo-signal or notation to "look at this item again."

10. *It.* "Never put an *it* on paper," said Cobbett (quoted by Gowers), "without thinking well what you are about. When I see many *its* on a paper I always tremble for the writer." Gowers provides the following as an example of too many *its*:

It is to be expected that it will be difficult to apply A unless it is accompanied by B, for which reason it is generally preferable to use C in spite of its other disadvantages. (C is generally preferable, in spite of its disadvantages, because application of A without B is difficult.)

When you see a heavy peppering of *its* on a page, you, too, can tremble for the reader, because he will surely have to pick his way among many *indefinite antecedents, anticipatory subjects*, and weak phrases. Let's look at these things.

(1) *Indefinite antecedents*, Davis (in Weil's *The Technical Report*) gives these examples of an indefinite antecedent for *it*:

The gage was attached to the tank, but it was found to be defective. (Which was defective, the gage or the tank?)

Do not blow out a pipet. It is not precise. ("It" has no definite antecedent.)

To these we can add the gems we find in writings that are supposed to be more official or more authoritative, because they begin with, "It is requested that . . ." (*Who* is making the request?)

(2) *Anticipatory subjects.* "The use of the anticipatory subject, so dear to the heart of some report writers," says Douglass (*Communication Through Reports*), "delays action in the sentence and multiplies the number of words. . . ." Take these examples:

"*It will be seen that* in the northwestern region . . .
"*It appears also from the above table that* . . .
"*It is estimated* that the total stand of . . .
"*It is necessary* to build new facilities . . .
"*It is obviously impossible*, however, to forecast . . ."

Should you never use "It is requested that . . ." or "It appears obvious that . . . , etc."? No, because there are times when the vague, bureaucratic phrasing fits the purpose, or because you are too busy to think of something better. But ration yourself on the number of *its* and *it is's* you permit yourself per page.

(3) *Weak phrasing.* "Like a kickoff when the ball bumps end over end instead of taking flight to the opponents," says Douglass, "the snub-nosed 'it was' sentence fails to start the communication game with excitement." Take a few of the endless examples:

"*It should be noted* that the amortization costs are overstated.
"*It is not likely that* the annual demand will exceed sixteen million boxes.
"*It is evident* . . .
"*It is planned* . . .
"*It is expected that* . . .
"*It is noteworthy* . . ."

Incidentally, you don't gain anything by substituting "This is" or

"There is," "This was," or "There are" for an "It is," or "It was" construction. (See *This* on page 188.)

The next time you find a page of writing that keeps you checking back to see what the writer meant, try circling every *it, this,* and *there,* and double circle every *it is* and *there is.* If you find more than a total of any five of them or combination of them per page, you will have found the trouble with the writing.

11. *Literally.* Literally is all too often used to mean the opposite of its *literal* meaning. For example, when a person gushes, "I literally died. . . ." then he means he actually did die and his ghost must be doing the talking. A person may *figuratively* die, turn green with envy, or see the greatest sight since creation, but to do something *literally* means that the matter is a real occurrence, not a figure or metaphor of speech. *Literally* is often a "padding-word" like the words listed with *actually* on page 181.

12. *Only.* Gowers says that the "sport of pillorying misplaced *onlys* has a great fascination for some people, and only-snooping seems to have become as popular a sport with some purists as split-infinitive-snooping was a generation ago." Gowers advises us: "So do not take the only-snoopers too seriously. But be on the alert. It will generally be safe to put *only* in what the plain man feels to be its natural place."

As example of the ambiguity a misplaced *only* can cause, Gowers gives the following:

His disease can only be alleviated by a surgical operation.

Does this mean: (1) Only a surgical operation will work, nothing else will do; or (2) a surgical operation can only alleviate, that is, not cure him but just help the patient to some extent?

13. *Realistic.* This is a word to watch carefully because it can be used in a very *realistic* way—and mean what? Sometimes it appears merely as padding or as a not too accurate substitute for *feasible, practical,* or *sensible.* After you have written *realistic,* look again to see if one of the other words would fit better. More serious is the possibility that you are trying to sway the reader into thinking you have more factual evidence than you really have. That is, what you like to think is true or reasonable, you call *realistic.* But is it real outside your mind and emotions?

Many people, too, find the contrasting *academic* vs *realistic* irresistible. What doesn't fit their prejudices is "academic," what they like to believe, is "realistic." But before you smear an idea by calling it academic, or praise a notion by saying it is realistic, check these words in a large dictionary and make sure how you intend to use either of them.

14. *Relatively.* See *Actually.*

15. *Same.* Long after the rest of the population has quit using *the same* or *same* as a pronoun (in place of he, she, him, her, they, them, or it), business men and Government officials keep on using and overusing *the same!* Perhaps they think it sounds more official and legal-like. Gowers says that it "is now by general consent reprehensible because it gives an air of artificiality and pretentiousness."

Succumbing to the temptation to use same	*Avoiding the temptation*
We have not received that order for more nuts and bolts you promised. Please advise me relative to the same.	We have not received that order for more nuts and bolts you promised. Please advise me about it.
Enclosed are the new contracts. When you have signed same, please have notarized and return same to me at your earliest convenience.	Enclosed are the new contracts. When you have signed them please have them notarized and return them to me.

16. *That* and *Which.* In addition to snoopers for misplaced *onlys* and *split infinitives*, there are "which-hunters"—people who catch you using *which* where you should have used *that* and vice versa. The grammarians, the purists, and even the non-sticklers like Fowler and Gowers explain the use of *which* or *that* on the basis of restrictive and nonrestrictive clauses and phrases, or commenting or defining clauses. For myself, I have never been able to remember these grammatical rules. When I do remember them I am not sure how to apply them. Fortunately for me, most people are in the same boat. Over the years, I have found that three simple rules will take care of 95%—if not 100%—of the occasions when one has to choose between *that* and *which.*

These rules are:

(1) Dispense with *that* whenever it can be done without loss of clarity or dignity. (Gowers)

(2) Use "who" and "which" where the meaning is "and he," "and it," "for he," "for it," "and they," and "for they"; otherwise use "that." (D. S. Davis, Chapter 5 in *The Technical Report,* edited by B. H. Weil.)

(3) When your page is piling up with too many "thats" and "whichs"—don't look to grammatical rules, try rewriting the page. (Dyer)

The first rule is pretty obvious. Gowers gives an example of it in action as follows: "I think that the paper that he wants is that one." This is a grammatically correct sentence showing *that* used correctly as a conjunction, a relative pronoun, and a demonstrative pronoun. (But who—20 years out of school—knows what a conjunction, relative pronoun, or demonstrative pronoun is?) Gowers rewrites the sentence with fewer *thats,* thus: "I think the paper he wants is that one."

The second rule works beautifully about 90% of the time. On the occasion when it does not seem to work, I am not sure why, or what should be used, so I follow the rule anyway. Davis gives the example, "Economic surveys which are poorly written should not appear in the journal." Does this mean that all economic surveys were poorly written and that none should appear in the journal? Of course not, so try substituting "for they" in place of the *which.* "For they" does not make sense, and therefore the sentence should read: "Economic surveys that are poorly written should not appear in the journal."

For examples of the third rule, see any of your own pages whereon too many *whichs* and *thats* appear. Apply first the Gowers rule and then the Davis rule. If the page still has too many *whichs* and *thats* about which you are not sure, try rewriting that page.

17. *This (These).* At least 5 men of every 20 whose writings I edit or review have the *this* habit. They begin every other paragraph and every other sentence with *This,* and they sprinkle *this's* and *these's* all through their clauses and phrases. *This* constant repetition of *this* leads to three faults: (1) the small one of boring a reader with *this* overused word; (2) the more serious one of using too many weak, vague constructions—"this is," "this was," "these are," etc.; and (3) the ultimately quite serious fault of letting oneself be trapped into a monotonous thought and speech pattern built around the word *this.*

The next time you think you discern an unusual number of "this's" of "these's" on a page—particularly if a lot of "it is's" and "it was's" also abound—circle them in pencil and count them. If there are more than five per page, you (or the writer you are reviewing) have become too dependent on the word. While there is nothing ungrammatical about many "this is's," the reader feels he is reading dull, vague, monotonous, stiff bureaucratic language. (See *It* on page 184.)

18. *Unique.* *Unique* belongs to a class of words that do not have comparatives—they just don't go with "more" or "less." Unique means the-only-one-of-its-kind-in-the-world, so a thing cannot be more unique, or rather unique, or pretty unique. It's either all the way unique, or not at all. Similarly, a thing can be perfect, or half perfect, or almost, or nearly perfect, but it cannot be more perfect than perfect. People are also careless with *essential* and *vital.* If you take away an essential part from a thing, that thing no longer exists— the essence of something is that which makes the thing what it is:— hence, if you have three essential parts, one cannot be more essential than the other two, nor can one be the most essential. A vital element or part is that which enables something to live. Remove a vital part and the creature dies. Hence, one part cannot be more vital than another vital part.

Misusing these words is not massive crime, but a goodly number who hear you say "rather unique" or "the most unique" thing will jump to the following conclusions: (1) you lack education; (2) you have no ear for language, and no sense of the meaning of words.

19. *Very.* There are two simple rules to remember about *very*: (1) Use it sparingly; a mark of the amateur writer (or gushing sort of speaker) is the sprinkling of *verys* all over his pages; and (2) don't use it with the past participle (use *much* or *greatly* if you need a stronger expression).

Typical Very's	*Very's Cut Out*
She is very beautiful.	She is beautiful.
I am very pleased to meet you.	I am pleased to meet you.
He was very inconvenienced.	He was inconvenienced. (He was greatly inconvenienced.)
Sales were very enhanced by good weather.	Sales were much enhanced by good weather. (Sales were greatly enhanced by good weather.)

20. *Wise.* Don't use terms like "time-wise," "money-wise," "weather-wise," and so forth. Not that the terms grammar-wise are incorrect, but prestige-wise they don't enhance you; and pattern-wise, they get you into the bad habit of sticking a "-wise" onto the end of a word to avoid the momentary effect of thinking of a better way of speaking or writing—effective English-wise, that is.

SUMMING UP THIS CHAPTER

The following paragraph can serve you both as a summary of the main points of this chapter and as a paragraph on which to practice what you have learned.

So as to make very sure that you have obtained the most unique and vital information from this chapter, let's review the more essential elements. Actually this chapter has covered the words that basically are simple in meaning, but relatively important in daily speech. Since the businessman has many cases in which, good English-wise, it is important for him to utilize correct grammar, this chapter fundamentally has sought to highlight aspects of words that often show up where business writers are concerned. Terms such as nouns, verbs, adjectives, adverbs, prepositions, pronouns, conjunctions, etc., are literally beyond the powers of comprehension of even the very well-educated businessman. Hence, it has been the purpose of this chapter to discuss same, but as they show up in realistic every-day speech and not from academic standpoints. To do this, it has focused on 20 words (and some of their synonyms or close relatives) which cause trouble more relatively often than others.

Now, see how you can rewrite the foregoing so that it reads more smoothly and clearly.

19

HOW TO BRIEF A REPORT, ARTICLE, OR OTHER DOCUMENT

Top Management Requires the Ability to "Conceptualize"

At the working level a man operates a machine, fills in forms, or repeats a sales pitch he has been taught. At the supervisory level and middle management levels a man must learn the company's policies, how to get along with people, and how to train and motivate subordinates. At the top management level a man must be able to "conceptualize"—that is, to be able to think, to visualize, and to plan for several departments or divisions.

Mr. Francis H. Boland, Jr., executive vice-president of George Fry and Associates, management consultants, refers to this ability as: "The capability of understanding and implementing by means of integrated administration the whole of management's separate functions, as contrasted to possession of outstanding expertise in a single or a few restricted functional areas." Dean W. T. Jerome, III, of the College of Business Administration, Syracuse University, says that the important skill for an executive will be "Knowing how to deal with complexity."[1]

Many men can do a good technical job and can handle people with great success, but they cannot present quickly the gist of an idea, or a program. They cannot even report on what they have been doing without bogging down into detail. They find themselves at a loss when told to bring a mass of information into a quick summary. Quite often, the man's failure to "speak to the point" is simply from lack of practice, or because no one has ever shown him what to do.

[1] Both Mr. Boland and Dean Jerome are quoted from the *Nation's Business,* article "Executive Skills You Will Need Most," February, 1961, p. 74.

Unfortunately for him, if he flops the first time, he may not get another chance.

Hence the importance of this chapter. The techniques described in it are applicable not only to briefing a report in order to save the time of the people who have to read or hear it; they are also applicable to the carrying out of most executive responsibilities. Most, if not all, of a manager's job is to transmit information: his ability to collect it, package it, focus it, and expedite it in a form useful to the people above or below him, marks him as an executive who can "think small" and can "think big." Moreover, after a man has learned how to get the gist of a report and to state it in summary fashion, he finds that this skill can be applied in other areas of his executive life. He learns to read faster and more efficiently, and to write and speak in a more organized and to-the-point fashion. Then, by developing a reputation for being able to "layer off" the right information in the right "packages" to the right "echelons," he gains more opportunities to do just that—and so his executive ability and his reputation for being able to "conceptualize," to integrate, to coordinate, and to synchronize is enhanced.

The Five Basic Steps to the Briefing Process

One. Read the whole report, or material quickly, skimming, to get an idea of its purpose and general content.

Two. Read it more slowly noting the key sentences and underlining them. Your time is more important than the costs of paper, so type or "burn" or "fax" or "zerox" an extra copy—or order another copy—so that you can mark one up. Even a long document will rarely cost more than $10 for an extra copy, and an hour of executive time is worth far more than that.

Three. Have your secretary type the sentences you have underlined. This is a mechanical job you should delegate. You can be doing something else while the material is being typed; and your subconscious mind can be mulling over the information or resting up for the next step.

Four. Combine the underlined sentences into a rough draft.

Five. Smooth the draft into your final brief. Don't be afraid to put it into your own words, but do be sure to highlight what the consumer (boss, subordinate, or customer) wants or needs to know. Be sure not to twist the meaning of the original author or authors—this can be a temptation when the information is inconvenient or disappointing to you.

An Example of Briefing—and a Lesson at the Same Time

For an example of the briefing process we'll use the explanation of *précis, paraphrase, summary,* and *abstract* given by Dr. Paul Douglass in his book *Communication Through Reports* (pp. 179-180). Thus, we can explain those terms at the same time we demonstrate the underlining and combining process.

Here is the section with the key sentences underlined:

Every report writer constantly digests statutes, regulations, reports, speeches, and documents. He summarizes points of view for incorporation into his text. Methods of abbreviating materials for accurate statement in shorter form are referred to in terms of the way the work is done as (1) a précis, (2) a paraphrase, (3) a summary, and (4) an abstract. Although in practice these forms overlap, they have individual characteristics.

The précis is a literary device widely used to produce abbreviated but exact statement of the substance of a matter in clear, concise, readable, and accurate form. Originating in diplomatic correspondence as an economical and effective form of reporting, it takes its name from the French *précis,* meaning "to cut down a statement." The précis selects the important facts and ideas in a passage, condenses them into a brief and lucid pattern, and restates them in the writer's own language. The précis is careful to preserve the organizational pattern, idea structure, mood, tone, and viewpoint of the text on which it is based. To write a good précis, a writer takes his pad and pencil and jots down the pith of the material, being faithful to include every essential point in the original. Then he summarizes the material orally in his own words before he writes down the substance in his own shortened restatement. He reproduces the emphasis which the author gave in his original material. The writer follows the plan of that original; he does not rearrange thoughts. He reproduces them accurately in condensed form. He uses his own words, being careful to leave out nothing which is essential to make the restatement correspond in content to the original. . . .

The paraphrase gives the accurate gist of a passage or work by a freely rendered restatement. One of the most useful of all techniques, it presents the sense of a text in the writer's own words and in his own style. It allows him greater liberty than the précis. . . .

The summary, like the précis and the paraphrase, achieves brevity by the restatement of essential data and tie facts together for working purposes. It is, however, a more mechanical performance concerned with a recapitulation in shorter form of the substance of a document. . . .

(The series of dots here and in the paragraphs above on *precis,* represent examples quoted by Douglass, which I have left out to save space. The paragraph on the *summary* comes before the others in his book; I have transposed it to save additional explanation.)

An abstract briefly summarizes the findings made, facts presented, conclusions drawn, and recommendations offered in a report. A précis or a paraphrase may be incorporated in the text, but an abstract stands as a separate unit and should be as brief as possible. It may be prepared merely by omitting words from the original text, or it may be written by concise and faithful restatement in the writer's own vocabulary. The American Institute of Physics suggests that an abstract should be written concisely for the reader in normal rather than highly abbreviated English, with the assumption that the reader has some knowledge of the subject but has not read the paper.

You will note that Douglass assumes that a writer will use pencil and paper and then summarize orally in his own words before he writes his version on paper. This method will work very well; and obviously is intended for a student who does not have an extra copy of the material to mark up, nor a secretary to type the underlinings.

Now let us suppose you have read through the foregoing passages and have decided that the author, Douglass, had two main purposes: (1) to explain the meanings of the terms; and (2) to recommend a method of making a précis—a method which can be applied to other types of briefings. On your second reading you made the underlinings which already appear on the copy quoted here. You give the pages to your typist with instructions to type the underlined words and to show the deleted materials by a series of dots—three dots if within a sentence; four dots if the deletion included the end of a sentence (see Chapter 17).

When typed up, the material might look like the following:

Methods of abbreviating materials are . . . (1) a précis, (2) a paraphrase, (3) a summary, and (4) an abstract. . . .

The *précis* is a literary device widely used to produce abbreviated but exact statement of a matter . . . it takes its name from the French *précis,* meaning "to cut down a statement." The précis selects the important facts and ideas . . . condenses them . . . and restates them in the writer's own language. The précis ... preserves the organizational pattern ... tone ... and viewpoint of the text on which it is based ... a writer takes his pad and pencil and jots down the pith of the material being faithful to include every essential point.... He summarizes ... in his own words before he writes down the substance in his own shortened statement ... follows the plan of the original; he does not rearrange thoughts. ...

The paraphrase gives the accurate gist of a passage or work by a freely rendered restatement ... it presents the sense of a text ... it allows ... greater liberty than the précis. ...

The *summary* ... achieves brevity by the restatement of essential data and ties facts together for working purposes. It is ... a more mechanical performance concerned with recapitulation in shorter form of ... a document. ...

An *abstract* briefly summarizes the findings made, facts presented, conclusions drawn, and recommendations offered in a report ... an abstract stands as a separate unit.... It may be prepared merely by omitting words ... or it may be ... concise and faithful restatement in the writer's own vocabulary. The American Institute of Physics suggests ... should be written ... in normal rather than highly abbreviated English, with the assumption that the reader has some knowledge of the subject but has not read the paper. ...

Making the smooth draft. Already the job begins to look easier: you now have only to add an introductory statement and a closing statement, and smooth all the phrases and sentences. First off, you notice that the words "faithful," "accurately," and "concise" are not needed; obviously the reader expects any précis or summary to be those things. He does not want to be exhorted to achieve such goals, he wants to be told how to do so. Similarly, you perceive that by recasting some of the sentences you can tighten up the brief and at the same time make it read clearly and smoothly.

You dictate your changes to your secretary, or you mark them on the rough draft; and when she completes the next draft, it might appear like the following:

BRIEF OF INSTRUCTIONS BY PROFESSOR PAUL DOUGLASS ON TYPES AND METHODS OF ABBREVIATING WRITTEN MATERIALS (*Communication Through Reports*, pp. 179-180.)

To help our junior executives improve their skill in digesting the voluminous information they must funnel to top management, I am passing along briefly what Professor Douglass has written on the subject of abbreviating written materials.

Four methods of abbreviating materials are:

(1) *Précis* (from the French "to cut down")—you should preserve the original author's organization, tone, and viewpoint; however, the briefer should select the important things and condense or restate them as necessary.

(2) *Paraphrase*—the gist is given but in the words of the briefer with no effort made to follow the original author's order or maintain his style.

(3) *Summary*—in essence a recapitulation of what has gone before.

(4) *Abstract*—a separate entity which summarizes the finding, facts, conclusions, and recommendations of a report.

Douglass recommends that you jot down the pith of the material, keeping to the original order of presentation, then summarize it in your own words. Douglass also quotes the American Institute of Physics as suggesting you write an abstract in normal, not highly abbreviated English, with the assumption that the reader already knows something about the subject but has not read the document in question.

Avoid a Telegraphic Style

Some men think dropping words to make like telegrams, save much time reduce size brief. Not so. A telegraphic or headline style all right for 50 words or less in telegram, or for three words at top of newspaper column, but for longer passages such style becomes burden to reader. (See what I mean?)

A good brief or abstract is already a highly condensed presentation of complex and important ideas which the reader will have to study. Don't add to his labor by making him puzzle over a telegraphic code. Most of the time, too, the problem is not one of getting the words on one page or in a narrow space—you can easily add another paragraph or page—but of saving the reader's time. He is better off reading 600 words of clearly phrased "standard English" than trying to decipher 100 words of telegraphic style.

Nor will you be more "businesslike" if your writing becomes so terse and clipped that it contains no verbs and no words like "the," "a," and "for." You may be able to train yourself to write in such a fashion, but will all your readers have learned to read such a code with ease and pleasure?

Six Rules for Making Briefs

1. Read the material all the way through to get its scope, content, and "feel."

2. Go through it again underlining what appears to be important sentences and phrases. Leave out the extras and asides, but keep anything that tells what the paragraph or section is about.

3. Have the underlined sentences and phrases typed in the order in which they appeared in the original; show where the deletions are by series of dots. . . .

4. Condense the excerpted material. Eliminate nonessential words; substitute one sentence to do the work of two or three; discard anecdotes and illustrative examples; and summarize data and statistics by general statements. Use for example, statements like "Chapter 27 presents 30 tables and 10 charts, the gist of which is that sales have not kept up with the growth of population. Chapter 31 presents the mathematical computations and the graphs which indicate that the sales lag has amounted to a 3 percent drop each year."

5. Read your condensation with the eyes of your future readers. What does the digest tell you? Does it tell the full story? Check back to the original to make sure you are accurately and appropriately reflecting it in your condensation.

6. Tie the material together using your own words and transitional phrases as necessary. A series of unrelated statements make for difficult reading. Too clipped style makes hard reading as said above. So make your sentences complete and don't leave out the verbs. Put the author's materials in words understandable to the future readers whom you represent.

SUMMING UP THIS CHAPTER

How would you brief this chapter?

Why not make a stab at it before reading the summary provided below? (Go ahead and mark up the text, you can always buy another copy!)

This chapter has pointed out the importance of being able to brief quantities of information into précises, paraphrases, summaries, and abstracts. The précis keeps to the original wording but "cuts down" the size of the report; the paraphrase is a restatement in one's own words; the summary is a quick recapitulation; and the abstract is a separate account in brief of what the matter is all about.

The average person cannot hold all the contents of a report in his mind at the same time, nor can he juggle them around, reorganize them, restate them, and edit them by a *tour de force* of brainpower. At the same time there is no reason why he should try; instead he should "mechanize" the job as much as possible to save not only effort but also give his mind a better chance to "pull back" and see what is really important.

This chapter, therefore, recommends that you:

1. Read the whole material to get the gist.

2. Underline the probable important points.

3. Have these typed up—while you deal with other things, or rest.

4. Prepare the final smooth version from the typed excerpts.

5. Keep the readers in mind—the briefing should be designed for their needs, not yours.

20

READABILITY FORMULAS: HOW TO MAKE THEM WORK FOR YOU

THREE EXECUTIVE USES FOR THE FORMULAS

The readability formulas—explained later in this chapter—are wonderful inventions because they provide a method for looking at one's writing more objectively. They will not make you, or anyone else, write great *literature*, but they will help you write more clearly and more interestingly.

Some men get on their high horses when you mention a Flesch or Gunning readability formula. They say, "Did Shakespeare need a slide rule?" Well, a Shakespeare may not have, but many a lesser author could have used the formulas to the benefit of his readers.

Many newspapers and publishers, and business, government, and professional organizations have employed Dr. Flesch or Mr. Gunning —and other, if less well-known, experts— to help improve their publications. As an executive you will be interested in the formulas for improving your own writing and that of your subordinates. Here are three uses for the formulas:

1. *Check the level of your own writing.* Suppose you have been writing briefs for the legal department or reports for a financial journal, and then are asked to write some sales letters or an article for the company magazine. Are you sure you can switch easily and accurately from a style suitable for one audience to a style for a mass audience? Wouldn't it be a good idea for you to check your writing on the readability scale and see if your style is appropriate for most readers or just for college graduates?

2. *Think of readability and human interest scores in terms of loudness, legibility, and "people stories."* When a speaker talks just loudly enough to be heard, people listen to him for a while but gradually

they tire and finally allow their attention to wander. Hence, an experienced public speaker usually pitches his volume about 25 per cent louder than that required to be just heard, and thereby helps his audience pay attention.

A man can read with pleasure for a longer time and with less fatigue when the printing is in large clear type. An audience pays better attention to a speech that is directed at them and contains many anecdotes and stories. "But," you ask, "how do I know when my writing is loud enough and clear enough and contains enough human interest?" To answer this, the readability experts have studied many audiences and have measured what those audiences have liked in the way of sentences, syllables, and personal words per sentence.

Therefore, just as your voice should be louder than that barely required to be heard, or the print on the page should be blacker than that just barely required to be read, so your Readability and Human Interest Factors should be pitched to a level *easier* and *more interesting* than that which just barely qualifies. In other words, while a college graduate can read at the academic and scholarly level, he will not sustain the effort, or his attention will not be held as long as when the writing is at the easier and more interesting levels. This does *not* mean at a lower level of *intelligence* or *knowledge*, but at a more *popular* level of writing style.

3. *When reviewing and editing.* The readability formulas can come in handy when you run into a sticky case of author's pride or when you know there is something wrong with a piece of writing but are not sure where the trouble lies.

When you tell an author, "Your writings are hard to read," he may get his back up and claim that his style is wonderful and the readers are stupid—or are not willing to read what is good for them. He may challenge you to point out the parts which are not composed in clear, beautiful prose, and you may find yourself bogged down in endless discussions of the meaning of words, clauses, and punctuation. However, if you can apply the Flesch or Gunning formulas to his pages and show him a low Reading Ease Score or a high Fog Index, the burden of proof shifts onto him. He has to disprove the formulas, or agree to some changes. In other words, you put him in the position of not arguing solely against you, but against a host of well-known experts.

Or, when you read a report or letter that doesn't seem to "jell" or to "fit the picture," try the Human Interest or the Reading Ease Score or Fog Index on it. Often they will indicate the spots which need touching up to bring new life to the piece.

HOW THE READABILITY FORMULAS WORK

The best known readability formulas are the Flesch *Reading Ease Score*, the Flesch *Human Interest Score* and the Gunning *Fog Index.*

The formulas for calculating these scores have been printed in many books and publications and covered in most of the courses and texts listed in Appendix B. Up-to-date versions by their authors are in *How to Write, Speak, and Think More Effectively* by Rudolf Flesch (Harper & Brothers, New York) and *The Technique of Clear Writing* by Robert Gunning (McGraw-Hill, New York).

1. *Flesch's Reading Ease Score.* Flesch's *Reading Ease Score* is based on counting the average number of words per sentence and the average number of syllables per 100 words. You multiply the average sentence length by 1.015 and the number of syllables per 100 words by 0.846 and add the results. Subtract this sum from 206.835 and the final figure is your Reading Ease Score, which can range between 0 (unreadable) and 100 (easy for anyone who can read). The table on page 203 shows how different types of publications stack up according to this formula.

Note that, in essence, the Flesch *Reading Ease Score* measures the average length of sentences in words and the average amount of "big words" or many-syllabled words in a passage. The theory—and practical discovery—behind the Flesch formula is that long sentences and long words are more complex and more intricate and therefore harder for the reader to plough through. That's been known for years, but Flesch and Gunning (and some others less well-known) have provided measuring devices to tell us how much more complex and therefore how much more difficult a piece of writing is *on the average* than other pieces of writing, and which levels of complexity can be read with ease by people in the United States.

2. *Flesch Human Interest Score.* The Human Interest Score is based on the concept that the more "personal" words are, the more "interesting" the writing will be to the average reader. Put briefly, this means that people like to read about people more than about things. Newspaper men have for years expressed this theory in the phrase "names make news." Professional writers describe even the most technical subjects in terms of how they are seen through a reader's eyes and how they affect human beings.

To find the Human Interest Score you count the number of "personal words" (names of persons, personal pronouns, etc.) in the text, or in 100-word samples of the text, and multiply the number of "personal words" per 100 by 3.635. Then you count the number of "personal sentences" per 100 sentences—either of the whole text or of 100-sentence sample of it. "Personal sentences" are those of spoken speech (direct quotations: "What you doing about the budget?"); questions, commands, and requests directed to the reader or audience; exclamations like "How terrible!"; and sentence fragments like "No, no, never." You multiply the number of "personal sentences" per 100 sentences by 0.314 and add the result to the figure obtained for "personal words." The total is your Human Interest Score, which can range from 0 (no human interest to 100 (full of human interest). The table on page 204 shows how some well-known publications stack up on the Human Interest Score.

3. *Gunning Fog Index.* The Fog Index also is based on the length of sentences and the number of polysyllables (words of three syllables or more). To find the Fog Index you take a sample or samples of at least 100 words and determine the average number of words per sentence, treating independent clauses as separate sentences (i.e., clauses separated by semi-colons are treated as sentences). Next count the number of long words—three syllables or more—but don't count them if they are capitalized, made up of short, easy words like *manpower*, or verbs of which the third syllable is the ending -es or -ed. Add these two figures and multiply by 0.4. Drop off any numbers after the decimal point. The resulting figure is the Fog Index for the passage.

The Fog Index is related to years of schooling; thus any Fog Index higher than 17 is put simply as 17—on the assumption that few readers have more than 17 years of schooling. A passage with a Fog Index of 12 can be read by a high school graduate; one that has a Fog Index of 16 can be read by college graduates, but it will be hard going (foggy) for the man whose schooling stopped with the 12th grade.

Note: The higher the Flesch score the easier the reading; the lower the score the harder the reading. But the higher the Gunning Fog Index the more difficult the reading; the lower the Fog Index the easier the reading.

Study the tables on pages 203 and 204. You will see that *The New Yorker* magazine has a score of fairly difficult in Reading Ease or Fog Index, but it ranks high in Human Interest. This shows how writing with a strong human interest factor can pull the reader through a more complex style than he would normally be willing to read.

READING EASE AND FOG INDEX COMPARISONS

Flesch Reading Ease Score	Examples	Level of Style	Average Sentence Length in Words	Syllables Per 100 Words	Schooling Equivalent	Percent of U.S. Readers Able to Read it.	Gunning Fog Index Score
0-30	Very technical reports and bureaucratese.	Very difficult	29 (plus)	190 (plus)	College graduate	6	17 (plus)
30-50	Academic: textbooks, science magazines, "deep-think" periodicals.	Difficult	25	167	Some college	35	14
50-60	Quality magazines and literary books: *Atlantic Monthly, Harpers, New Yorker, Fortune.*	Fairly difficult	21	155	High School graduate	55	12
60-70	Mass media nonfiction: *Time, Sat. Eve Post,* newspapers, digests.	"Standard"	17	147	Graduate Grade School (Some H.S. or equivalent.)	85	8-10
70-80	Slick fiction: *Sat. Eve Post, McCall's, Woman's H. Companion, Ladies H. Journal, Reader's Digest.*	Fairly easy	14	139	Seventh Grade	89	7-8
80-90	Pulp fiction.	Easy	11	131	Sixth Grade	93	6
90-100	Comics.	Very easy	8	123	Fifth Grade	95	5

FLESCH HUMAN INTEREST TABLE

Human Interest Score	Description of Style	Typical Magazine	Percent "Personal Words"	Percent "Personal Sentences"
60-100	Dramatic	Fiction	17	58
40-60	Highly Interesting	*New Yorker*	10	43
20-40	Interesting	*Time*, Digests	7	15
10-20	Mildly Interesting	Trade magazines	4	5
0-10	Dull	Scientific and Professional	2	0

An Easy Way to Get Immediate Benefit from the Formulas

Put the theory to work for you. Obviously, the theory behind the readability formulas is that a word stands for an idea. A "big" word contains several ideas; a sentence contains a number of ideas. The "ideas" you hand the reader in one dose, or the more *complexly* you present them, the more trouble he has grasping the central idea of your sentence. So, for a quick check simply circle every word of three syllables or more on a page and then stand back and look at the page. The average typewritten double-spaced page of 8 by 11 inch stationery contains about 300 words. If you see the page full of circles—two or more to a line—you had better try to simplify some of the words.

Next, circle all the sentences with more than 20 words. If there are more than 5 to a page, you had better look again to make sure you are not rambling, and that the sentences do not make unnecessarily hard going for the reader.

Finally—perhaps using a colored pencil—circle all the "personal" words and "personal sentences" (as described on page 201). If you don't average at least a circle every third or fourth line, you might read the page again to see where you can add some human interest.

SUMMING UP THIS CHAPTER

One or more of the following problems can arise every day:

1. You want to make sure your style will apply to a different audience.
2. You have an assistant who writes in a "muddy" or "dull" style and who won't admit it.

3. You want to make your own writing more interesting and more readable.

4. You want to be sure you know what people are talking about when they refer to the "readability," the "fog index," or the "human interest score" of a report.

Accordingly, this chapter has explained what the formulas are and how they work, and has pointed out the ways in which an executive can put them to use quickly and effectively.

In particular, you should:

1. Think of readability and human interest in terms of loudness, legibility, "people-stories" and "names-make-news."

2. Check your work—or any writing in question—for unnecessarily long sentences, too many big words, and not enough of the "stuff of human nature"—personal names, personal pronouns, direct quotations, questions, and exclamations.

The formulas can not do the whole job of making you a good writer. The next two chapters will discuss some ideas and methods for improving your writing style and also your speaking style.

21

TWELVE KEYS TO GOOD WRITING

Added to the points made in Chapters 17 and 18 on punctuation and trouble-making words, the twelve "keys" in this chapter will help you take care of over 90 per cent of the questions that will arise in regard to *style-improvement* in business writing. These twelve keys cover such questions as sentence length, split infinitives, elegant variations, and the avoidance of "weak" constructions. Let's begin with the question of sentence and paragraph length.

FOUR KEYS TO GOOD SENTENCES AND PARAGRAPHS

1. *Think in rambling sentences, but write in short ones.* Most books on readability and most business writing courses emphasize the importance of *short* simple sentences. Obviously, then, most people must naturally tend to write in long sentences. This point is worth thinking about, because so many people accept two assumptions which apparently are not true: (1) that simpler sentences are easier to read and therefore they are easier to write; and (2) by telling a person to simplify his sentences, you thereby make it easy for him to do so. Since these ideas are not true, our practical conclusion is: Don't hamper your creative flow or burden your mind with the effort to write in short sentences, just let your mind operate the way it wants to. Later, when you polish your writings, try to recast the sentences into the forms recommended by the experts.

2. *The key to professional style is rewriting.* The beginner wants

to write perfect prose from the top of his head; when he finds he cannot do it, he gives up, saying, "I'll never be a writer." The professional, however, knows he will have to rewrite and therefore he schedules time and energy for that purpose.

John Gunther (author of the famous *"Inside"* books) describes his method of writing—after a lifetime of success—thus:[1]

> I write almost everything three times ... I ... can never get anything right on a first attempt. First I do an insanely hurried rough draft. If I have organized my notes properly I can type out ten pages, say 2,000 words in about three hours.[2] Then this must be revised—often rewritten. My experience is that revision takes as long as the original writing, perhaps longer. If it took me three hours to write a section, it will take me three or four to revise it. Sometimes hardly a word of the original script survives ... then my secretary ... types all this out and makes a clean copy. Then I go over this again and make almost as many corrections and emendations as on the first draft.... Draft No. 3 does not need so much work as No. 2 ... but then I do a great deal of work on proofs—almost enough to warrant the galley proofs being called Draft No. 4.

The key to your own good writing will lie in being willing to allocate as much time and energy to the rewriting and polishing as to the original dictation or scribbling. Does that double the time and effort required? No, because (1) you can save time by doing the first draft in rougher fashion; and (2) you can accomplish good writing more easily by planning on several "improvement increments"—several drafts—than by straining to be perfect the first time.

3. *The key to sentence length.* While you are rewriting and recasting your sentences, what lengths should you shoot for?

Here are the recommendations of the experts:

Author	Recommended Length
Rudolf Flesch	17 words
Newsweek editors	18 words
Robert Gunning	Under 20 words
Porter Perrin	Check sentences that are all less than 20 words or more than 30 words.
Robert Warnock	Too many sentences under 18 words will result in missed connections between ideas; sentences of over 40 words will probably be too loose or rambling.

[1] *Harper's* Magazine, April, 1961, p. 75.
[2] Note how this corroborates the advice given in Chapters 11, 12 and 13.

It would appear that one should average between 15 and 20 words, with a few sentences going as high as 30 and 40 words, or as low as 5 and 10 from time to time. Too many short sentences give a choppy effect; too many long ones strain the reader's attention.

The secret of a good sentence is that it should contain one central idea expressed in a way that a reader can understand it at a glance. When a sentence goes to 30 words and over, the odds are it contains two or more major ideas; and they should be separated into different sentences. When there is a series of short sentences, the odds are that one of them contains the main idea, and the others qualify it, or "pin it down." If so, combine the little sentences to form one sentence.

4. *The key to paragraph length.* In general, short paragraphs are more pleasing to the eye, so it is usually better to err on the side of too many short paragraphs than on the side of too many long ones. However, a series of illogically short paragraphs makes for jumpy disconnected reading.

The secret of a good paragraph is that it should contain *one central thought* and the supporting ideas or details that prove it, describe it, or qualify it. Here, are two guidelines to follow:

(a) If a paragraph runs a whole page, you had better check it. Ask yourself, "How many central thoughts or ideas does this paragraph have?"

(b) If there are more than three short paragraphs on a page, ask yourself, "Do each of these little paragraphs contain a separate thought worth a paragraph to itself?"

These guidelines are based on the fact that language represents ideas; a long series of words should present several ideas; a short series should present a few ideas. The average typewritten (double-spaced) page contains 250-300 words, and therefore contains on the average enough wordage for at least two or three main ideas. Rarely will one idea require a whole page; and only occasionally will the same page be crammed with more than four main ideas.

As we said earlier, you should decide on the length of your sentences and paragraphs when you make the final rewrite. Don't strain during the first draft, whether the draft be purely in your mind, on paper, or by dictation. And, don't fall for arbitrary rules like the one that says every paragraph should be exactly 100 words, or 10 lines. Your pages might look like they had been "simplified," but they won't read more simply; rather they will lack a coherence and smoothness that most readers will immediately detect and dislike. Use the rough rule "average two to three paragraphs to a page and check if a page has only one paragraph or four or more on it" as a warning signal for possible trouble; don't use it as a rigid pattern by which to cut the cloth of your wordage.

THREE KEYS TO FORCEFUL WRITING

Certain constructions like the *passive voice*, the verb *to be*, and *indirect phrasing* cause writing to appear "weak." At times you may want to appear cautious and even vague; but if so, do it on purpose, not because your customary style—or that of your subordinates— tends toward the "namby-pamby." The following three "keys" to forceful wording will also show you the types of constructions to avoid.

1. *Use the active voice instead of the passive voice.* The passive voice is not *wrong*, and its use can give variety or a better "flavor" in many instances. However, too many business (and government) writers believe they are being more "objective," "impartial," or modestly "anonymous" by putting everything into the passive voice. Try circling every *is, was,* and *have been,* on a few pages and total them up. If you are averaging nine or more on a page, you had better look hard at your tendency to use the passive voice.

Try recasting every other sentence into the active voice. If you are averaging five *is's* or five *was's* a page, you should study your use of these verb forms. Or, to phrase it in the passive third person so depended upon by timid writers:

> *It is suggested* that a study of the use of the passive voice *be undertaken* by you and special concern *be directed* to what *has been determined to be* a less effective form of writing.

2. *Avoid overuse of all forms of the verb "to be" and particularly the "and is" and "is that" phrases.* The verb *to be* is a weak verb. The same writers who overuse it in the passive voice also tend to over-use it as a verb in its own right. Its weakness particularly shows up when the constructions *and is* and *is that* are used. Note how weak the following sounds:

> An important change in the business world today *is that* the major corporations are paying more attention to the anti-trust laws.

> This book has been designed for executives *and is* also useful for managers and supervisors.

3. *Avoid negative, hesitating, or vague noncommittal phrases.* Some writers don't like to speak out; they say everything in an indirect

fashion, overusing "rather," "not very often," "not much," and "nor." Here are some examples based on those given by Strunk and White (*The Elements of Style*):

Negative Way	Positive Way
He was not very often above bottom in production.	He usually was at the bottom in production.
The annual report is rather unclear in spots. The capital costs are not stated in full, nor are the depreciation rates the sort to leave the reader other than unimpressed with their completeness.	The annual report has weak spots. Some of the capital costs are missing, and the reader will see that the depreciation rates are incomplete.
He did not remember that many of the employees were not honest, nor was he ready to pay any attention to the cautions from the bonding company.	He forgot that many of the employees were dishonest and he ignored the cautions from the bonding company.

Vague Way	Specific Way
The latter period of the year was characterized by disproportionately higher losses.	During October, November, and December our losses were 20 per cent higher than normal.

FIVE KEYS TO A BETTER STYLE

There are five points of style that always arise, and, if well taken care of, will solve a good 90 per cent of the style-improvement questions you run into in business writing. These are:

1. Split infinitives
2. Final prepositions
3. Elegant variation
4. Dangling modifiers
5. Live vs dead metaphors

1. *The key to a split infinitive.* There is nothing grammatically wrong with splitting an infinitive; however, "to carelessly split" infinitives (see, there we did it) can impart jarring notes to your speech and writing. In some cases, as William Strunk and E. B. White (*The Elements of Style*, Macmillan Co., N. Y.) point out, infinitives improve on being split. They give the example: "I cannot bring myself to really like the fellow." Put the other way, the sentence becomes stiff: "I cannot bring myself (really) to like (really) the fellow."

In brief, don't go hunting for split infinitives. When one sounds all right and makes clear sense, let it stand. Unless, of course, you are writing to or for an old stick-in-the-mud who will be upset by a split infinitive. In that case, why fight over a point of grammar? Rewrite the sentence and avoid the infinitive altogether. For example: "I have tried not to, but I find that I really hate the fellow who splits his infinitives carelessly."

2. *The key to a preposition at the end.* There is a story that an officious clerk once rewrote a sentence by Winston Churchill so that it would not end with a preposition. Mr. Churchill angrily changed the wording back to the original and wrote beside it in the margin: "This is the sort of thing up with which I will not put."

Fowler says, "It is a cherished superstition that prepositions must, in spite of the incurable English instinct for putting them late . . . be kept before the word they govern." He explains that the belief that a sentence ending in a preposition is an inelegant sentence constitutes a misapplication of Latin syntax to English syntax. Fowler shows many examples from Shakespeare to the Bible of sentences which end in prepositions and are the more grammatical and elegant for doing so. His advice, and the advice of modern writers on the subject, is: Follow no arbitrary rule, but choose the ending that sounds comfortable to you.

3. *The key to elegant variation.* In his *Dictionary of Modern English Usage* Fowler excoriates the attempts at "elegant variation" as follows: "It is the second-rate writers, those intent rather on expressing themselves prettily than on conveying their meaning clearly, and still more those whose notions of style are based on a few misleading rules of thumb, that are chiefly open to the allurements of elegant variation. . . . There are few literary faults so widely prevalent. . . . The fatal influence is the advice given to young writers never to use the same word twice in a sentence—or within 20 lines or other limit. The advice has its uses; it reminds any who may be in danger of forgetting it that there are such things as pronouns, the substitution of which relieves monotony. . . . It also gives a useful warning that a noticeable word used once should not be used again in the neighborhood with a different application." But don't use ill-fitting words just to be different!

Here are some examples:

Unnecessary variation:

Americans spend more on chewing gum every *year* than foundations give away *annually.*[3] (Italics added.)

[3] This example is taken from the article "How to Run a Small Foundation" by Adam Yarmolinsky in *Harper's Magazine*, April 1961. Mr. Yarmolinsky is a professional writer of considerable reputation, and the editors of *Harper's Magazine* enjoy high literary prestige. But we all have lapses. I am sure that I will hear from

At least half the *stockholders* are willing to vote for the merger, but until two-thirds of the *owners* agree the directors cannot act. (Italics added.)

In these variations the reader is confused by the change from *year* to *annually* and from *stockholders* to *owners*. Did the writers just change for the sake of using different terms, or did they want us to understand something differently?

On the other hand, a sentence like the following certainly could be improved by avoiding the repetitions of *serious* and *qualified*:

The manager spoke seriously about the serious shortage of qualified personnel who could qualify for the jobs.

4. *The key to nondangling modifiers.* All the writers on the subject, old and new, castigate dangling modifiers. D. S. Davis (Chapter 5, *The Technical Report*) says that dangling modifiers are usually participles and infinitives. They "dangle" when they cannot be associated immediately and unmistakably with the words they modify. The following examples are based on those given by Davis and by Strunk and White (*The Elements of Style*).

Dangling	*Tied More Firmly in Place*
Being in a dilapidated condition, he was able to buy the plant at a low price. (Who? The buyer or the plant?)	Because the plant was in a dilapidated condition, he was able to buy it at a low price.
Finding no mention of a prior owner, a search of its title was initiated by the lawyer.	Finding no mention of a prior owner, the lawyer initiated a search of its title.

at least three readers who will point out at least three errors in this book, which being on writing, "ought to set a perfect example!"

For the sake of other writers and editors in this country who are caught in literary or grammatical errors, the following is quoted from the *Newsletter* of the American Council of Learned Societies (Vol. V, No. 1, 1955, page 27). It is an item translated from the Hankow *Chiang Jih Pao* (courtesy *Shanghai Commercial Press*):

In the course of printing a small part of the *Selected Works of Mao Tse-tung*, Vol. II, we found the first word, *hsi*, on the first line of page 490 was indistinctly printed but was erroneously changed into *chi*. This is a serious error. This error was caused by the fact that in carrying out this important task our attitude was not serious enough and our system was not perfect and thorough enough. We accept the profound lesson this time and will hereafter intensify ideological reform, maintain a solemn working style and raise our work efficiently, and pledge ourselves to make amends for the serious mistake by taking concrete action. We hereby tender our apology to the readers and make the above self-examination.

And we think we have nit-pickers in the United States! Note the repeated use of the word "serious" in the paragraph, and the variation (if inelegant) of "mistake" for "error."

5. *The key to live metaphors.* For our purposes we will consider a metaphor any figure of speech, and not go into the technicalities of similes, synecdoches, metonymies, etc. A mixed metaphor (often derided in *The New Yorker* under the heading "Block That Metaphor") occurs when you use metaphors that present the reader with conflicting images; for example: "Let's face the crisis with our heads held high, our eyes on the road, our shoulders to the wheel, and our hands on the plow." Can you do all those things at the same time?

However, a more important point from the standpoint of long-range improvement in style than the ability to catch mixed metaphors is the understanding of the difference between *live* and *dead* metaphors.

A live metaphor is one that still creates an image in your mind; a dead metaphor is one whose original image has been forgotten. For example: When you say: "The *final countdown* for the presentation of the budget to the board of directors has begun," you are using a live metaphor. Your hearers can envisage a space-rocket team or a nuclear weapons testing team tensing for the start. But suppose you write: "That's a case of Hobson's choice," or "We'll hoist the opposition on their own petards." What reader knows who Hobson was? Or, what a *petard* is?

From the context a reader guesses that by *Hobson's choice* you mean that you take what you get; and that hoisting a man on his own *petard* probably means giving him tit for tat (another dead metaphor, by the way). Hobson was a stable keeper in England who made people take the horses as they happened to be placed in his stable, and not as the customer desired; a petard was an explosive device used for breaching walls. Hence, the reader must use the context to figure out what a dead metaphor means, and therefore such a metaphor adds no "oomph" to the writing. On the other hand, a live metaphor provides the reader with an image which helps him to understand what you are trying to tell him.

A metaphor need not be old to be dead. Suppose you use phrases like "bull pen," "three-bagger," and "a walk with four on" before an audience that knows nothing about baseball. They may be able to figure out what you mean, but even so, your metaphors amount at best only to padding.

A test, then, to apply periodically to your writings and speeches is to examine the similes, comparisons, and other figures of speech, and ask yourself: "Do my audience or readers know the original, the literal, reference well enough so that they will get mental pictures which will help them visualize what I'm trying to say? Or will they guess the meaning of my metaphor from the context of my message?

When a metaphor is overused—whether dead or still live—it becomes *hackneyed* (or *jejune*, or a *cliche*) and loses impact; it bores, or even annoys the reader. (Perhaps in some places the use of "countdown" has already been overdone?)

Metaphors can give life and color to speech and writing; but to do so they must be alive and colorful to your hearers and readers.

SUMMING UP THIS CHAPTER

This chapter has explained the following twelve keys to good writing:

1. Go ahead and think freely in long rambling sentences, but later rewrite them in clear, compact ones.

2. The key to professional writing is rewriting.

3. Each sentence should contain one idea; your sentences should *average* between 15 and 20 words, but range as short as 10 words and as long as 30 words from time to time.

4. Each paragraph should contain one central thought; on the average you should shoot for two to three paragraphs a page.

5. Use the active voice in preference to the passive voice.

6. Avoid overuse of the verb *to be* and constructions based on it.

7. If split infinitives bother you or others for whom you write, recast the passage to avoid the infinitive altogether.

8. Avoid negative, hesitating, or noncommittal phrasing.

9. End sentences with prepositions as often as you like; but not when the sentence sounds weak or peculiar to you.

10. Vary words to avoid monotony—but not when you obtain elegant variation at the expense of simplicity and clarity.

11. Avoid dangling modifiers.

12. Use live metaphors—that is, use figures of speech that give your readers clear mental pictures and not figures which they have to unravel from the context.

All these rules seem quite obvious, and yet they are rarely followed. Why? The next chapter will give you some suggestions why the average human opposes improvements in his speech and writing.

22

IMPROVING YOUR SPEAKING AND WRITING STYLE

Why the Effort to Improve is Painful

Why do people go on writing and speaking badly when they know it is to their advantage to improve?

> The biggest untapped source of net profits for American business lies in the sprawling, edgeless area of written communication where waste cries out for management action . . .
>
> A really effective knowledge of the techniques that make business writing clear, fresh, forceful, interesting, and terse cannot be superimposed as a brittle veneer. Such knowledge must become part and parcel of the man. It must work from the inside out.
>
> —Langley Carleton Keyes
> "Profits in Prose,"
> *Harvard Business Review*, Jan-Feb 1961

When the French writer Buffon said that *style is the man himself*, he pointed a psychological truth. A man is what he is, and it shows through in his speech and writings. To change one's style, one has to make changes in oneself, and that means to face up to criticism.

Pride of authorship is a powerful, instinctive reaction that flares up at the first hint of criticism. When a man or woman asks you:

215

"What do you think of this page?" Or, "What did you think of my speech?" they usually mean: "Tell me how good a writer or speaker I am." An editor, teacher, and professional writer dreads having someone say to him: "Now tell me the real truth about my writing (or speaking)." If the editor or teacher dares reply, "Well, it seemed to me that you were too . . . ," the humble author suddenly becomes the outraged artist and launches into long explanations about what he intended to say or what he was trying to do when he wrote or spoke such and such words.

In his book, *The Silent Language* (Doubleday & Company, 1959), Mr. Edward T. Hall proposes the theory that people operate on three cultural levels: (1) *formal*, (2) *informal*, and (3) *technical*. (Mr. Hall gives his own special meanings to these terms.) In general, the *formal* level includes the things we are unaware of and normally do not question; they have been molded into us at an early age by adults who themselves have never questioned them. The parent says, "Boys don't do that," or "You can't do that!" The *formal* patterns are almost always learned *when a mistake is made and someone corrects it* in a manner and with a tone that implies no other form is conceivably acceptable. Thus the adult corrects the child's speech "Not 'goed!' But went!" Most grammar is taught in this manner and hence, many people *feel* that having correct grammar is a sacred and unquestioned duty. When you disturb or question a *formal* element, the person feels the very foundations of society are threatened.

Informal learning, according to Mr. Hall's terminology, comes from imitating models. The child imitates older students, his parents, his teachers, and so forth. The person being imitated rarely notices it, and, indeed, the learner does most of it unconsciously. A characteristic of *informal* activity is the absence of awareness: a person drives a car, types, or plays music without having to think about what his fingers and feet are doing. Only when we consciously question or observe an *informal* activity do we realize all the things that go to make it up. For example, a typist who starts thinking about how her fingers should be moving, may disrupt the smoothness of her typing. When a man thinks about his golf swing in detail, he loses rhythm. Mr. Hall quotes a neuropsychiatrist as pointing out that it is enough to draw attention to one level of activity while a person is operating on another to stop all coherent thought. For example, a mother is berating her little boy. The boy looks up and says, "Gee, Mommy, your mouth moves funny when you're mad." The mother is apt to become speechless.

The third, the *technical*, level comprises conscious behavior. Learning at this level is analyzed in terms that can be clearly written out and is taught by a teacher who knows consciously (or should) what sort of model he is providing. There is a minimum of emotion involved: the professional and the technician keep their wits about them, and their temper under control. That is, so long as they stick to the technical level. But suppose the professional has to go to a tea party where he is not sure what type of social manners (formal and informal) he should display. Then he becomes nervous and anxious about his behavior.

People fight changes and they fight with the greatest emotion those changes which involve their formal and informal habits. Technical items can become informal or formal and vice versa. Hall gives the example of divisions of time: certainly the hours, days, weeks, and months are *technical* inventions by men. But men who grow up under one system tend to feel that it is the "natural," the right way to tell time. In England, in 1752, the people rioted in the streets in protest against the switch to the revised Gregorian calendar. You laugh? Haven't you noticed that every year when an area changes to daylight saving time, someone protests that men shouldn't "try to change God's time"?

Thus, when a person writes or speaks, he does so on three levels: the *formal* (which he learned as a child); the *informal* (which he has picked up unconsciously as he has gone along); and *technical* (which he has learned from conscious analysis and study—in schools, courses, and from books like this).

A man will be quick to make changes in things he has learned at the technical level, and he will be objective and unemotional about them. But when you criticize his way of speaking or writing, he may become hurt, angry, and resentful. You ask, "Why can't the guy see what he is doing wrong?" He can't because he is reacting at the *formal* or *informal* level.

Now you might take that big step and ask about yourself: "What am I doing wrong that I refuse to see—or to which I am blind but others are not?"

How to See Yourself in Action

We are all often reminded of Robert Burns' famous lines:

> O wad some Pow'r the giftie gie us
> To see oursels as others see us!
> It wad frae mony a blunder free us,
>   And foolish notion.

We see another man fumble a presentation, mispronounce words, make distracting gestures, and mutter "er-ahs," and we think, "If only someone would show him what he is doing wrong."

We can quickly correct another man's letter or report—because we see *his* errors so clearly.

But how do *we* look to others? What mistakes are *we* making?

Certainly the first step toward improvement is to identify the mannerisms, the phrases, the "style" that needs improving.

The American Management Association has installed television cameras for use in its communications courses so a man can see himself on a monitor picture tube or later on a video tape. And, of course, many offices and individuals own tape recorders which can record your voice mannerisms for future analysis.

Toastmasters Clubs and public speaking teachers help a man visualize his "style" by holding critiques or by having an observer count the number of times a man says "er"; or looks at the ceiling; or jingles keys in his pocket; and so forth.

Professor Henry Roberts warns that one should be careful in accepting the advice of fellow beginners; use critics who have had enough training to be able to discriminate between less effective and more effective speaking techniques. Thus, I have learned to call on several people for an opinion before accepting any one man's criticism of a speaker or writer. For example, a man completes a presentation and asks for suggestions. One man in the audience says, "You used too many gestures. You flailed with your hands." The speaker, making an effort to accept the criticism gracefully, replies, "Thank you. I'll try to cut down on my gestures."

At this point I interpose with the suggestion: "Wait, there are thirty other people here. Why not ask if anyone else thought you used too many or too few gestures?"

The speaker does so, and finds to his surprise that one man thought he made too few gestures, another did not notice any gestures at all, and the majority thought he made just about the right number and type of gestures.

But, assuming you do not have access to a TV camera equipment or a public speaking course, what can you do to see your strong and weak points with an outsider's eye? The three most helpful ways I know of are: (1) the *evaluation sheet* method, (2) the *murder board* technique, and (3) the *parody* method.

1. *The Evaluation Sheet Method*: Audiences are accustomed nowadays to "speaker evaluation sheets." You can design your own and

hand them to all or part of your next audience to fill out and return "unsigned." I regularly use a form like the following.

SPEAKER EVALUATION SHEET

.... Date ....
Place or Group

1. Please fill out this form while the details are still fresh in your mind. Be frank and specific; you need not sign it; however, check one or more of the boxes at the bottom so that your criticism can have more force.

2. *Content of Talk?* Was the content appropriate? Adequate? Convincing?

....

....

....

3. *Delivery by Speaker?* Did the speaker put the message across satisfactorily? Did he speak too fast? Too slow? Were his gestures distracting? Could you hear and understand him? Were his aids clear? Understandable? Useful?

....

....

....

4. *What Next?* Do you have any unanswered questions? Was there a topic or facet which should have been covered? Would you like to hear the same speaker again? What improvements in content or presentation would you suggest?

....

....

....

5. No signature necessary, nor need you fill in the following if you think it would identify you. However, in pitching a presentation to a future audience—or to this audience again—an idea of the type of person making the evaluation would be useful. Therefore, please check the boxes that describe you:

Man (....) Woman (....) Business (....) Professional (....)
Age: Under 21 (....) 21-30 (....) 31-40 (....) 41-50 (....) 51-60 (....)
Over 60 (....)
Executive (....)   Manager (....)   Supervisor (....)   Other (....)
Already experienced in subject (....)   Mostly unfamiliar with subject (....)
Average annual earnings: Under $10,000 (....) $10,000-$20,000 (....)
        Over $20,000 (....)

Few audiences will inform a man to his face that he was "terrible." Too often some members of the group will gather around the speaker and congratulate him on a fine talk (particularly when he outranks them). So he continues to make rambling, overly long, and frequently outmoded presentations, without waking up to the fact that his hearers are wondering: "Why doesn't someone tell him to shut up?"

Indeed, why doesn't someone tell him? Simply because they have no polite mechanism whereby they can do it. Moreover, a speaker should not accept as definitive just one or two criticisms from one or two friends—or outspoken persons. He should obtain a "spread" of comments. An evaluation sheet will provide such a private, but frank and representative criticism.

2. *The Murder Board Technique.* The murder board technique is a good one for obtaining criticism before you give a presentation to the audience that really counts. The board consists of one or more qualified persons who listen to your presentation with a "murderous attitude." That is, they look for the errors, "goofs," and "bugs." Knowing you want frank, even brutal criticism, they hammer on you and your presentation until you are sure it is ready for the real test.

A murder board is an excellent thing to use when preparing for a crucially important presentation. However, it does involve the time and trouble of other people. If they are expert enough to serve as effective critics, their time is worth money. When you use the murder board, remember to assure them of no reprisals—you really want them to tell you the bitter as well as the sweet things. Remember, you are looking for deep-cutting, even painful criticisms, not gentle praise—otherwise, why use the murder board?

3. *The Parody Method.* The parody method has not, to my knowledge, been given the publicity is deserves. It has the advantage of being flexible and often times will reveal weak points more quickly than any other way. Moreover, it is applicable to one's writings as well as to one's spoken presentation. In essence, it consists in getting someone to mimic, to imitate, to caricature; i.e., to parody one's "style."

The efforts of your family, friends, or colleagues, to mimic you will stimulate them to detect the basic patterns of wording, enunciating, and gesturing in your "style." They will help you see the worst that others see in you. They do not have to be good mimics; in fact, the worse their imitations the more they will show up your mannerisms.

Two Ways of Applying the Parody Method to Writing Improvement

a. *Read some parodies.* Most nonprofessionals and probably few professional writers can see quickly and clearly the distinctions between the various styles of writing which fill the millions of pages of newspapers, books, periodicals, and business writings which flood our desks. Therefore, you should take advantage of the sharp-eyed critics and humorists, who have made parodies of many types of writing. A few hours spent on parodies can show you some of the secrets of the great writers more quickly than long and serious analysis could. (Try reading some of the examples in Mr. Dwight Macdonald's book *Parodies: An Anthology from Chaucer to Beerbohm—and After,* (Random House, N.Y., 1960), and see what insight you gain into the styles of other writers—and at the same time see what not to do yourself.

b. *Ask someone to mimic one of your letters or reports.* Ask your secretary, your assistant, a friend, your wife—almost anyone who has reason to read your stuff—to imitate your style. Then study the patterns that show up in their exaggerations of your repetitions, confused phrasings, and so forth. In my experience most businessmen attempt to improve their styles by intermittent efforts to "correct their spelling," "enlarge their vocabulary one word a day," or "use more forceful verbs." But because they can't see the continuing patterns to their strengths and weaknesses, their improvements are hit and miss. When, however, they see themselves as others see them through the exaggerations of mimicry and parody, they are able to work wonders of improvement.

Two Ways of Applying the Parody Method to Speaking Improvement

a. *Ask someone to do an imitation of your public speaking voice, mannerisms, and "stage presence."* If there is no one with the gift of mimicry handy, ask anyone—friend, colleague, or enemy—who is willing to try, but don't ask him for a full-fledged imitation of everything you do. The ordinary person doesn't have the ability to detect all the patterns in your style nor will he have the ability to portray them clearly. But even the stiffest and clumsiest friend can indicate how *one part* of your behavior appears to him. One friend or fellow worker can imitate your vocal mannerisms, another your gestures, and another your way of putting words together. You don't have to have all these done at the same time; spread them over months and years; just remember to take advantage of the opportunities that arise. And don't overlook members of your family—

children, in particular, can with unconscious art do shrewdly accurate take-offs on almost any adult who is willing to let them do it!

b. *Mimic or parody yourself!* Stand in front of a mirror and try to do a take-off on yourself as a speaker. Sit down and write a letter or a page from a report parodying your usual style. These efforts can provide you with an amazingly fresh and useful insight into your style as a speaker or writer. You don't have to be a good mimic or professional parodist to gain valuable results, because the essence of the mimicry and parody lies in the *exaggeration* and the *highlighting* of your mannerisms. Equally important is the mental "breakthrough" which occurs. That is, you begin to see yourself, not with grim defensiveness and many justifications, but with good humor and resolutions to improve.

SUMMING UP THIS CHAPTER

This chapter has explained some of the psychological habits or "defense mechanisms" which prevent a person from seeing himself as others see him, and which hinder his insight into his self-improvement needs.

Five methods or approaches to self-evaluation are:

1. Recordings of one's appearances by video and audio equipment.

2. Participation in a class or practice group of speakers or writers.

3. Speaker evaluation sheets—to be filled in by the audience.

4. "Murder boards"—critiques by colleagues or consultants who know the requirements of the subject and of the audience.

5. Parodies or imitations and caricatures by others or by oneself.

These methods can help you ensure your own improvement and that of your subordinates. Appendix A and Appendix B, which follow, provide lists of books, courses, and institutions which answer a specific writing or speaking need, which have not been covered here.

APPENDIX A

No man can be expert in all things. The executive, or future executive, who has learned how to give a technical presentation may not have had time to develop ease in a conversation or skill in the type of after-dinner speech which is used when presenting a gold watch to a faithful employee or when introducing a lecturer to a club meeting. But even if you were a paragon of a speaker, presenter, speech writer, or conversationalist, you might have colleagues or subordinates with special problems for which help can be found in the sources in this appendix or in Appendix B.

Books

1. *Public Speaking as Listeners Like It* by Richard C. Borden; Harper & Brothers, New York. This little book (four chapter, 111 pages) is a classic in its field. Its chapter titles are: "Listeners' Laws for Speech Organization"; "Listeners' Laws for Speech Substance"; "Listeners' Laws for Speech Phraseology"; "Listeners' Laws for Speech Delivery."

2. *Putting Yourself Over in Business* by Dyer, Evans, and Lovell; Prentice-Hall, Inc., Englewood Cliffs, N. J. One of the first of the modern books on presentations and business conference techniques, its Chapters are: "What Are You Going to Get Across"; "When to Be Doubly Sure of Your Presentation"; "Most Important: How to Look—Really Look—at People"; "How to Handle Your Nervousness: Use it, If You Can't Cure It"; "How to Use Your Body, Legs, and Hands"; "How to Get the Most Out of Your Voice"; "Getting the Other Fellow Into the Act"; "How to Select Presentation Aids"; "How and Where to Get Your Aids Easily"; "What to Do When You Need Aids in a Hurry"; "How to Handle Suggestions and Gripes"; "How to Use the Basic Types of Conferences"; "How to Run a Conference Successfully"; "Secrets of Good Timing"; "How to Deal With Younger Men"; "How to Deal with Older Men"; "How You Can Avoid Pitfalls of Bias"; "How to Bargain Successfully and Pleasantly"; "A Few Final Useful Words."

3. *The Toastmaster's and Speaker's Handbook* by Herbert V. Prochnow, Cardinal Edition, Pocketbooks, Inc., New York. This book is based on his earlier books *The Toastmaster's Handbook, The Successful Speaker's Handbook,* and *The Speaker's Treasury of Stories for All Occasions.* Chapters in it are: "Responsibilities of the Toastmaster"; "Techniques of the Toastmaster"; "Ten Fundamentals for the Toastmaster"; "Effective Public Speaking and Leadership Training"; "Everyday Speaking Is Not Difficult to Learn"; "Taking the First Steps"; "What to Talk About"; "Determining What You Want to Say"; "Developing the Plan of Your Speech"; "How to Use Anecdotes and Stories Effectively"; "Illustrations of Actual Introductions"; "Illustrations of How Speakers Respond to Toastmasters"; "Interesting Stories from Introducions and Speeches"; "Epigrams and Witticisms"; "Quotations for Many Occasions"; "Humorous Stories for All Occasions."

4. *Showmanship in Public Speaking* by E. J. Hegarty, McGraw-Hill Co., New York, explains the use of showmanship in holding and convincing an audience. Includes advice on testing materials, handling notes, use of charts and other aids. Also contains a quick resume of information for a person who has to prepare a speech in a hurry.

Note: From the title, *Showmanship,* you might get the impression that the book deals mostly with the histrionics on the platform. To my regret I allowed this impression to delay my reading of the book for all too many years. The greater part of the book is on the behind-the-scenes work for preparing material and organizing and handling it. When I am asked, "What *one* book on public speaking would you recommend for the man who had no time for another, or for the man who wanted just *one* book on the subject?" I answer: "Hegarty's *Showmanship in Public Speaking.*"

5. *Successful Sales Presentations* by Charles B. Roth, Prentice-Hall, Inc., Englewood Cliffs, N. J. Chapter titles are: "Why a Standardized Presentation Will Increase Your Sales"; "What A Good Sales Presentation Must Be"; "What to Cover in Your Presentation"; "How to Start Building Your Presentation"; "How to Make Your Presentation Sincere and Persuasive"; "How to Make It More Convincing"; "How to Work in Resistance Chasers as You Go Along"; "How to Deliver Your Presentation Most Effectively"; "How to Use a Presentation Before a Group"; "Why it is Important to Keep on Improving a Presentation."

6. *How to Win the Conference* by William D. Ellis and Frank Siedel, Prentice-Hall, Inc., Englewood Cliffs, N. J. This 211-page book is divided into 27 short chapters. Among the chapter titles are: "How a Conference Becomes a Hassle"; "Uncommon Sense in the Internal Meeting"; "Imagination in the Conference"; "Some Masters of the Conference"; "The Empty Chair"; "Humor in the Conference"; "Some Auto-

crats of the Conference Table"; "Is This Conference Necessary?"; "The Irate Delegation"; "How to Close a Conference."

7. *The Club Member's Handbook,* by Lucy R. and Harold V. Milligan, Barnes & Noble, Inc., (paperback); Doubleday & Company, (hardcover), Garden City Books, New York. Chapters are: "How Clubs are Organized"; "How Meetings are Conducted"; "Constitution and By-Laws"; "Duties and Qualifications of Officers"; "How Motions are Made and Amended"; "How Resolutions are Made"; "How Minutes are Kept"; "How Votes are Taken and Counted"; "How Elections are Conducted"; "How Papers are Prepared"; "How to Speak in Public"; "Customs and Etiquette in Woman's Clubs"; "Customs in Men's Clubs"; "Appendix —Summary of Parliamentary Terms—and Laws."

Courses on Public Speaking

1. *Toastmasters, International* is a nonprofit, nonpartisan, non-sectarian, nondiscriminatory—but men only—*educational* organization devoted to speech, parliamentary procedure, and personal development on a "learning by doing basis." Toastmasters does no advertising but its more than 500,000 members of "graduates" provide word-of-mouth volunteer promotion. It operates through local clubs which are chartered by the Home Office in Santa Ana, California. Many of the clubs list their telephone number in the local telephone directory and can receive inquiries and new applicants by phone.

The average length of membership is about two years; many men have been members for more than 20 years; and it is easy for a member to reaffiliate with a Toastmasters Club when he moves to another area. Total membership in 1961 in the United States and 43 foreign countries ran over 80,000.

A Toastmasters Club usually meets weekly for dinner; the meeting including the dinner lasting about two hours. A Toastmaster of the evening presides over the program which includes four to six short speeches. The members assigned to make these prepared speeches do so in accordance with the *Basic Training Manual* of the Toastmasters. All the other members present are given an opportunity to speak extemporaneously on a "Table Topic" or during the business part of the meeting; each main speaker is assigned a personal evaluator, who also gives his evaluations orally. Evaluator assignments are rotated; each member is evaluated by every other member.

Initiation fees range between $5 and $10, and monthly dues are $1. Members receive *The Toastmaster,* the monthly magazine of the organization, and notices of other publications and services that are or become available. For more information write: Toastmasters International, Santa Ana, California.

2. *International Toastmistress Clubs, Inc.,* is similar in organization and purpose to Toastmasters International; however, Toastmistress Clubs are for women only—there are no "coed" groups (as of 1961), and no affiliation between the two organizations. In 1961 there were about 900 Toastmistress Clubs with about 16,000 members. For more information write International Toastmistress Clubs, Inc., 6829 Rita Avenue, Huntington Park, California.

3. *Dale Carnegie and Dorothy Carnegie Courses* are available in cities and towns throughout the country and are advertised in the local newspapers as well as listed in the telephone books. Their cost ranges around $175 and from what their graduates say must be well worth it. The Carnegie Courses can do wonders for a man or woman who wants to improve his or her ability to speak in different ways and before different groups.

4. *American Management Association.* The AMA conducts in New York City and certain other locations, a wide variety of courses in public speaking, presentations, conference techniques, and so on. For further information write: American Management Association, Inc., 1515 Broadway, New York 36, New York.

5. *Markus-Campbell Company Self-Study Courses.* The Markus-Campbell Company, 835 Diversey Parkway, Chicago 14, Ill. provides two self-study courses (texts with lesson equipments and guides). These can be particularly useful to men or women who cannot attend a course or club program. These are:

a. *Effective Speech Course*—consisting of six books and twelve lesson assignments. The books cover nearly every phase of public speaking (except use of visual aids) and include breathing, voice control, speaking over the radio; argument and refutation, speeches of dedication, acceptance; and so forth. The lesson assignments include additional explanatory materials as well as exercises and review questions. (Price $11.50 or $12.80, if taken on a monthly plan.)

b. *Conservation Studies*—The Ethel Cotton Course in Conversation which consists of 12 lessons on guiding conversation, getting acquainted, overcoming irritation, revitalizing interest, humor, overcoming complexes, discussing books and plays, interesting descriptions, home and business conversations, brief conversations, long conversations, and the do's and don'ts of personality development. (Price $13.95; or $15.75 monthly plan. Optional 7-day free trial.)

6. *Schools and Courses.* Most universities and technical schools, the YMCA, and other organizations provide "adult education." *Tip.* Be sure the class is "adult." You or your subordinates will get much more out of any public speaking class if the students are mature, responsible persons who can establish the same climate and conditions you face in the business world.

APPENDIX B

MATERIALS AND ORGANIZATIONS THAT CAN HELP YOU
IMPROVE YOUR WRITING ABILITY

Books

1. *Reader Over Your Shoulder,* by Robert Graves and Alan Hodge, Macmillan Company, N. Y., contains a wonderful explanation of the different kinds of English one encounters, and then demonstrates how to write and rewrite for clarity and gracefulness.

2. *Plain Words: Their ABC,* Sir Ernest Gowers, Alfred A. Knopf, Inc., N. Y., lives up to its billing as a "charming guide through the thickets of gobbledegook and out to the clear sunlight of plain words."

3. *Communication Through Reports,* Paul Douglass, Prentice-Hall, Inc., Englewood Cliffs, N. J., contains more than its title implies. It covers letters, memos, and legal documents, as well as scientific, accounting, and annual reports. The chapters on tables and charts are alone worth the price of the book.

4. *How to Write, Speak, and Think More Effectively,* by Rudolf Flesch, Harper & Brothers, N. Y., and *The Technique of Clear Writing,* by Robert Gunning, McGraw-Hill Co., N. Y., explain their famous readability formulas and provide much additional useful information about writing as well.

5. *A Guide to Technical Literature Production,* by Emerson Clarke, TW Publishers, River Forest, Ill., is an excellent, and to my knowledge the first, manual on how to organize, staff, and manage a writing department, including how to estimate costs, and how to evaluate and train writers and editors. Mr. Clarke's explanations and descriptions almost exactly parallel my own on-the-job experiences. (Had I known his book was going to be published, I could have saved myself much research and compilation of information.)

6. *The Elements of Style* by William Strunk, Jr. and E. B. White, Macmillan Company, N. Y., *The Presentation of Technical Information* by Reginal O. Kapp, Constable & Co., London; and *A Dictionary of Modern English Usage* by H. W. Fowler, Oxford University Press, London, are too famous to need more than a mention here to remind you of their titles, authors, and publishers.

7. *How to Make $18,000 a Year Free-lance Writing* by Larston Farrar, Hawthorne Books, Inc., 1957. How to write salable articles and sell them.

8. *Executives' Guide to Handling People,* by Frederick C. Dyer, Prentice-Hall, Inc., Englewood Cliffs, N.J., is not a "writer's manual" as are the foregoing books. However, like the *Guide to Technical Literature Production,* it is valuable to the executive who has to manage and motivate others to produce promptly writings that are imaginative and effective. Chapter 4, "Ten Rules for Generating Creativity and Productivity"; Chapters 3, 5, 6, and 7 have information of particular use to the executive who must deal with the creative person.

9. *The Working Press of the Nation* consists of three volumes:
Volume I   The Newspaper Directory. Lists all the daily newspapers of the country and over 1,000 important weekly newspapers. Names the editors, requirements, syndicates, features, etc., and lists the personnel for the departments from Art to Farm, from Fashion to Veterans.
Volume II   The Magazine Directory. Lists over 2,700 magazines, their addresses and editors, and provides alphabetical groupings of service, trade, professional, industrial, agricultural, and consumer publications. Also lists the magazines in their specialized fields—as Finance, Travel, etc. Includes information about deadlines, page size, and column width, illustration requirements, charges or payments for copy or pictures, readership analysis, and subscription rates.
Volume III   The Radio and Television Directory. Lists all the major radio and TV stations in the United States, and gives information about their power, news services, executives and program directors, broadcast times, and types of programs.
These books are primarily designed for public relations executives who have the job of placing publicity in U.S. media. However, any person interested in writing will find these books extremely useful guides to possible publishers of one's writings.
The Working Press of the Nation is issued annually in November, and each volume is priced at $25; the current price (1961) for the set of three volumes is $49.50. They are available only from the National Research Bureau, which, incidentally, publishes the *Blue Book of Magazine Writers* (also for use by public relations personnel), the Businessmen's Record Club, Direct Mail Idea Library, and the Public Relations Idea Library. Address, The National Research Bureau, 415 North Dearborn Street, Chicago 10, Ill.

Periodicals of Use to Writers

Most people interested in writing are familiar with the following monthly magazines which are sold at most magazine stands; reading them regularly can provide a person with what amounts to a course in modern writing techniques. They are listed here to provide their titles and addresses:

The Writer, 8 Arlington Street, Boston 16, Mass.
Writer's Digest, 22 West 12th Street, Cincinnati, Ohio.
Author & Journalist, 3365 Martin Drive, Boulder, Colo.

Institutes and Writing Courses

The American Management Association, Inc., (1515 Broadway, New York 36, New York) and the Industrial Education Institute (221 Columbus Avenue, Boston 16, Mass.) both conduct programs in report writing and in writing improvement for businessmen.

Many universities and adult education centers provide similar courses. The University of Chicago, for example, provides a correspondence course in writing, and the Famous Writers School (Westport, Conn.) provides several. A college course costs from $35 to $175; each of the Famous Writers courses (which take three years to complete) costs around $420. These charges include the texts and study guides, and are not only reasonable but necessary—you cannot obtain the proper level of instruction and materials without paying for it. Other courses are regularly advertised in the writer's magazines already listed.

Professional Writing Societies

There are many writer's clubs and associations, national as well as local. However, for the businessman the following are probably the most likely sources not only for information about the "state of the art," but for advice about the availability and the costs of writing services.

The Society of Technical Writers and Publishers, Inc. (STWP), (P.O. Box 3706, Beechwold Station, Columbus 14, Ohio) is the result of a merger of three national groups of technical, engineering, and scientific writers and editors. The magazine *STWP Review* and bulletin *STWP Newsletter,* and its national conventions and local meetings, all provide information and assistance with regard to standards and practices in technical writings (books, manuals, periodicals, releases), as well as agencies and individuals qualified in preparing or teaching technical writing. (Memberships dues range around $10 a year.)

The American Business Writers Association (ABWA), 1007 West Nevada Street, Urbana, Illinois) is an organization composed largely of professors of business writing and training managers in industry. Through its *The ABWA Bulletin,* national conventions, and other meetings it provides information about standards and practices of and the teaching of business writing. (Dues range around $5 a year.)

The Authors' League of America includes *The Author's Guild* and *The Dramatist's Guild* (6 East 39th Street, New York 16, N.Y.). These are associations of professional authors who have published a certain number of things. However, since Pfizer employed John Gunther to do its annual report, and other corporations have hired "big-name" authors to prepare company histories, special reports and addresses, the Authors' League should not be overlooked as a possible source of information with regard to "name" authors, standards of publishing contracts, use of copyrights, going rates of top professional writing, and so forth. (Dues range around $25 a year.)

INDEX